EDGAR CAYCE

ON
CHANNELING
YOUR
HIGHER SELF

BY HENRY REED
UNDER THE EDITORSHIP OF
CHARLES THOMAS CAYCE

WARNER

A Warner Communications Company

WARNER BOOKS EDITION

Cover design by Karen Katz

Warner Books, Inc.
666 Fifth Avenue
New York, N.Y. 10103

 A Warner Communications Company

Printed in the United States of America

First Printing: May, 1989

10 9 8 7 6 5 4 3 2 1

Table of Contents

Introduction

Channeling is a fascinating mystery. It has captivated people for thousands of years, providing them with a taste for things beyond the limitations of physical life on earth. In recent years, channeling has taken on a particular meaning that, though fascinating to some people, is even more mysterious to most.

The electronic age has brought channeling out from behind the secret door of consulting rooms into the living rooms of a nation. Television has provided channeling a medium never before available to spread its spell. Regardless of one's attitude toward it, witnessing channeling in progress creates a reaction.

Edgar Cayce's name is so often associated with being a channel that it is appropriate to review the large body of his own channeled material on this subject. The task of presenting his view has been put in my hands. The result of that trust is this book.

I've written two previous books outlining Cayce's teachings— *Awakening Your Psychic Powers* and *Mysteries of the Mind*. In contrast to ESP, or the power of visualization to affect the functioning of the body, there is not much scientific research that directly bears on the phenomenon of channeling. It's not because of lack of study. It is because channeling is more a perspective, a way of looking at the nature of reality, than it is any single phenomenon inviting validation. With regard to the reality of spirits who might speak through living persons, Cayce indicated that it's not something that can be scientifically validated. Science has come to agree with Cayce's assessment.

The psychic aspect of channeling is perhaps the best documented, but the word psychic includes being able only to pick up information, not in understanding the information, or in being able to make suggestions about what to do with it. As a channel in trance, Cayce was not only able to see into the workings of a body hundreds of miles away, but he also understood what he saw, he could describe it for others, and he knew what to suggest to improve the functioning and the health of that body. He evidenced wisdom beyond mere knowledge.

Inspiration and creativity are also aspects of channeling. Being able to elevate others to higher states of consciousness, and bring out the best in other people, are facets of channeling. There are many sides to channeling besides talking with the voice of a disembodied spirit. Edgar Cayce demonstrated all these aspects of channeling.

Cayce gave a perspective on channeling that shows how all these facets relate to one another. He provided a viewpoint that will help you learn what significance channeling, in all its aspects, has for your life. His approach, and the value system he respected, is reflected in the term, *higher self*. It is part of this book's title and is a major theme throughout the book.

In preparing this book, I had much assistance, for which I am grateful. Many others have gone before me to explain Cayce's concepts and some of the enigmas of channeling. Their work made my job easier. Among the many who provided me with direct support, I want to thank Henry Bolduc. The hypnosis sessions he provided me helped me find my own way toward trance channeling. Thanks are also due to Daniel Clay, Al Minor, and Ray Stanford for their openness in sharing with me their experiences in developing the trance channel. I must give thanks to the cardinal in the oak tree who supervised many of my dictation sessions in the backyard, and who may also have impressed certain thoughts upon me. To my imaginary servant in the tuxedo, who always was able to pull the right book out of my ethereal library for me to read during sessions of dictation, I also give thanks, even if I didn't always write down what I read there. I appreciate Rob Grant's excellent work transcribing my dictated cassettes and for his generous help in finding my way through some little-known passages in the Cayce readings. I especially want to thank my wife, Veronica, for the tireless editing of my writing, for helping me prepare the illustrations, for the even harder job of keeping my spirit intact, and above all for showing me what it means to channel from the heart.

All of these sources contributed to my attempt to make Cayce's perspective on channeling clear to you. They did so because, like Cayce, they know that behind the sometimes confusing world of channeling phenomena, there lies something of great value and importance for you. I hope that this book contributes in some small way toward your finding your own way of channeling your higher self.

CHAPTER ONE

What Is Channeling?

"Not my will but Thine, O Lord, be done in and through me. Let me ever be a channel of blessings, today, now, to those that I contact, in every way. Let my going in, mine comings out, be in accord with that Thou would have me do, and as the call comes, 'Here am I, send me—use me!' "

—**Edgar Cayce, 262–3**

"When it works, it's like . . . *freedom*! Suddenly these things are coming out of you. You're in control, but you're not. The characters are coming *through* you. . . . It's *channeling with call waiting*!"

—**Robin Williams**

Stephen King, the author of such demonic novels as *The Shining*, tells us in *The Writer's Handbook* that when he was a high school sophomore, he wrote and distributed a devilishly satirical newspaper that gave the teachers no mercy. After he had been properly punished, his guidance counselor got him a part-time job as a writer for the local newspaper. It was, in his words, "a more constructive channel for my talent."

It's easy to appreciate King's story. You can recognize the common wisdom that creative energy needs an outlet, it is hoped through a *constructive channel*. I'm sure you have an intuitive understanding of the term, *channel*, when it's used in this way. It makes sense.

You do have a basic understanding of our topic. Whenever necessary you can remind yourself of that understanding by simply imagining someone channeling his energies in some manner. *Channel* and *channeling* are good words and refer to something that we all appreciate and value. Get your own everyday example of channeling fixed in your mind and keep it ready for use. It will help you maintain clarity in the sometimes confusing world we're about to enter.

Out on a Limb

Perhaps you were among the millions of television viewers to witness Shirley MacLaine play herself in her autobiographical miniseries. Watching her *Out on a Limb*, viewers accompanied her into the strange realms of metaphysics. We were like flies on the wall as she welcomed into her home the *channel* Kevin Ryerson. For many viewers, it was their first experience with trance channeling.

Kevin informed Shirley that as many as four different *entities* spoke through him. Did he mean that he was a spokesman, delivering messages on behalf of others? No, he meant that these people *literally* spoke through him. These entities were *spirits*, people without bodies, and used Kevin's body to communicate.

As if he were going away, Kevin said to Shirley, "See you in a little while." Along with Shirley, we watched Kevin take off his coat, loosen his tie, close his eyes, and go into what he called a trance. Shortly, Kevin's head turned back, his body jerked, and out of his mouth another voice, a whispery one, announced, "Please identify self and state purpose of gathering."

Shirley's reaction suggested that she was now communicating with someone else other than Kevin, someone perhaps far away. She looked up, as if peering into a television monitor projecting a satellite transmission from outer space, and introduced herself by saying, "I am speaking to you from Santa Monica."

The voice referred to itself as "We." Shirley asked about the identity of the "We." She learned that it was a spirit, a guide. The voice explained that we all have such guides. It also indicated that human beings are more than bodies, that we have a spirit that we must recognize by something other than our senses.

Shirley reacted skeptically. "On what do you base this information?" she asked. The voice then gave Shirley a lesson in metaphysics. He described the *Akashic Records* as an invisible dimension, a Hall of Records, where *all* thoughts and experiences are stored. The information there can be contacted psychically. As if to convince her of its ability to know things, it asked her about an unusual event that took place at the beach. Shirley was amazed that it could know about that. The voice indicated that it could read Shirley's mind.

Abruptly, the voice announced, "Pause, entity desiring to speak." With his eyes still closed, Kevin jerked his head, cleared his throat and then another, different voice, one with a heavy Irish brogue, announced, "McPherson here. How you be doing out there?"

Shirley noted that she could really feel the presence of another personality coming through. McPherson asked to be blindfolded to keep the light out of *the instrument's* eyes, referring to Kevin. Apparently the instrument's mouth needed refreshing and McPherson asked if it might have a drink. When Shirley offered to get it something, it volunteered to get it himself. This blindfolded stranger in Shirley's house then proceeded to walk over to Shirley's bookcase, find and push a lever, and revealed the bar hidden behind. Shirley was amazed at this demonstration of his psychic ability. There was more to come.

In their brief discussion, McPherson made reference to a

statement Shirley's friend had made to her some time ago. Shirley had told no one of the incident. McPherson then went on to name the friend and explain some of the psychology of their relationship. He acted as a counselor with a psychic connection to the relevant facts.

As abruptly as he appeared on the scene, he left, leaving the whispering voice to say good-bye. Tossing his head to the side, Kevin then raised his hands to his eyes, rubbing them as if coming out of a deep sleep. When he opened his eyes, he asked, "How did it go?" Shirley explained about the entity McPherson finding the bar behind the bookcase. Kevin seemed surprised that the entity had such command of Kevin's body, but otherwise seemed indifferent to the events. He bid a farewell and left Shirley, and the audience, to ponder what had happened.

Television Channels Channel Channelers Channeling

In interviews about her show, Shirley explained that the channeling segment wasn't an act. During rehearsals, Kevin actually channeled the two entities. John, the first spirit to speak, and Tom McPherson, the Irishman, had even contributed to the script, and followed it during the filming. What was filmed was also an actual channeling session. The spirits became TV stars.

Shirley's show elicited quite a bit of commentary, much of it humorous, as in Robin Williams's joke about *channeling with call waiting* referring to the abrupt, "Please, there's someone desiring to speak." Some of the jokes were a bit derisive. Johnny Carson, for one, got a lot of mileage out of Shirley's revelations. The commentaries and jokes indicated that Shirley had touched a nerve. The humor was a way of dealing with the emotions her show elicited. She brought something out into the public arena that couldn't just be ignored. It was something that cried for explanation.

Talk shows and television magazine shows tried to help out. They were expressions of the public's curiosity about the phenomena. Many familiar television commentators interviewed various channels and investigated the unfamiliar presences that spoke through them.

On the Merv Griffin show, for example, actor Michael York and his wife introduced Jack Pursel, who channels the entity, Lazaris. Although they had little to say about Jack himself, the Yorks spoke at length about Lazaris as a valuable friend. Unlike Kevin Ryerson's Tom McPherson, who claims to be the spirit of an actual person who lived in the past, Lazaris is simply a spirit, and has never been a flesh-and-blood human being.

Jack soon shut his eyes and went quickly into his trance state. Jack's eyes remained closed as a voice, not unlike Jack's own, spoke and greeted the Yorks and Merv by name. With a humorous reference to his own long-windedness, Lazaris invited Merv to ask a question. Merv asked Lazaris to explain why he, and other entities like him, have come. His question certainly suggested the arrival of alien beings from a faraway place. In his answer, Lazaris didn't reject this implied notion. In fact, he gave four basic reasons for their coming.

First, he assured us, he and the others haven't come to save our planet. We're capable of doing that ourselves, he indicated, if we will only remember our power and ability to do so. Their mission is to remind us of our powers. The second purpose is to remind us that we create our own reality, through love, choice, and the power to change. The third reason is to remind us to find out how completely and profoundly we're loved, and what profound powers of love we have ourselves. Finally, he reminded us to dream, to remember our dreams, and to value them, as a creative power. Merv didn't have anything to say in response to Lazaris's message.

On the show "Entertainment Tonight," hostess Mary Hart showed many examples of channels in the act of channeling. To investigate the phenomenon in more depth, she interviewed Daryl Anka, who channels an alien from outer space named Beshar. Anka explained that channeling is actually a normal process that we all engage in. He defined channeling as any type of creative expression (an idea we will explore in more detail in a later chapter). Upon meeting Beshar, Mary asked, "How do we know you're who you say you are?" Beshar's answer was provocative:

"You do not, and that is not the purpose at this time. The idea is not for us to prove we are who we say we are. We would prefer, in actual fact, that you not *care* who we are in that sense . . . that you focus on the idea of the information itself. If the information serves you, use it. If it doesn't, do not."

Afterward, Mary Hart's cohost asked her if she was able to keep a straight face during the interview. Mary noted that she did enter the interview as a skeptic, but she admitted that she found the presence of Beshar to be very powerful.

Another powerful presence to make the rounds on the television networks was Ramtha. On the "Good Morning America" show, for example, Joan Lunden presented clips of Ramtha seminars and of the opulent private life of Ramtha's channel, J. Z. Knight. Viewers saw Mrs. Knight close her eyes briefly, then open them, get up and become Ramtha, a warrior who lived 35,000 years ago. In contrast to the other entities, this one was rather active onstage. The news correspondent interviewed a woman from the audience who said this seminar was the fourth one she had attended, at four hundred dollars each. The television camera later showed a profile of this woman, her mouth dropping open in a rather vacant smile, while a commentator pronounced that it's simply a hunger for easy answers to life's difficulties that motivate people to believe in this stuff. The impression given was that the woman was somewhat foolish.

Two experts appeared on this show to pass judgment on Ramtha and the channeling phenomenon generally. Each had about one minute to explain this perplexing phenomenon. Both dismissed Ramtha, and both indicated that channeling was old news.

One of these, Gerald Larue, a retired professor of biblical history and an expert on the scientific examination of religion, gave us three choices: (1) Ramtha is a real spirit, which would be real news; (2) J. Z. Knight is deluded; or

(3) she is a fake. His conclusion was that she did have a genuine experience—a hallucination. She then developed a profitable business out of it. His word for it was "scam."

The other expert, psychologist Larry LeShan, who is a respected investigator and author on the paranormal, indicated that the only thing we saw that was 35,000 years old was the channeling phenomenon itself. It's nothing new. Scientists like him who study this sort of thing have seen hundreds of such *cases*.

Dr. LeShan then made an interesting statement because of what he implied. He noted that there are *good* ones and there are *bad* ones. The good ones want to do something useful with the phenomenon, so they donate themselves to science, presumably never to be heard from again. The bad ones, he indicated, go public. In other words, he concluded, if you encounter someone who channels publically, chances are it's a bad one. Indirectly, he invalidated all that we have seen.

Yet, there's another message in what Dr. LeShan said. If there are good ones, what exactly are they good at? They make you think more deeply about yourself, he noted. Though he satisfied the skeptics by dismissing the phenomenon, he also dropped a subtle hint to the attentive viewer that there's something valid and worthwhile about the phenomenon. What are we to think? It would appear that we aren't being told everything.

Some of the entities that come through those who channel claim to be extraterrestrial beings—aliens. Is it possible that UFOs are making telepathic contact with our planet? Shirley MacLaine's television movie gave that suggestion. People have often suspected that UFOs have appeared on earth but that the government has covered up the facts. Is channeling a way for the aliens to bypass the usual channels of information and speak directly to the people? Is that the sort of thing that the scientists are secretly learning when they study channeling?

Among his statements, Dr. LeShan claimed that channeling was popular in Germany in the 1930s, which is an ominous reference. We might link that remark with other ominous current news reports that Satanic cults and demonic possession are becoming more common. Is channeling actually some kind of evil influence that's infiltrating the minds of unsuspecting people?

When Robin Williams joked that he was channeling his comedy, was he implying that he's possessed, that spirits are speaking through him? Or is his joke a subtle message that his type of improvisational comedy is a form of channeling, much like the definition that Daryl Anka's entity, Beshar, gave?

It does get confusing and the experts don't necessarily help, especially during brief media interviews. When television channels channel channelers channeling, the *medium* is the message: "Watch this channel to see a channel!" The possibility that spirits might exist and be talking through the channelers is more compelling than any message the spirits have to convey. The possibility of spirit contact is quickly rejected and any messages, such as Beshar's advice, goes unheeded. It would be a rare talk show where the commentator discussed the message rather than the medium, especially because, as Dr. LeShan indicated, the message seems to be the same from all the sources. Rather than suggesting that it is all the same *old stuff*, in other words, there's *no news*, it could be suggested that they're all *pointing out the same message* and that message *is important news*!

The History of Channeling

Although the news that channeling brings us is important, it's also true that it's not new. Varieties of channeling have existed since the beginning of recorded history. The message has been the same. Perhaps the best sourcebook on this history is Jon Klimo's *Channeling: Investigations on Receiving Information from Paranormal Sources*. Here's a brief outline of the documented history of humanity's contact with nonphysical sources that Klimo presents.

Belief in immortality has always been with us. Prehistoric and primitive people have had their *shamans* or healers who could make contact with the spirit world. The practices of shamans from around the world, and throughout the ages, show a remarkable consistency.

Dating back as far as 5,000 B.C., the Egyptian *Book of the Dead* details the ability of the human soul to leave the physical body and communicate with the spirits of the deceased. Around 2,000 B.C., the Chinese developed the prototype of the modern Ouija board. Two people would hold a forked branch while a spirit would guide the branch to spell out messages in the sand. Later, the ancient Greeks had their oracles, considered to be mouthpieces of the gods.

By 1,000 B.C., monotheism became a strong religious force in the origins of Judaism. The Old Testament contains many descriptions of channeling, beginning with the prophet Moses, followed by Solomon, Samuel, Daniel, Elijah, Elisha, Ezekiel, Jeremiah, and Isaiah. In the New Testament, if we skip over the touchy question of whether Jesus was a channel of God or God Himself, we have Saul's experience of Jesus on the road to Damascus as an experience of channeling. The event of the Pentecost, the descent of the Holy Spirit onto the followers of Jesus, began a historical sequence of channeling, speaking in tongues, that continues to this day. Perhaps the most profound example of channeling in the Bible is John the Beloved's Revelation.

During the Middle Ages, though the Christian church frowned on channeling, certain mystics nevertheless had communion experiences with divine beings. Saint Teresa of Avila described her experiences in the *Interior Castle* and Saint John of the Cross wrote of his in *Ascent of Mount Carmel* and *Dark Night of the Soul*.

Channeled experiences have given birth to new Christian sects. In seventeenth-century England, for example, George Fox's vision became the basis of the Society of Friends, or Quakers. In early nineteenth-century America, Joseph Smith's vision of the angel Moroni lead to *The Book of Mormon*. It was during that time that the Spiritualist movement was also born, again in America. We'll examine that period of the history of channeling in Chapter Nine.

Through These Channels:
The Psychic Experience of Edgar Cayce

While watching television interviews of channelers, one consistent thing to note is that almost every one mentions Edgar Cayce. He seems clearly to be a point of reference. In *Out on a Limb*, Shirley MacLaine tiptoes into a metaphysical bookstore and a book falls from the shelves into her hands. When she asks about it, the friendly and knowledgeable clerk tells her that it's a classic piece of channeled metaphysical literature. When Shirley questions her about the meaning of the word, *channeled*, the clerk explains the concept by referring to Edgar Cayce.

As his biographer, Thomas Sugrue, wrote in *There is a River*, the story of Edgar Cayce properly belongs to the history of hypnosis rather than to spiritualism. Thus we will postpone our synopsis of Cayce's development as a psychic until Chapter Eleven, where we examine hypnosis.

It was Cayce, in his psychic trance, who enlisted the word, *channel*, into metaphysical service. He didn't use the word to describe just the phenomenon seen on TV, but to describe a more general and basic fact about human existence. The heart of the message that came "through these channels," as Cayce often referred to himself when in trance, was that *we are all channelers*.

> "In the application of the physical forces as are
> manifested in a material world, individuals
> often lose sight of the fact that all force as is
> manifested in a material world emanates from
> that source that *brought* the world *into* being.
> Because there arises much that apparently
> is within the ken or scope of individual
> accomplishments, the credit is given to man's
> forces—or the lack of man's ability, or accredited
> in man's own making, rather than that man,
> or those men, or those conditions, are rather but

the channels of a manifestation of that One
Force as brought them into being.''

Edgar Cayce, 13–2

The Human Being: A Channel of Divine Energy

Ecology teaches us that all life is interconnected. The
energy of sunlight, the atoms of the air, the molecules in
plants and animals constantly recirculate among themselves.
Life is an integrated whole. The body of a human being
contains all these elements and is thus a reflection of the
whole. But how does a human being transform the atoms of
food, air, and sunlight into works of art? There's clearly
something more to a human being than physical, earthly
atoms.

It's easy in this age of scientific technology to assume
that we're just flesh and bones, or as someone put it,
animated meat. When Cayce focused his psychic ability on
understanding the true nature of the human being, where we
came from, and our purpose for being, what emerged was a
portrait of a truly cosmic creature.

Although we're hypnotized by our senses to believe only
in the reality of the physical world, it's energy that's the
essential reality. The essence of our nature is energetic. It's
a nonmaterial spirit. We are channels of divine energy.
That's the universal message of all mysticism and religion,
it's Cayce's essential message, and contemporary channelers
repeat it.

You can develop the awareness of your spirit through
intuition, but not through the senses. Through meditation
and your dreams you can be guided to these intuitions. Your
imagination is also a very powerful tool that needs to be
cultivated.

Many of these ideas are more than two thousand years
old. They certainly didn't originate with Cayce. But Cayce
did provide the first detailed description of these concepts,
within an integrated framework that's proving to be quite
compatible with modern psychology and philosophical

concepts. What had been a mystical claim in the past, or based on religious faith, Cayce was able to express in terms quite compatible with the thinking of modern psychology.

The channeling phenomenon today appears to give us a double message. On the one hand, the voices coming through the channeler identify themselves as disembodied spirits. Their message to us seems to be that the presence of such spirits or entities should prove to us that we're more than just bodies, that we ourselves are spirits. On the other hand, they tell us to ignore who they are and focus on their message. But by basing the proof of their message on their claim that they are spirits, we find ourselves in a bind.

We naturally focus on the nature of these disembodied spirits. The spirits are the marvel and that's what makes their message interesting. On the other hand, we can't verify their claim as being spirits and thus we don't know whether or not we should believe their message to us.

There's a way out of this predicament. When we study the message carefully, we realize that they're also saying, and Edgar Cayce said this as well, ''Don't take my word for it that you are spirit, but find out for yourself. Don't take the word of all the religions of the world that you are a soul, don't rely on the reports of the mystics who have had this experience themselves. Rather, *find out for yourself*. Until you've experienced yourself the reality of spirit, it's just a concept, one idea among many.''

Learning that you, *too*, are a channel of spirit can be a means of spiritual awakening. The highest psychic realization, Cayce declared, is that God talks directly to human beings. It's a realization that many of us have already had. According to a recent Gallup poll, 50 percent of the American population have experienced God's speaking to them through an inner feeling or impression.

What is Channeling?

It's very likely the case that no one would use the word channeling to describe the various forms of inspiration, prophecy, and ministering going by that name if it weren't for Edgar Cayce. It's a fair approximation of truth to say that it was Edgar Cayce who first used the word *channel* to describe the human being as a source of psychic and spiritual transmission. By his visionary use of the word, in a variety of suggestive ways, he imprinted it upon the imagination of those who would follow.

Cayce didn't restrict the term to describe contacts between the living and the deceased, or between the physical personality and the realms of the infinite mind. He didn't restrict it to refer to those individuals whose psychic powers were clearly active. He indicated that every person, as a manifestation of divine energy, is a channel. The question is what a person would channel and for what purpose.

The constructiveness of the channel was what was of special interest to Cayce. To understand channeling, and to make it a constructive process in our lives, Cayce would have us first understand it in its broadest perspective.

Consider this analogy. A young child asks his parents, "What's sports?" Football, a particularly popular sport at the time, happens to be playing on television. The parents say, "Look at the television. What you see there is a sport."

The child watches the football game for a while. He watches the playing on the field, the people in the stands, he listens to the commentators. The child turns to his parents and says, "Is sports fighting over a ball? People are hitting one another, trying to steal the ball away, throwing it around. People knock one another down. A lot of people are excited and are yelling. Some are very happy, some seem really angry. Is that what a sport is, like a big fight?"

The parents might agree that, yes, sometimes it is, but sports has a broader meaning. Understanding this broader meaning we can see how football is an example of a sport. We can understand what to look for to appreciate how playing football exemplifies the concept of sport as well as how the commercial football industry can crush and defy good sportsmanship.

The same kind of thing holds with channeling. Judging from what we see on television, we receive a very narrow vision of what it means to be a channel. It would seem as though it's a matter of closing one's eyes and speaking in a strange voice, trying to be someone other than who you are, perhaps the mouthpiece of a spirit. It would seem that it's a way to attract large audiences that would otherwise not listen to you, or a scam to make a lot of money.

Few of us would want to talk in our sleep to a large group of people. But channeling isn't limited to making inspirational speeches from an unconscious state. That's just one aspect of a much larger picture.

In the most general sense, a channel is a means of transmission. It receives and passes along. For example, when an idea comes to you, and you share it with someone, you're being a channel of the idea. Go up to your friend and give him a hug. You're a channel of love.

A channeler receives something that might otherwise be invisible to others, shapes it into a transmittable form, and presents it to others. With our lives, for example, we make visible our thoughts and motivations.

A channel also involves a specific focus of application. We may experience our love for a person in the form of good feelings. When we channel those feelings, however, they may manifest in something specific, such as making dinner for that person, or helping someone with a problem.

Channeling has the special implication of transmitting something from beyond the channeler's personal self. A channeler brings forth information that's not part of the channeler's own learning or experience. There are psychic components, or creative, spiritual, and inspirational dimensions to channeling that transcend the channeler's ordinary abilities or knowledge. Sometimes a channeler serves as an oracle of wisdom.

A channeler may receive communications from a disembodied spirit, from God, from an angel, from plants or animals. The channeler may simply have an intuition. The channeler may then transmit what's received verbally, in writing, by painting or other artwork, by actions, through community work, or by a smile. The channeler may be asleep, in meditation, in a trance, or awake while channeling.

From the perspective of the Cayce material, the type of channeling that's a fad today, the kind that's shown on TV, is but one special instance of a very general phenomenon. Speaking with the voice of a spirit is only one example of channeling. It's a form that Cayce used only rarely. Although Cayce gave his readings from an altered state of consciousness, it wasn't his only mode of channeling. He was also psychic and inspiring in the waking state.

Every day, in countless ways, you and I are channels of spirit, of ideas, and of resources that come from beyond our conscious personalities. Our channeling abilities have profound impact on our own lives and the lives of those around us. We can become aware of this fact. We can realize that we're channelers and can consider which types of channeling we wish to perfect and use. Cayce indicated that there are as many ways of channeling as there are individuals. Rather than channeling without awareness of what we're doing, we can take a more active, creative role in our channeling. By doing so, we assume our birthright, our mission in life, to become a channel of blessings to others by the way we willingly choose to channel our energies.

PART I

Channeling in
Everyday Life

CHAPTER TWO

Listen to Your Intuition: The Channel of Your Guardian Angel

"The divine is within self. Hear the voice within, not the temptor from without."

—**Edgar Cayce, 5018–1**

"Thy body is indeed the temple of the living God. *There* He has promised to meet thee, to commune with thee. *There* is the psychic development, the psychic phenomena that ye seek!"

—**Edgar Cayce, 1598–1**

". . . the *intuitive* forces that arise *with* same make for rather the safer, the saner, the more spiritual way, with the less aptitude of turning to forces from without . . . Hence, *intuitive* force is the better, for in this there may come more the union of the spirit of truth with Creative Energy; thus the answer may be *shown* thee . . . in *whatever* manner or form . . . there are many channels, many manners. . . ."

—**Edgar Cayce, 261–15**

Have you ever had the experience where you just *knew* something about a person the moment you met? There are some people you instinctively trust, and others you distrust. Did someone ever say to you, "trust me" and you had a gut reaction that you shouldn't? Have you ever trusted such a person and later regretted it?

Sometimes we have feelings about a situation that we just can't explain. Maybe you are shopping for a used car. You find one you really like and the price is right. Yet you have this unexplainable feeling: "No, don't buy it, there's something wrong here." Have you ever ignored such a feeling and later wished you hadn't?

These feelings are like hunches. I haven't met a person yet who hasn't had a hunch. Neither have I met anyone who doesn't have a sad, or even tragic, story to tell about ignoring one. Hunches are often right, even if they don't often make sense. Sometimes we just have a feeling about something that we can't explain on the basis of anything we've learned. The knowledge just seems to come from the inside. Strange as it may seem, the knowledge is *usually accurate*.

I'm talking about intuition, of course. We often define it as knowing without the use of the senses or reason. In other reasons, it's *direct knowing*. The knowledge is simply there. Out of nowhere, uncanny knowledge comes your way, asking you to accept it, even if you can't explain it.

Intuition is a common, everyday word. Yet it hides a mystery. Intuition has always challenged thinkers. It suggests a reality that's somehow different or hidden from what appears obvious to the senses or reason.

Your own intuitions may have made you wonder how you can know things that you have no apparent basis for knowing. Perhaps your intuition can also help you understand Cayce's view that the human being is naturally a channel. Some of our exploration of channeling will challenge your reasoning mind. No matter how hard I may try to explain things in a clear and reasonable fashion, you'll still need your intuition to see what reason can't grasp.

Intuition as a Channel of Guidance

Intuition is a channel of knowledge that comes through you from a seemingly invisible and unknown source. You may experience it as a gut reaction, or you may feel it "in your bones." An intuition may give you a nudge to do, or not to do, something. It may give you a feeling about something, an inclination or an inspiration. Intuition is a natural channel of guidance.

One use of intuition that I value is my inner defensive driving program. Sometimes I find myself pausing when entering an intersection, only to see a car running a stop sign and crossing my path. I regularly get hunches about intersections and specific cars that I should watch carefully. Sometimes I intuit that a particular car may suddenly turn in front of me or do something else that might affect me. These hunches are usually right.

I also find intuition to be a reliable channel of guidance in my business affairs. On certain days, for example, I'll feel an urgency to discuss a proposition with a member of one of the organizations for whom I do consulting work. Yet I'll have a hunch that I'd better not. If I ignore the hunch, and proceed anyway, things don't work out. Then a day will come when I'll get the feeling to "act now!" The feeling usually proves valid. Sometimes I will have nothing particular in mind when I'll get the urge to visit a particular organization. I'll arrive and run into someone who'll say, "What a coincidence, I was just thinking about you." The person has a project to discuss and my being on the scene at the time makes me a ready consultant.

I'm certainly not the only one who finds intuition helpful in business. Years ago, Douglas Dean and his associates at the New Jersey School of Engineering published *Executive ESP.* Their research demonstrated that the corporations that were doing the best economically had leaders who scored high in ESP tests. These corporate executives were even quite willing to express a belief in ESP and they admitted relying heavily on their intuitions in making decisions.

Judging today from the number of books on intuition in the business section of the bookstore, there's a bull market for learning to use intuition.

The Psychic Side of Intuition

Edgar Cayce called intuition the highest form of psychic ability. He paid it this compliment because intuition never comes randomly with odd bits of information. Intuitive information is never simply idle gossip about something of no concern to you. Intuitive knowledge comes to you because the information is useful for you at the moment.

Intuition is also more than psychic ability. It draws a conclusion and directs your actions. It's holistic: Cayce explained that intuition compares psychically obtained information with your ideals, your needs, and your purposes, and then searches for an appropriate response. Intuition works like the faithful guide dog's nose. It can sniff out situations, locate quarry, or alert you to danger.

In her well-researched and documented book, *Psi Trek*, sociologist Laile Bartlett gives a number of examples of how intuition has saved lives. She tells the story, for example, of a nineteen-year-old girl, Elaine, getting ready to board a bus for an important trip. Suddenly, Elaine had an overwhelming urge to visit her mother instead. She switched buses and headed in the opposite direction, toward her parents' furniture store. All the way on the trip she found herself anxious to get there. When she arrived, she found her parents sitting in some chairs near the store's front window. She felt silly about her bizarre feelings of apprehension. Yet she managed to convince her surprised parents to leave the store to get some lunch with her. As they left through the back of the store, a car crashed through the front window, demolishing the chairs where her parents had been sitting.

Perhaps you have heard a story similar to this one. There are many such stories of trips postponed or canceled on the basis of foreboding feelings, but for no other apparent reason. That is, no reason was visible until later. This type of incident happens often. An interesting study, in fact, suggests there's an uncanny, intuitive wisdom at work in the traveling population.

W. E. Cox studied train accidents. He compared the number of people on trains on the day of an accident with the number of passengers on other days. Sometimes these differences were very pronounced. "The Georgian," for example, had only *nine* people aboard for its accident on June 15, 1952. Yet the day before it had sixty-eight passengers, and the day before that, sixty. Each day that week, except the day of the accident, it carried an average of sixty passengers. The day of the week the accident occurred was not usually one with few passengers. On the same day of the four preceding weeks there were thirty-five, fifty-five, fifty-three, and fifty-four passengers. The overall statistics confirmed his hunch that wrecked trains carried significantly fewer passengers than trains that had a normal trip. People have some intuitive way of avoiding accidents.

Cox termed the source of this effect "subliminal premonition." It suggests that intuition often guides our actions without our knowing it. Intuition often operates through a subliminal channel of guidance.

However we wish to define or explain intuition, its invisible hand does seem to guide our actions. We can be thankful for it, even if we don't understand it. Edgar Cayce provides a way, however, to understand intuition so we can cultivate this everyday channel of guidance to our advantage. His approach also gives intuition a higher purpose in our lives, to help us realize something even more important.

All Knowledge Is Within

Cayce valued intuition as a channel of both guidance and inspiration. He also valued it because it operated in a purposeful manner consistent with a person's values. Most of all, he valued it because using intuition directs our attention within ourselves.

Cayce defined intuition as *knowing from within*. Learning intuition required turning within, looking within, and sensing information that came from within oneself. Knowing that all knowledge is *within* us, and learning to *look within* were two keystones of Cayce's teachings. Understanding and developing intuition puts us on the path to those important lessons.

Perhaps you already have an intuitive grasp of what makes intuition possible. My first experience with an intuitive understanding of intuition came from the book, *Zen in the Art of Archery*, by Eugen Herrigel.

The author, a German philosopher, traveled to Japan to learn about Zen. The Zen masters wanted nothing to do with him, assuming his interest to be an intellectual one only. By consistently demonstrating his personal sincerity, however, he finally was able to begin instruction under Master Kenzo Awa, the revered archer.

For four years Herrigel found himself engrossed in the challenge of learning how to draw the long and very stiff Japanese bow. How to release the arrow smoothly was even more difficult. Like learning ballet, Zen archery required both extreme physical effort and learning how to move gracefully through unfamiliar and awkward gestures. It required learning the mysterious secret of getting out of his own way and letting the movements flow. There was also the matter of disciplining his breath. He was learning that Zen archery is a form of meditation.

During this time, he shot at no target. The target, he learned, was an inward one—a state of mind. Learning to draw and release the arrow properly required developing this state of mind. It was truly a spiritual discipline.

Finally, during the *fifth* year, the master brought out a target and demonstrated shooting at it. Herrigel saw that his master could repeatedly hit the center of the target without apparently aiming the bow. He watched closely and confirmed that his master's eyes were barely open and that he did *not* take aim. He joked that his master had learned to shoot in his sleep.

Herrigel's remark resulted in an invitation to return to the master's studio that night. The master then revealed an amazing secret about the Zen art of archery. In pitch blackness, the master quickly loosed an arrow, and then another, at the target some sixty feet away. When Herrigel found his way to the target, he discovered that the first arrow had hit the center. The second arrow had penetrated and split the first!

Herrigel wondered how a person could hit the target without being able to see it. If the first arrow was some combination of luck and experience, what about the second arrow?

The master explained that we believe we need our eyes to see because we believe the world is out there beyond us. If you separate yourself from the target you then have to learn the trick of how to hit it with the arrow. He advised that the art is to become one with the target, allowing the arrow to return to its natural home.

He said that an archer who aims the arrow at the target is merely a *trick* shooter. The archer who *becomes* the target is on the path to realizing Zen's great Secret.

The years spent practicing drawing and releasing the arrow was to learn how to let *It* shoot. The archer becomes merely a channel for the art of archery to manifest the spirit of Zen.

Like the Zen archer, Cayce knew how to hit the bull's-eye by turning within himself to contact the source of all knowledge. Like the Zen master who taught Herrigel, Cayce teaches us how to turn within to hit the targets in our lives. Like Herrigel, we will learn from Cayce to shun "trick shooting."

In contrast to the archer's use of concepts from Zen Buddhism, Cayce's teachings draw upon biblical concepts. He reminded us of Jesus' teaching that the Kingdom of God is within. If God is within, then everything is within. Cayce's advice was to follow the principle given in the Bible to seek first the Kingdom within. Everything else will be naturally forthcoming.

Concerning the workings of intuition, Cayce approached it like the Zen master approached archery. He didn't practice it to become a good shot. He practiced it as a way to truth. Don't develop intuition to produce a good performance, such as becoming *psychic*. Follow the path of intuition because it leads to our true nature, One with God. To Cayce, this discovery, like Zen's great Secret, is the true prize, and the main value, of developing intuition.

The Secret of Unitary Oneness

Cayce's perspective on intuition also provides a vision of how intuition operates and what makes it possible. Intuition is not a creation of the conscious mind. The conscious mind separates us from the rest of life so that we can analyze it with our senses. The conscious mind, which reasons on the basis of the senses, assumes knowledge must come from without. Such an assumption is self-evident to the conscious mind. Intuition, however, operates on another assumption. Intuition presupposes an underlying unity to all life. Until recently, this intuitive appreciation of unity has usually been restricted to a mystic's awareness. As our century comes to a close, however, science itself is coming to adopt a similar point of view.

Science is the ultimate expression of the viewpoint of the conscious mind, using its intellect to perfect a method of knowing. Using its own favorite methods, however, science has discovered their fundamental limitations. Browse the New Age section of your local bookstore and you will find a variety of recent books on the emerging *new* science. Such books as *Sympathetic Vibrations*, *The Tao of Physics*, and *The Dancing Wu Wei Masters*, all explain how modern scientific concepts are approaching a worldview similar to mysticism. Here is a nutshell version of the story of that new science.

We traditionally assume that separate atoms with space in between them make up the world. We assume that it requires a chain reaction, atom bumping into atom, to transmit an effect over space.

When modern physics, however, examined the atom at

very close range, it discovered that the atom evaporates. It appears to be more like *energy*. We think of an atom like a thing, but it's really more like an *event*. It further appears that atom-events can have an instantaneous connection with one another, as if there were no time or space between them. This seemingly impossible connection also holds for the mind that observes them. Atomic energy is so strange it even responds to the consciousness of the observer! The conclusion is that mind and matter make an indivisible, unitary whole. Think about that—mind and matter are one, single, indivisible dance of energy.

Cayce's term for what modern science is coming to accept is *Oneness*. There is *one spirit*, or energy, that unites all of Creation. It permeates everything. It unites all the atoms of the universe. It connects all human beings with one another and with everything else in creation. Although we may appear to one another as separate, disconnected beings, we are each extensions of the Creator's spirit. What happens to one of us touches us all. There is a unified, psychic ecology among all events in creation.

Cayce explained that God created human souls out of the Creator's own being. Each soul is a projection of God, in the same way that our thoughts and images are projections of our mind. Although each soul has its individuality, all souls are of one spirit.

Moreover, each soul reflects the whole of creation. Each soul is a miniature universe, a model of the larger universe. Cayce likened the soul to a drop of water from the ocean. The drop is a miniature ocean with all the ingredients of that ocean. Within each person, therefore, is intimate knowledge of all of creation.

Cayce's statement that each of us is a miniature model of the universe is a restatement of an ancient mystical teaching. It's also becoming a recurrent theme in the *new* science. The modern jargon states that creation is *holonomic*, a term based upon the properties of the laser hologram. It has become a way of thinking about the unity of life. You'll find it discussed in most of the New Age science books.

The development of laser holography has made unity

concepts such as Cayce's teachings concerning oneness more vital and exciting, while less philosophical or mystical. Unity is real, even if still hard to grasp or believe.

When you aim a laser beam at a holographic plate, the beam bounces off the plate and projects a three-dimensional picture into space. You can walk about this picture and see the object from all sides—it looks solid and real.

The holonomic property of the holograph becomes evident when you take the plate and break it into many small pieces. Even the smallest piece will still re-create the entire three-dimensional picture in space! In some mysterious fashion, every tiny piece of the holographic plate contains the entire picture!

In Cayce's language, a soul is a piece of the complete holograph we call creation, or God. Each soul has knowledge of the whole. That's why, Cayce explained, being psychic is an inherent, natural attribute of the soul. Intuition draws upon this universal knowledge that is psychically available to the soul.

The Superconscious Mind

Obviously, from this description of the soul, our minds must be more than what appears to consciousness. In Cayce's model of the mind, the conscious mind is the lowest form of mind. It has the sharp sensory focus for detail, like a mouse, but lacks the farseeing vision of the eagle. The mind does have its eagle, though. It's not the conscious mind, but what Cayce called the superconscious mind.

Cayce once had a dream where he saw the mind pictured as a funnel. Its open end descended from infinity and stretched down to form a separate little mind (see Figure 1). The little mind is the conscious mind, what a soul uses to focus on physical reality. In another instance, he envisioned the mind as a multi-pointed star, each arm of the star being a funnel growing out of the universal mind to become the tip of a soul's conscious mind (see Figure 2).

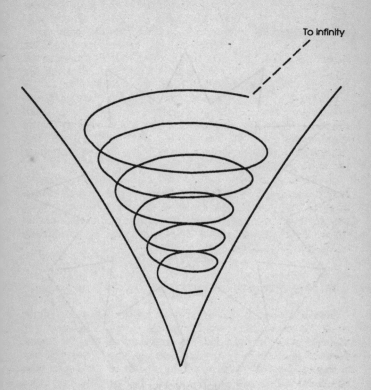

To Infinity

An Image of the Mind
from Cayce's Dream

Figure 1

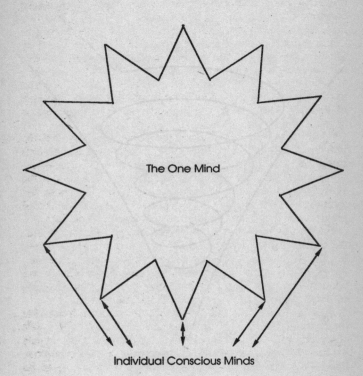

The One Mind

Individual Conscious Minds

The Relation between Individual
Conscious Minds and the One Mind

Figure 2

Cayce's vision of the mind has some startling features. First, there is *only one mind*. This single, living reality is a universal mind that we all have in common. It's a hard concept to grasp. The modern terminology calls the mind *transpersonal*. That means that except for your conscious mind, mind is not a personal thing, but something shared by all. Mind is like the air we share. Although we each have our separate lungs to touch that air, there's only one air.

Second, this mind remembers everything. Cayce referred to this aspect of the mind as the Akashic Record, or the Hall of Records. Everything that humanity has ever experienced is imprinted on the Akashic Record.

Third, between the level of the universal mind and the individual conscious mind lies the region of the subconscious mind. We each have our own portion of the subconscious mind, but there are no boundaries in the region of the subconscious mind. All subconscious minds, of both the living and the dead, are in contact with one another. We'll learn more about the implications of that startling fact.

Fourth, as important as it is for dealing with the world, the conscious mind is only the very tip of the whole mind. It's highly focused and specializes in sensations concerning the physical world. The conscious mind has a very sharp boundary around itself. Through the conscious mind, each of us appears distinctly separate from one another.

Finally, these different levels of the mind each provide their own channels of information (see Figure 3). The conscious mind is a channel of sensory information. It gets its knowledge from outside the person. The subconscious mind is a channel of telepathic information. It gets its information from other people's thoughts and experiences. The superconscious mind is a channel of clairvoyance, or universal knowledge. It gets its information directly from the oneness of all life.

Intuition is a *super*-channel, taking advantage of information coming through all the other channels. When intuition uses the imagination as its vehicle of expression, it will speak through visions and symbolic impressions. When it uses feelings and the emotions, it will speak through urges

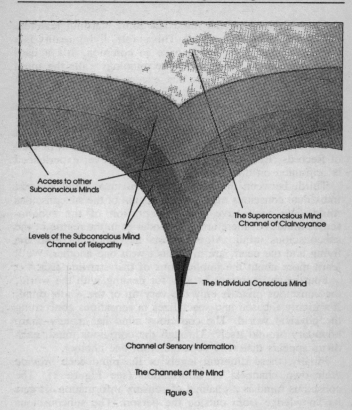

Access to other
Subconscious Minds

The Superconcsious Mind
Channel of Clairvoyance

Levels of the Subconscious Mind
Channel of Telepathy

The Individual Conscious Mind

Channel of Sensory Information

The Channels of the Mind

Figure 3

or promptings. When it uses thoughts, it may speak through a voice that we hear inside us.

As we explore ways we can channel psychic information, inspiration, wisdom, and guidance, we'll refer to this basic vision of the mind. From these basic premises about the mind, Cayce has provided a way for us to understand what can be both intriguing as well as confusing about the channeling phenomenon.

Developing Intuition

For most of us, our intuitive experiences have come unbidden. They have been unexpected and spontaneous. Cayce encourages us, however, to learn to develop our intuitive capacity. To do so, he would suggest we remember these major principles:

1) Intuition exists through our essential oneness with creation. As you become consciously one with life, you become more consciously intuitive.

2) Intuition arises from our sympathetic attunement with the object of our intuition. Empathy is a form of attunement. Love is the highest form of attunement.

3) A need to know something, usually for protection or guidance, stimulates intuition.

4) Intuitive knowledge comes from within. Look within for intuition.

5) Intuition requires an acceptance of what spontaneously comes from within. It's usually our very first thought, feeling, or image.

6) Genuine intuitions are consistent with our highest values or ideals.

7) The best way to honor our intuitions is to act on them.

Cayce bases his approach to developing intuition upon this sequence: *need, attunement, and application.* Intuitions come to guide us. There needs to be something we can do with the information for intuition to deliver it. Putting the intuitive information into service, applying it, is an important part of the process of developing intuitive awareness.

Imagine that your channel of intuition is like a lightning rod. The lightning up in the sky is the infinite intelligence, the energy that seeks expression when it's needed. You want to bring the lightning down from the sky. If you don't provide a ground, however, a connection with the earth, the lightning won't come down your channel. Being prepared to put intuitions into service provides the necessary grounding.

Spend Time in Nature

Cayce often suggested that to begin to develop intuition, spend time in nature. It's an excellent method for cultivating the experience of oneness with life. Nature has a time-honored history of elevating people's consciousness to an awareness of God and of their relationship to all life. In surveys of spontaneous religious experiences, nature ranks as the number one temple where such revelations occur.

In her book, *Ecstasy*, Marghanita Laski provides many examples of personal accounts of special experiences induced by nature. In one case, a young woman in a state of deep depression pulled off the road to rest at a picnic site. When she got out of her car a blue jay flew down right in front of her. With its insistent calls it got her attention. When the woman noticed it, the blue jay starting hopping away, stopping, looking back, as if it wanted the woman to follow. She did and she followed the bird quite a way into a clearing that revealed a beautiful view of Mount Hood. The sight of the snow-covered mountain struck a chord with the woman and she felt somehow comforted. She broke into tears and soon she had flushed her depression out of her system. Then she heard the blue jay calling again. Once again she followed the bird. It led her back to her car. She drove away a different woman.

This woman's story reflects one of those old phrases describing intuition: "A little bird told me." Birds are a common symbol of telepathic and intuitive messages. Birds are expressive of the soul's spirit. In the Bible the Holy Spirit appears as a dove. In pictures of other religions' symbolism they often sit on top of a tree, the place of superconscious awareness (see Figure 4). The symbolism of birds is but one of many examples of humanity's intuitive awareness of the channels of communication between nature and human beings.

Ron Carey is the channel of *The Starseed Transmissions* and *Return of the Bird Tribes*. He tells an interesting story of

Aztec Tree of Life (Corn Plant):
Bird (Higher Self) Sits on Top

Figure 4

how he became a channel for this inspirational source of intelligence. He moved his family out to live in nature for seven years. While living in harmony with the elements, and with no television or newspapers for distraction, Carey became more sensitive to nature's vibrations. His intuitive resonance with nature grew into communion with higher levels of intelligence. Waves of knowing came over him and he allowed those feelings to blossom spontaneously into words. He thus became a channel of what he calls intuitively received transmissions.

Intuition Is Empathy

The description of Ron Carey's experience contains some of the words expressive of Cayce's concept of oneness: harmony, resonance, and communion. Cayce taught that intuition, as well as psychic ability, operates through such expressions of oneness. Intuition is not knowing through the senses or analysis, but through the *sympathetic vibrations of empathy*.

The word Cayce most often used was *attunement*. When we attune to something we become one with it. Through an affinity of sympathetic vibrations, we resonate with the knowledge we wish to obtain. The knowledge becomes us.

What is an intuitive understanding of a rose? You can look at the rose, observe its parts and analyze them. That will give you an objective understanding. If you meditate on the rose, you can empathically merge with it to become a rose yourself. You will begin to feel as a rose feels. From within yourself, imagery will arise that expresses your affinity with the rose. Thus you will come to know the rose intuitively.

Questions also have their own vibrations and contain the seeds of their own answers. You too will learn that when you pose a question to yourself, you can become aware of an answer that intuitively presents itself from within. As Cayce reminded us, "Ask and you will receive." Develop asking into the art of attunement, of empathy with your core being, and you'll learn that the answer is a spontaneous response that happens within.

Hearing Voices

Socrates, the ancient Greek philosopher, had a voice that spoke to him. He called it his Daimon, a divine voice. He noted that it never told him what to do, but often warned him against doing something that he was about to do. He learned to pay attention to its warnings.

Intuitions often come as feelings. Sometimes they come as voices. Among her documented cases, Dr. Bartlett tells of a woman who heard such a voice. She was driving a car when she heard a loud, male voice yell in her ear, "Stop!" She was so startled she slammed on the brakes. She found herself at an intersection. Although the light was green for her, just then a car running a red light sped across her path.

Pat Rodergast is a channel for a source that calls itself Emmanuel. She describes the experience as somewhat like intuition, an inner knowing. She remains in a normal state of consciousness. She turns within and she hears the voice of Emmanuel speaking.

Hearing voices sounds like something that happens to the mentally ill. It's true that some people do suffer from psychological disorders that involve hearing voices. Hearing voices, however, doesn't necessarily mean a mental disturbance. We might say there are good voices and bad voices.

In his book *The Natural Depth in Man*, Wilson Van Dusen shared his experience counseling people in mental hospitals who suffered from hearing voices. These people reported hearing different voices, voices that spoke with different tones and spoke different things. There were voices that were highly critical and said terrible things. He coached the person to speak back to those voices, to tell them to stop. They also heard voices that spoke kind words and had encouraging things to say. He helped the person to learn how to listen to those voices. These inner helpers could offer advice about the person's recovery. As mental health returned, the bad voices went away, but the good voices remained as helpers and guides.

Hearing voices can be a symptom of madness or a channel of intuition. Cayce indicated that a person who hears voices may be closer to the universal than the person who stands by to comment, yet through imbalances the voices are not helpful. Here is but one of several examples we'll see in this book concerning some "good news" and some "bad news" about channeling.

Exploring the range of channels available to us puts us at risk. We can gain from learning to become active channels, but we'll also confront dangers as well. Here is where Cayce's perspective proves to be quite helpful. He teaches us to anchor our channeling in ideals and purposes. We will learn that by basing our explorations upon a standard of excellence, an ideal, we direct the receptivity of our channel. By having some purpose focused on serving a real need, we direct the active part of our channel in a constructive manner.

We'll learn that the subconscious mind is like a strong crosscurrent that we have to swim through as we reach upward to the superconscious mind. Whenever dealing with the subsconscious mind, be prepared for both "good news and bad news." Ideals and purposes help us filter what the crosscurrents of the subconscious bring us. They also help us to reach the superconscious mind of our higher self. Our ideals help us attune to the highest source of guidance.

Learning to Listen to the Still, Small Voice

When the Society of Friends gather for their religious service, they sit in silence. There is no one singled out as the minister who delivers a sermon. Instead, all meditate and wait upon the *still, small voice* within. As a person feels prompted by that voice, that person speaks it aloud. Sitting together, sharing with one another messages from the still voice from within, the Quakers find the spiritual communion they value.

Cayce gave us a way to introduce ourselves to the still, small voice within, a term he identified with intuition. Cayce's method is learning by doing, making practical use of intuition even as we learn to recognize its voice. You'll learn how to enlist the aid of intuition in making decisions while learning how you personally experience intuition operating within you.

Begin with a difficult decision you have to make. Think through the alternatives, consider your values and purposes, and make your best decision. Make a tentative commitment to follow through on that decision. Making that commitment is necessary to arouse your entire being in the contemplation of that decision. Hypothetical thoughts don't excite the intuitive faculty, for it's of a more practical bent.

Cayce suggests that you next sit down and get as quiet as possible within yourself. This step is the attunement. Focus on the feelings evoked by your highest values and your ideals. When you are in the frame of mind that is resonating with your ideals, ask yourself if your decision is a good one. There will be a response to that question within you, a "Yes" or a "No." That response is the voice of intuition. You may experience it as a voice or as a feeling or as a thought.

An answer will be there. It's usually the very first thing that comes to mind.

Learning to Trust Intuition

Accepting the first thing that comes to mind is often one of the hardest aspects of learning intuition. It involves trust. It involves acceptance of one's natural, spontaneous impulses. Most of us have trouble with that level of trust and self-acceptance. One of the reasons working with intuition pays spiritual dividends is that it forces you to work on the issue of self-trust. It requires you to make contact with that part of you that is trustworthy.

Suppose I have a question that I need answered. I try to notice what's the first thought to come to my mind. That will be the intuitive answer. I find, however, that I can't even tell what the first thing is. As soon as anything comes into mind, I react to it, I evaluate it, and I judge it. I do that so fast, I can't even find the original thought anymore.

Those evaluations and reactions are the functioning of the logical, rational mind. They jump on and modify the intuitive response so quickly it's hard to catch the intuition in its raw form.

Part of learning to trust intuition is learning to accept your first response and save the evaluation for later. One way to learn to identify your first, spontaneous response is that it is unpredictable. That's what makes it individual, unique to you, and special. Your other responses are much more of a habitual nature. They are more predictable. Unlike intuition, the voice of conscience can be predictable. If you're not surprised when your conscience bothers you, it's not likely to be your intuitive conscience. When your conscience surprises you with its interjected remark, it's more likely to be the intuitive dimension to your conscience and not simply habits of evaluation. The intuitive conscience is like a loving friend because rather than simply criticize or condemn you, it sees your underlying motives and helps you face yourself. Better pay attention!

The Guardian Angel

Intuition guides and guards us. It inspires us. It brings us experiences of spiritual meaning. Sometimes it speaks to us as an inner voice, sometimes it creates feelings or desires within us. Sometimes it simply nudges us and guides us without our awareness. Its promptings are both subtle and loud. It is one face of the higher self.

Intuition performs all the services we might expect of the guardian angel. Cayce indicated, in fact, that within each of us is a guardian angel.

Cayce explained that our guardian angel resides where

our portion of the superconscious mind becomes the one, universal mind. Cayce described the guardian angel as that part of us that hasn't forgotten our oneness with God and knows of no separation from God. The guardian angel thus has no free will of its own, but serves only the will of God.

The actions of our intuition aren't the response of our free will. They are involuntary, spontaneous responses of our guardian angel, drawing us ever closer to the experience of oneness. Our guardian angel part of ourselves is one of the images we can have for the term "our higher self."

By day, when we are awake, we experience our guardian angel through intuition. By night, when we sleep, Cayce indicates that we drop the consciousness of separation and attune more to the consciousness natural to the guardian angel state. In sleep, we become pure intuition. Out of that state of consciousness, we give birth to dreams, a nightly channel of the higher self.

CHAPTER THREE

Dreams:
The Nightly Channel of the Higher Self

"Forget not that . . . the Creator, the gods and the God of the Universe, speak to man through his individual self. Man approaches the more intimate conditions of that field of the inner self when the conscious self is at rest in sleep or slumber, at which time more of the inner forces are taken into consideration and studied by the individual. . . . It is each individual's job . . . to understand his individual condition, his individual position in relation to others, his individual manifestation, through his individual receiving of messages from the higher forces themselves, thus, through dreams."

—Edgar Cayce, 3744–4

"Dreams which come to a body are of a different nature and character, dependent upon the channel through which these are brought to the physical consciousness."

—Edgar Cayce, 903–5

On June 10, 1976, I recorded the following dream in my journal: "I am watching the building of the pyramids.

Someone is showing me the secret of their construction. There is an empty box-shaped form made of heavy, stiff paper. It sits right in the place of the next stone. Someone places bits of porous rocks into this paper form. The person adds water and the mixture turns to concrete. It has become the next stone, perfectly shaped and sized. The old mystery of the pyramids vanishes—there were no weighty stones to carry or carve.''

More than eight years later, in the November/December 1984 issue of *Equinox*, there appeared a report on the work of the French chemist, Joseph Davidovits. He had developed a ''geopolymerized limestone cement,'' a man-made material that closely resembles quarried rock. The Egyptians had readily available the ingredients necessary to make this type of cement. Davidovits proposed that they could have easily cast the pyramid stones right in place. Analyzing actual pyramid stones, he found them to have a lighter density than natural, quarried stone, but of the same substance as the synthetic stone he produced in his laboratory. They contained elements that aren't in natural rock. He also found traces of human hair and organic fibers within the pyramid stones, which would seem possible only in cast stones.

What about my dream? Was I peering back into the lost secrets of the Egyptians or was I foreseeing an intriguing scientific discovery? Edgar Cayce sometimes delved into the ancient past as well as provided prophecies of the future. My unusual dream had to have been performing one of these two feats of channeling.

Cayce showed that dreams are perhaps the most profound channels available to the average person. In his book, *Dreams: Tonight's Answers for Tomorrow's Questions*, Mark Thurston explains six ways that Cayce demonstrated dreams function as a channel. (1) They are themselves real experiences in the spiritual dimension. (2) They provide ''readings'' on our current life. (3) They provide us with a way to contact God. (4) They are inspirational, teaching us lessons. (5) They are creative, presenting solutions to problems. (6) They are psychic, seeing into the future.

Extraordinary dreams, in fact, are often people's first encounter with something suggesting the existence of a larger intelligence at work within the mind.

Dreams as a Channel of Psychic Experiences

If you have ever had an ESP experience, the chances are it happened in a dream. Ian Stevenson, of the University of Virginia, presents in *Telepathic Impressions* a careful study of 9,300 documented cases of psychic experiences. He tabulated that 57 percent of these ESP events occurred in dreams. Dreams are clearly a channel of psychic awareness.

Many people have had a dream that came true. A survey conducted through *Psychology Today* (March 1978) found that 8 percent of the population—over two million Americans—have had dreams that foretold, in explicit detail, of an event that later happened. Cayce revealed, in fact, that *anything of importance* that would ever happen to us we would first preview in a dream. Dreams are a channel by which we obtain important information about the future.

Many such dreams provide important warnings. In *New World of the Mind*, for example, Dr. J. B. Rhine details many substantiated cases of dreams that saved lives. In one instance, a woman dreamed that a palm tree fell on her son's tent. It was during World War II and her son was in the Pacific Islands. She awakened frightened, calling his name out loud. At the same time that she had this dream, her son was sleeping in a tent. He awakened at what he thought was his mother's voice calling to him. He walked out of his tent and looked around. As he did so, a palm tree fell on his tent and crushed his cot.

I have a friend whose dream saved her from being confronted by a burglar in her home. During an afternoon nap on her living room couch she dreamed of a man who crawled in the window of her house. He stood in front of her as she lay there. She took one look at him and woke up. The dream made her nervous so she decided to spend the night with friends. When she returned home the next day, it had been burglarized—the robber coming through the same window as in her dream! The police apprehended the man, who had committed several robberies and rapes. When she went to identify her property, she recognized the man the police had arrested as the man in her dream, dressed in the very same clothing.

Dreams: The Health Care Channel

Dreams are also an important channel of preventive health care and healing. While we sleep, our own inner physician is always in attendance. Dreams have warned people of a developing illness within the body, given advice about treating health problems, and even provided direct healing services.

In Ancient Greece there were temples devoted to the god, Asklepios, who healed people there while they slept. A patient would make a pilgrimage to an Asklepian temple and spend a night sleeping there. In the morning the patient would awaken with a memory of a strange event. During the night, Asklepios himself, or one of his animal spirit helpers—a dog or a snake—visited the person in the temple and performed an operation. Sometimes Asklepios touched the person, the snake bit the infected area, or the dog licked the wound. The experience seemed real, the person felt awake. Was it real or was it a dream? The strangeness of the event suggested that it was a dream. Whatever the nature of the visionary experience, however, what was remarkable was that upon awakening, the medical problem was healed!

In Asklepios's temple medicine, therefore, the dream itself was the healing factor. As the years went by, however, temple medicine lost some of its power. Visionary dreams that provided direct and immediate healing became rare. Instead, people would experience more ordinary dreams that required interpretation. A temple attendant would interpret the dream to devise an approach to treating the person's illness. As diagnostic and prescriptive aids, the dreams were still valuable but no longer healing experiences themselves.

The mystery remains alive, however. In response to an inquiry about inspiring dreams, I received a letter from Calvin Hall, an eminent dream researcher at the University of California, Santa Cruz. He told me that he once had visited Carl Meier, the Swiss psychiatrist whose book, *Ancient Incubation*, documented the Asklepios's temple medicine. Dr. Hall admitted that he was quite skeptical about the possibility of healing in dreams. Soon after his visit, however, he dreamed that a dog bit his shoulder. When he awakened, he noticed that his shoulder, normally stiff in pain from chronic bursitis, no longer ached. He said it never bothered him again. He remained a skeptic but was glad to be free of the pain.

We know today from research that the mind can affect the body, especially through imagery. Perhaps a particularly powerful dream could have a healing effect. Ernest Rossi, in his book, *The Psychobiology of Mind-Body Healing*, outlines the evidence showing that during the dream state the body is receptive to new programming. The synthesis of new DNA molecules while dreaming could spark a reversal in a disease process. We may soon see a revival in temple medicine.

In the meantime, dreams are valuable for their advice on health matters. Cayce himself was quite accurate in his physical medical diagnoses. He claimed we could all do as well ourselves by studying our own dreams. Many of the dreams he interpreted for others gave evidence of providing information on the health and functioning of the dreamer's body. Joan Windsor, a professional counselor and psychic, tells in her book, *The Inner Eye: Your Dreams Can Make You Psychic*, how a dream suggested an alternative to surgery for treating a cyst. As a result of this dream, she became acquainted with the Cayce readings and worked further with her dreams to develop psychic counseling abilities. Her book contains many examples of people receiving medical guidance from their dreams.

Dreams as a Channel of Many Mysteries

Name any psychic ability and it's easy to find someone who's channeled that ability in a dream. The reference books I've mentioned contain many examples. For any other profound ability that you might associate with being a channel, you can find an example in *Our Dreaming Mind: History and Psychology*, by Bob Van de Castle, of the University of Virginia Medical School. This book is an encyclopedia of documented cases of wondrous dreams that have shaped the course of history.

Religious experience is a prime example. All the major religions have been born or prefigured in dreams. There were dreams that alerted the wise men, as well as Mary and Joseph, about the birth of Jesus. The mother of Buddha learned in a dream about the significance of the son she was to bear. Mohammed had his experience of religious calling in a dream. Since the beginning of recorded history, people have had a glimpse of the spiritual nature of reality through dreams. The Bible is full of examples of God talking to people in their dreams.

Creative inspirations are another example. Dreams have provided the basis of works of art, literature, and poetry. Musicians have dreamed music that was ready for them to transcribe upon awakening. Dreams were also the channel of many scientific discoveries and technological inventions. Even politics has its history of influential dreams!

Psychic, religious, or inspirational dreams happen to more than just illustrious individuals of the distant past. Edgar Cayce interpreted hundreds of dreams of ordinary people. The dreams and his interpretations form a two-volume collection, *Dreams and Dreaming*. Many of them show the same kind of extraordinary channeling as in history's influential dreams.

Cayce makes clear that only some dreams are *spaghetti dreams*, caused by indigestion, and other trivial sources of stimulation. He granted that some dreams were the result of unintentional suggestions from the conscious self to the subconscious mind. Also, many dreams express the subconscious fears and wishes of the dreamer. He noted, however, that remembered or not, every night we also have dreams coming from the superconscious mind. They're the work of the higher self.

Meeting the Higher Self

Have you ever had a dream where you encountered someone with magical powers, someone who seemed especially wise, a teacher? Such people may be symbolic representatives of your higher self. I'll always remember my first dream encounter with my higher self.

In my dream I'm camping in a sacred forest sanctuary and am standing face-to-face with the sanctuary's caretaker. He is a rather plain-looking old man, but I feel his presence as a powerful energy. I feel very fortunate to be with him on this land.

I notice nearby an empty bottle of wine. I realize there's a drunkard sneaking into the sanctuary to have his drinks. I point out my discovery to the caretaker. I am very righteous and indignant. I say, "We must find him and get rid of him. We cannot allow such a person on such holy grounds."

In response to my outburst, the old man says, "Henry, I know that fellow. I have invited him here. He is my guest. In fact, he has been here much longer than you. It is I who put that wine there—to lure him in so that I might feed him."

The old man's statement puzzles me. What is he doing encouraging a drunkard to drink? I look to the old man for an explanation. His eyes meet mine and he seems to know me to the very depths of my soul. I experienced through his eyes my judgmentalness and my criticalness of the drunkard. I felt very ashamed to have these feelings be so obvious. Who was I to condemn the drunkard? Obviously the old wise man loved him and cared for him. But what was his plan, what was the purpose in encouraging this fellow to drink?

The dream hit home. With my own first drink at age eighteen, I became an alcoholic. I had been drinking steadily for several years by the time of this dream. I had climbed on and fallen off the wagon many times and tormented myself with guilt. The effect of my encounter with the old man, however, was to create a drastic revision in my attitude toward my alcoholism. I couldn't understand what the purpose of this disease might be. I could, however, try to adopt the same compassionate attitude toward it that the old man had shown toward the drunkard. The purpose became evident later.

I didn't know it at the time, but such can be the impact of an encounter with the higher self. It leads the dreamer through surprising turns into a deeper understanding of the meaning of one's problems.

Who is the Higher Self?

The old man in my dream proved to be but one face of my higher self. This same source of wisdom, guidance, and spiritual values has appeared as a Native American medicine man, a Zen master, a doctor, a teacher, a gardener, or a valued friend. The higher self appears in many guises. It's something from within me that has an attitude, a wisdom, and a knowledge much broader and transcending that of my conscious ego. It understands that there is a purpose in all things. While we hate obstacles, criticize our failures, and deplore our weaknesses, the higher self views all these experiences as opportunities for growth and learning.

The more I worked with my dreams, the more I came to realize there was a larger intelligence at work directing my life. It's as if I am the driver of a car, but not its owner. At any time, however, I may hear a voice behind me declare, "Turn right here, Henry!" Such moments remind me that I am really only the chauffeur. Although I have to steer and brake the car, the true master of the vehicle is sitting in the backseat. The identity of the higher self is one of those mysteries that keeps us searching.

The psychiatrist Carl Jung studied the world's religions and mythologies, as well as the dreams and visions of many people. He found it's a universal pattern of human experience to encounter within a wiser part of ourselves. This larger *Self*, as he termed it, appeared as many different symbols. It could be a person or an abstract symbol. The most common abstraction is the circle, representing wholeness, and the cross, representing the conscious awareness of that wholeness. Jung argued, much like Cayce, that the cross points to the Christ Consciousness as the ultimate symbol of the higher self. It represents the conscious integration of a physical and a spiritual life into one being. It's the self-realization of the divinity of God that lives within us.

For Cayce, the higher self is like the seeing eye of the soul. The higher self is the soul's awareness of itself, that the soul is our true identity. Mark Thurston, a scholar of the Cayce readings, explained to me that he sees the soul as like the total house, the person's complete life. The higher self inhabits the house. The higher self knows the whole person—body, mind, and spirit—not simply what the ego thinks of itself.

Though the ego has the use of the conscious mind, the higher self has access to the subconscious and the super-conscious mind. Cayce's explanation of what happens in dreams suggests that whether or not the higher self makes a specific appearance, it's at work in many of them.

Cayce Explanation of the Dream

What is a dream? How can dreams be such a superior source of infinite intelligence, of wisdom, of creativity, and of other powers? If not from our own mind, where do dreams come from?

Cayce has answers to these questions. His view of what

happens as we fall asleep, and the nature of the dream, is quite intriguing.

Cayce explains that as we fall asleep, our body relaxes and our conscious mind dissolves. The sensory information the conscious mind relies upon to stay awake becomes muted. As the conscious mind dims, the subconscious merges to take its place and we become lost in our thoughts.

Drifting, dissolving, falling—these words picture something of what happens to the conscious mind as we enter sleep. Imagine a drop of water falling back into the ocean to become absorbed in the immense waters. Thus Cayce describes sleep as the shadow of death. It's a preview of what death is like.

As we fall asleep, our intuition, our sixth sense, not only remains awake but also becomes more expansive. Our entire body, our whole being, begins to function as an ear that listens intuitively. We merge with creation and resonate with all that we hear. There is no awareness of a separate self. There is simply being—deep, silent sleep, pure intuition, pure psychic oneness.

Try imagining what it's like to be in deep, dreamless sleep. If you dissolve into the universe, how do you come back in the morning as yourself? Fortunately, it's in this deep sleep that we are most closely attuned with our guardian angel consciousness. It guards us while we are asleep, protecting the pattern of our individuality. It "beams" us back to ourselves intact.

Out of that dark and deep sleep of pure intuitive being, our soul awakens. That part of our being that knows itself as an individual and yet is aware of its connection with its creator wakes up and looks upon our lives. It takes stock of what it surveys from the perspective of its superconscious awareness.

Although we ordinarily evaluate our lives by our hopes and fears, the soul evaluates our experiences from another vantage point. Its ideals, its memories of previous lives, of experiences and lessons learned, and its purposes for this lifetime in this body and personality shapes the soul's

Deep Asleep, Merged with Life.
Artist, James Yax

Figure 5

examination. The soul compares what we are experiencing in life to its expanded awareness.

It's somewhat like what happens when we watch a movie: We see the characters go through their drama, but we are aware of more than they are. We know who might be around the bend, we know where something might lead. Though the characters in the movie are relatively unaware of what we see, we experience their situation from our broader perspective. That's what it's like for the soul when it surveys our life.

The experience the soul has while we are asleep we remember as a dream. When we awaken, what we remember is the dream, not the *aha* or the *uh oh* that the soul experienced. The soul experiences a *goodness gracious*, the subconscious mind mirrors that experience symbolically, and what we remember we call the dream.

Whether or not our dreams reflect clearly the soul's experience depends upon the level of our personal development. Cayce guaranteed that the more we work on ourselves, the more we try to contact and cooperate with the soul level of our being by living according to an ideal, the clearer our dreams become.

Cayce's description of the role of our soul in dreams explains why dreams are such a far-reaching channel of intelligence and inspiration. Our soul has access to the superconscious mind, where all knowledge is available. The soul exists in the dimension of eternity, where time and space does not exist. Thus it shouldn't surprise us that often in dreams we find residues or footprints left behind that are clues to another order of reality.

In one of his most surprising statements about dreams, Cayce said that anything we might wish to know or experience we can safely obtain through dreams. We can safely experience what it's like after death. We can examine conditions on another planet. We can explore the superconscious mind. We can preview future events or learn our soul's intentions and purposes. Any other method of channeling the secrets of the universe contains risks, but dreams do not.

Cayce noted that we do not have to wait to have a dream help us. We can actively seek out a dream to help us with a particular purpose. Having a purpose for dreaming, in fact, is an excellent way to learn to understand the dreams that come.

Dream Incubation: Opening the Channel

My dream of the old man and the drunkard's wine led to my recovery from the active stage of alcoholism. It also led to the rediscovery of the mystery of dream incubation. I tell the entire story in my book, *Getting Help From Your Dreams*. Here I'm describing enough to help you understand how it's still possible to channel powerful visionary dreams.

Cayce suggests we can actively seek helpful dreams. I found Asklepian dream temple medicine as certainly a case in point. I also found several other examples of *incubation*, or the ritual of seeking a dream of divine origins. The Native Americans have their vision quests. Their youths go out to a certain spot to seek a vision giving them their mission in life. Dream incubation still exists among the Moroccan Jews. They make yearly pilgrimages to the shrine of a Jewish saint, or *saddiq*, Rabbi Shimeon Bar-Yohai. Many report being visited by Rabbi Shimeon in a visionary dream.

What these rituals have in common are two symbols. The first is the special place—the sanctuary or shrine. The second is the benefactor—the spirit or god. The special place induces a feeling of reverence, it evokes our highest ideals. We enter a specially receptive state of consciousness. We feel protected and can open ourselves up to a special receptivity. In the sanctuary we hope to encounter a revered presence. We await the benefactor, the source of the cure, the wisdom, the inspiration—in effect, the higher self. The universal pattern of dream incubation reflects Cayce's model of channeling the higher self (see Figure 6).

As a research project, I devised a modernized ritual of dream incubation. I performed this research for several

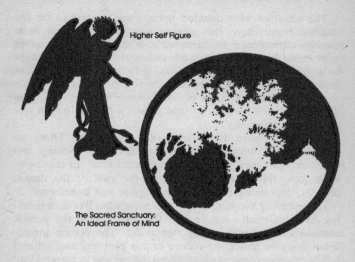

Higher Self Figure

The Sacred Sanctuary:
An Ideal Frame of Mind

Dream Incubation as a Model of Channeling

Figure 6

years at the A.R.E.'s summer camp in the mountains of southwestern Virginia. I used the two symbols to re-create a frame of mind among modern dreamers similar to what might have existed among pilgrims to the ancient incubation sites.

I used a round, dome-shaped tent to serve as a "blank slate" around which the dreamer created a sanctuary. The person decorated it to resemble their own special place. It could be a nature shrine, whether a mountaintop, an ocean or riverside scene, perhaps a cave. It was the spot the person imagined being the most sacred, powerful place possible. The person spent an entire day in isolation within the imagined sacred space, thinking about the purpose for incubating a dream.

The dreamer also decided upon some person to be the awaited benefactor. This person was someone who most closely represented the dreamer's highest ideal, someone who could bring the needed assistance. This person might be a historical figure like Jesus, a fictional character like Superman, or a special person from a previous dream. It was to serve as a symbol of the dreamer's higher self. The dreamer created a mask of that person's face to use in our incubation ceremony.

At dusk I joined the dreamer in the sanctuary. There we enacted a visionary drama on the theme of seeking and receiving guidance from a revered benefactor. In this symbolic skit, the person played both the role of the dream pilgrim, and using the mask, the higher self benefactor.

Role playing the higher self was somewhat like a channeling exercise itself. Acting like the higher self, the person assumed a wise and loving mental set. The person improvised insights about the nature of the problem and offered helpful encouragement. It required the person to pretend and use imagination, yet it provided genuine inspirations. This exercise, by the way, is the first of several you will find in this book as you learn more about the value of role playing and the imagination as a form of channeling.

The ceremony concluded with the person making a commitment to carry out some part of the advice that came through the higher self character. This promise was to demonstrate sincerity of purpose in trying to solve the problem. It also honors Cayce's wisdom that the intention to apply what you already know is the seed of further inspiration.

It was now time for the person to go to sleep. Dreams grow from what is on the mind while falling asleep, so I helped the person maintain the desired focus with presleep suggestions. The person imagined being asleep in the sacred sanctuary and that the benefactor was nearby. The person imagined awakening in the morning to recall a helpful dream from the benefactor.

The next morning I returned to the tent sanctuary to hear about the dream. I remember, for example, one fellow who was a very bright fourteen-year-old. He found school boring

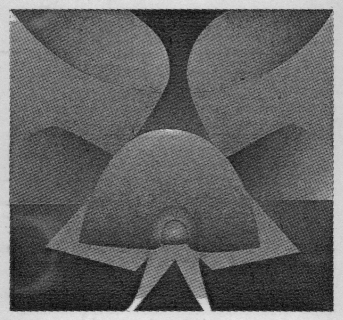

The Dream Tent

Figure 7

and he was an accomplished drug abuser. He came to the dream tent looking for a fresh outlook on life.

In his dream he was walking along a dry and dusty road. Alongside the road there was a deep forest. He decided to leave the road and enter the forest. He soon lost himself in the dense growth. He despaired for a while, then decided to climb a tree. From that height he saw an ax in the distance. He climbed down the tree, got the ax, and cleared a path through the forest.

When we looked at this dream, he felt its meaning was obvious. He found going through life along the road prepared by others was a stale trip. He had been seeking deeper meaning in the use of drugs but lost himself in the forest of the mind. By climbing to a higher perspective, he could look at the world from the viewpoint of his ideals. There he could find the means to discover his own cutting edge, his particular talent, that would help him find his own way.

That fall he successfully arranged, with his parents' support, to create his own curriculum at school. He designed his own program of studies. He left drugs behind. Many years later, he has become a successful theater director and award-winning playwright, writing and directing his own scripts.

This boy's story is more than an example of the success of dream incubation. It's also a testimony to the true value of dreams and speaks to my own history as well. Before I started working with my dreams I felt condemned to choices prepared and packaged by others. Once I began working with my dreams, I had the means to create my own path in life. Dreams help us to become ourselves, to create our own lives.

The dream tent provided many such solutions as this one. Something else happened as well. Several people had experiences during the night reminiscent of the original visionary mystery of dream incubation. These were dreams whose events happened right there in the sanctuary tent itself.

One woman, for example, reported in the morning a very strange experience from her night in the tent. She said that she woke up in the middle of the night and the tent had blown away! A very strong wind was blowing, frightening her. Then she heard a voice call her name. A small, elderly woman sprightly jumped out from behind the bushes, laughing and saying to her, "Let me show you!" She took the girl by the hand and they floated up into the sky. The woman pointed to a giant tablet. The girl saw written upon it all the events of her past lives and of her current life. She saw her future written there, too, but couldn't read what it said. Then she woke up again. The tent was there as it was supposed to be, but a strong wind was blowing.

This woman had a visionary dream of inspiration that

happened right where she slept, as in the visions of Asklepios's temple. Her experience, and others like hers that occurred during this research, demonstrated that the visionary quality of the dream is still quite alive and well. With the proper preparation, dreams continue to be a profound channel of spiritual inspiration.

Preparing to Channel a Dream of Guidance

Most of us do not have the time or desire to endure such an intense dream incubation ritual. There must be an easier way to prepare for channeling dreams of guidance. Many people have since found, in fact, that getting dreams to answer questions can be quite a simple task.

For example, Gayle Delaney, in her book, *Living Your Dreams*, teaches what she calls the "phrase focusing" method. In her effective method, you first write out your feelings about your question, to get all your thoughts out on paper. Then reduce your question to a single phrase that expresses the heart of the matter. Repeat this phrase to yourself as you fall asleep.

One struggling artist asked, "Should I get a job?" He awakened with a dream of seeing an admission ticket to financial security. It cost twenty dollars. He realized that twenty dollars was the price he charged the students who took his art class. Even though the income was sporadic, he decided to stay on his present course.

Delaney gives many other examples in her book to show that it's easy to get dreams to solve problems or present guidance on the question proposed. One benefit of working with this simple method is that you will soon discover that your dreams *do respond* to your questions.

I developed a self-paced program, *The Dream Quest Workbook*, to help people prepare for and work with dreams of guidance. One technique it teaches is the "dream pillow letter." Write a letter to your dreams asking for their advice. In your letter, outline what you already know about the problem, and what you are *going to do* about it. Invite your dreams to show you a better way. Put the letter under your pillow when you go to bed that night. As you fall asleep, imagine yourself following through on your own plan.

I once tested his method among participants attending an A.R.E. conference on the theme of psychic guidance. They submitted a set of questions to two psychics for advice. They also used the pillow letter technique to get for themselves a dream's answer to one of the questions. Afterward, they rated each source of guidance for its helpfulness in answering their questions. Only 40 percent of the participants recalled a dream when we conducted the pillow letter part of the study. Two out of five of these people found the dream they recalled to be at least as helpful as the psychic readings. We didn't expect that dreams would score nearly as high as the professional psychics, but we were surprised at the large proportion of relatively inexperienced people who did find their own dreams to be at least as helpful as the psychics.

With minimal effort, you, too, can channel helpful guidance from your own dreams. Ask of your dreams and you shall receive—at least if you don't forget them.

Learning to Recall Dreams: An Exercise in Channeling

Many people, of course, don't remember their dreams. Like most of us, I remembered more dreams when I was a child than I do as an adult. It took me a lot of effort to learn once again how to remember my dreams. If you don't remember yours, you too can learn how. Learning to recall your dreams can even be a good exercise in developing your channeling ability.

Cayce declared that forgetting dreams is simply a matter of negligence. With sufficient desire and attention devoted to the task, he said, people can remember their dreams. The kind of attention required seems to be the crucial matter.

I followed the usual advice of leaving a pad and pencil beside my bed. With those procedures as my only aid, it took me over three months before I was able to remember a dream! I studied the problem further by examining all the laboratory research on the topic and practiced many techniques. The most important thing I learned is that dreams occur in a particular stage of sleep. When we dream our bodies are paralyzed. Later, every time we move, we erase part of our dream memory. It's therefore important not to move your body when you wake up in the morning until after you've recalled a dream. Then you can roll over and perhaps recall another dream in that posture.

What happens as you lie still in bed, trying to recall a dream, is a good exercise in channeling. Your mind isn't blank, but you have no distinct images, either. There may be some subtle feelings present, and it takes time to allow them to blossom into images or memories. It requires some trust, I've found, some bravado, to simply allow yourself to know what you dreamed. The information is there in how you are feeling, if you will simply let it flow forth. That's what makes it good practice in channeling.

I've found that for many people, it isn't actually the recall process that's difficult, but taking the time in the morning to let the dream memories appear. It requires patience to fish for dream memories, to wait for the feel of the fish's presence, hook it, and bring it to the surface.

If you're serious about learning to remember your dreams, you would do well to conduct this experiment to see if you pass the patience test: Make a commitment to yourself that for one week, every morning when you wake up but before getting out of bed, you'll write a full page of your thoughts. Regardless of whether you believe you remember a dream, write down whatever comes to mind, no matter what it may be. Everyone I know who has completed this test was writing down dreams before the week ended.

This experiment makes sure you are making enough time available for dream recording. It also speaks to the issue of following through, which is important in all forms of channeling. We see it in the dream incubation ritual and the pillow letter method, and it will appear in the other channeling techniques we'll learn in this book. Channeling often does not begin to flow until you are already making active efforts of your own toward the goal you hope to achieve through channeling.

It's also one of Cayce's principles that you need to be ready to apply what you channel before you can expect to channel it. If you want to learn to recall dreams, show that you're prepared to spend the time it takes to write them down.

Channeling Dreams into Action

Edgar Cayce's son, Hugh Lynn, used to say, "The best interpretation of a dream is the one you apply." There is sound wisdom in this provocative statement. It's a rephrasing of what I like to call "Cayce's Law." It states, "In the application comes the awareness." To understand something, act on what you know, and through that experience you'll gain real understanding. Cayce's Law has a surprising implication for dream interpretation.

Cayce was the first person to go on record asserting that anyone can learn to interpret their own dreams. Today there are many fine books available to help you learn this skill. They didn't exist in Cayce's day, but he didn't feel that we really needed them anyway. As Hugh Lynn said, "The best book on dreams is the one you write yourself." He was referring to Edgar Cayce's simple secret to learning to interpret dreams.

First, have a purpose for dreaming and write it down. That in itself will make the rest easier. Second, when you recall a dream, write it down. Third, find something in the dream—*anything*, it doesn't matter—that you think *could* be a clue relative to your purpose for dreaming. Fourth, think of some way to test the validity of that clue, or your understanding of it, by some practical application. In other words, find, or make up, an insight from the dream. Then *do something* constructive about it. Write down the results of your experiment and compare them against your own standards. He promised that if you apply your understanding, no matter how tentative your understanding might be, you'll receive a follow-up dream. It will correct any errors of interpretation. Through this trial-and-error approach your dreams will teach you how to understand them. It's a simple method, yet quite profound in its implications. Our higher self *does* want to cooperate with us if we will but demonstrate our willingness to do our part.

This principle was Cayce's most frequent teaching about seeking guidance. It's also the one too rarely followed. Dreams, as well as any form of channeling, do their best work when we have done our homework and take action to apply our insights.

I had the opportunity to test Cayce's idea with a group of two hundred A.R.E. members who used my *Dream Quest Workbook* for a special experiment. For twenty-eight days, they used this workbook at home and kept a record of some of their daily habits. In particular, they noted whether or not they meditated that day. They recorded whether or not they applied a dream insight that day. They also made careful records of their dreams. They rated how well they recalled them and how clear, or easy to understand, their dreams appeared.

At the end of the month, I received their records and analyzed them statistically. I found, as in earlier research, that when people meditated, their dream recall improved the following day. More to the point, when people applied a dream insight one day, the dream they recalled the next morning was clearer and easier to understand! Dreams do respond to our efforts to understand them. In particular, they respond to our *putting into practice what we think we understand* of them!

Even if you have never recalled a dream, much less tried to interpret one, here is an easy method to get started on the path. It's a method taught the children at A.R.E. camp. First, record your dream. If you don't remember a dream, write down whatever comes to mind when you first wake up. Second, find something in your dream, or in your recorded thoughts, that you can make come true that day. Then *do it*! It can be something very simple. If the color red, for example, appears in your dream, wear something red that day. It's simple as child's play, yet it will lead to something big.

Dreams are experiences of our higher self, creations of our soul. To begin channeling the dream wisdom of our higher self into our lives, there has to be a first step. Doing something in real life on the basis of a dream is a good first step. Bringing something of our inner experience outward into our lives completes a circuit of energy. Learning to complete such circuits is itself part of learning to be a channel.

CHAPTER FOUR

The Creative Channel of the Mind: What We Think, We Become

"How develop the psychic forces? So live in body, in mind, that self may be a channel through which the Creative Forces *may* run. How is the current of life or of modern science used in the commercial world? By preparing a channel through which same may run into, or through, that necessary for the use in the material things. So with the body mentally, physically, spiritually, so make the body, the mind, the spiritual influences, a channel—and the *natural* consequences will be the manifestations."
— **Edgar Cayce, 5752–2**

"As sex is that channel through which creation in the material world brings forth that which is of creating itself, so are the organs of same—the centers through which all creative energies— whether mental or spiritual—find their inception in a material world for an expression."
— **Edgar Cayce, 911–2**

". . . those who consider the manner of being channels through which souls may enter are taking hold upon God-Force itself . . ."
— **Edgar Cayce, 281–55**

If you've ever felt restless, you know it's not a comfortable feeling. It's the experience of energy that you don't know how to channel.

Being a channel is more than being intuitive, psychic, or inspired. It involves receptivity, to be sure, but there's also an active side to being a channel. Besides receiving input, there's also the matter of producing output.

When we feel restless, we fidget and feel uneasy because we've no outlet for our energy.

What's the problem? You don't feel like doing anything in particular, but then again, you don't feel like doing nothing, either. You can't just sit still or relax. Something wants satisfaction, but nothing satisfies.

How does restlessness resolve itself? We imagine various projects, things we might do, should do, could do, perhaps even enjoy doing. Our mind entertains a number of images of activities, sampling the possible experiences. The psychology of restlessness suggests that the energy arises from a desire, but one we can't quite acknowledge. In some cases, for example, we may *feel* like doing one thing, but think we *should* do something else. The stalemate is the experience of restlessness. Gradually, however, as we mull over our options, one thought begins to have some predominance over the others. Soon we find ourselves involved in an activity. Our restlessness has now been absorbed. We've found a way to channel the energy.

We live our lives as channels of energy. Every day we exercise this role. We make choices about how to channel the life force into actions. We work and play, keep house, interact with our friends and associates, amuse ourselves, and deal with emergencies. We do what we have to do and, at other times, think of things to do. There's nothing particularly mysterious about being such channels in everyday life. At least not on the surface.

There are three components of being the channel that we call a human being. On the input side, there's energy. It comes from being alive, the air we breathe, the food we eat. It's the given. By the word, *given*, we stress an important fact: Energy isn't ours to own because it belongs to life itself, but it's ours to use, to channel.

On the output side of this channel, there are the experiences we make for ourselves, our actions or behavior, the things we do. We channel and transform life energy into our physical bodies and the things we do with them.

In the middle, between the input and the output, there's the psychology of the mind. We have ideas about how to spend our energy. We have values about what's worthwhile. We make choices. We exercise our will. With the mind, we shape our channels. With the mind we regulate the incoming energy and focus it toward our choice of outgoing activity.

As simple and familiar as this image of a channel may be, it nevertheless points to a creativity that's basic to our lives. The mystery of life creates us as flesh and blood. In response, we create our human lives and touch the lives of those around us. Cayce would have us understand that as channels of the life energy, we have an important role to play in the ongoing story of creation.

The Formula of Creation: Going Through Channels

A river is a source of energy. The human mind conceives a mill and channels the energy of the moving water to grind grain, saw lumber, or generate electricity.

Electricity is another form of energy. Create the appropriate pattern of parts and the electricity will make a clock keep time. It will allow a television station to transmit sound and pictures to the TV set in your home. It can also electrocute a criminal.

The forces that hold an atom together is another source of energy. Depending upon how you pattern the release of that energy, you can generate enough electricity to power a metropolitan area, or to blow up a piece of the world.

Energy is energy. It's a raw potential. It's a neutral force. How the energy is channeled determines its effect. It's channeled by the patterns through which the energy is applied. Energy combined with a pattern of application creates the effect. This is a basic and familiar process in nature, in engineering, and in our daily lives. Cayce indicated that it's the fundamental process of creation. It originates with the Creator. It's how the Creator, or God, the supreme channeler, created all that exists.

God's love, or Spirit, is the one, single force in the universe. It's the basic energy of creation. There's no other source of energy. To manifest the various forms of nature, God patterned this one energy. A multitude of patterns arose out of the mind of God and channeled that one energy into the forms of nature.

We can appreciate the intricate beauty, the recurrent and interlocking patterns, and the unbelievably intelligent interrelationships among life forms. We've paid tribute to the mind of God as a divine mathematician, divine musician, and divine architect. Even scientists who claim to be atheists must admit that the design of the universe is comparable to a masterful intelligence. Human beings have been able to improve upon nature, perhaps, but only in one small area at a time. These improvements, however, usually prove to create unanticipated side effects down the line. The original design of the universe, whatever its source, managed to embrace all aspects of nature in one interlocking masterpiece. This superior design intelligence is what many people call God the Creator.

Cayce expressed it as this fundamental lesson: "Spirit is the Life, The Mind is the Builder, and the Physical is the Result." It's Cayce's formula for creation and it's the basic process of channeling.

There's perhaps no better way to visualize this formula than in the analogy given by Herbert B. Puryear and Mark Thurston in their book, *Meditation and the Mind of Man*. They explain Cayce's formula by way of reference to a film projector, as shown in Figure 8. The light bulb in the projector is the source of energy. It shines a neutral light and is like spirit. Place film in the projector and the patterns on the film pattern the neutral light, shaping and coloring it.

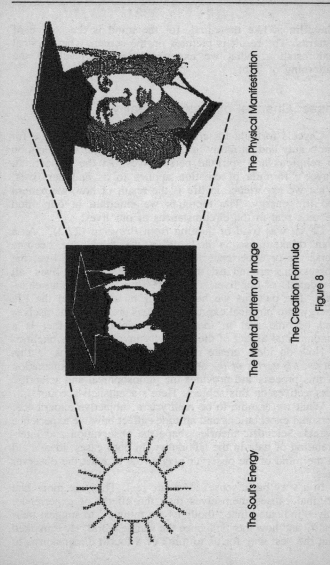

The Physical Manifestation

The Mental Pattern or Image

The Soul's Energy

The Creation Formula

Figure 8

The film is like the mind, for the mind is the source of patterns. The result is pictures on the screen. The physical manifestation, what we experience, is the result of the patterning of light.

Ideas: Channel of Material Reality

Cayce's formula for creation expresses the reverence for the beauty and harmony in God's handiwork that's common to religious and spiritual perspectives. At the same time, Cayce's formula of creation applies to us and our lives. What we experience in life is the result of how we pattern the life energy. The thoughts we entertain in our mind become real in the circumstances of our lives.

Cayce was fond of quoting from *Proverbs* (27:3), "As a man thinketh, so is he." What we think, we become ourselves or experience in our lives. The life we live, the possessions around us, the circumstances of our lives, all the details of our lives, are expressions of our being channels. The patterns we hold in our minds channel the life energy into physical expression. Ideas are real in themselves and become real in the physical world. This fact is a fundamental aspect of the creativity involved in channeling.

How do ideas create reality? My previous book in this series, *Mysteries of the Mind*, explores Cayce's explanation of this process and provides the philosophical and scientific perspectives on this subject. Here's a nutshell account.

What we assume to be reality is a subjective experience. Personal expectations and attitudes affect how we experience events. Scientific theories shape the observation and interpretation of data in the laboratory. In both cases, ideas held in the mind of the observer play a role in what the observer sees.

In a very basic sense, ideas are real. They are more like original causes themselves than the effects of experience. Cayce indicated that "thoughts are things," to suggest their reality and how they influence the visible world. He remarked that the best way for us to think of a fourth dimension is to think of an idea! Others have had similar notions of a fourth dimension.

The psychiatrist Carl Jung, for example, upon observing the dreams of patients and studying the world's mythology and religious literature, concluded that there must exist universal psychic patterns called *archetypes*. He said these archetypes live within a universal mind, or a *collective unconscious*, as he called it. According to Jung, these archetypal patterns govern *both* the forms of nature and the experiences and behaviors of human beings.

The biologist Rupert Sheldrake, in his books, *New Science of Life* and *The Presence of the Past*, argues a similar theme. He presents extensive evidence to show how both the forms and laws of nature are the result of life energy being patterned by invisible force fields. Like ideas existing in another dimension, these *morphogenetic* force fields, as Sheldrake calls them, are the reason a particular plant or animal assumes its given shape and displays its particular characteristics or behavior.

What these influential theories, from a psychiatrist and a biologist, have in common is that they both state that ideas are real in themselves. Ideas exist in another dimension. They're the underlying reality that become the original causes of what we experience in the visible, physical world. Ideas have their effect through their patterns. Ideas create physical reality.

Cayce's notions about the existence of a universal mind, in which ideas, or patterns, govern the visible world, are therefore not that unusual. Intellectual thought is moving in the direction presaged by Cayce's channeled source. His notions, of course, if we're to accept Cayce's own psychic account, came directly from that universal mind, rather than from speculation or observation. Thus Cayce presented the mind's own version of its role in creation. Apparently we should listen to what that mind has to say.

We normally believe that ideas are something that we obtain through experience. Cayce, however, would have us understand that ideas exist in another dimension, that they exist outside of space and time. We tune into ideas. As we tune into an idea, it begins to shape our experience. Every moment of our lives we're acting as channels of energy, shaping events through the ideas we hold.

Cayce's formula for creation was the origination of the now popular New Age slogan, "You create your own reality." This slogan, although it's true, is also misleading. Cayce's statement that mind is the builder means that it is ideas, the patterns in the mind, that create the reality. Ideas don't belong to us but exist within the universal mind. They're not ours to own, or to possess. We can't assume responsibility for the ideas themselves, or their consequences. Instead, our role is to choose which ideas or patterns we will hold within our mind. It's more accurate to say that our choices determine which ideas will create our reality. We're responsible for our choices.

Ideals: In What Spirit Will You Channel?

What ideas will you channel into reality? Because the thoughts that we entertain are so influential in our lives, Cayce would have us consider carefully which thoughts we let grow within us. It's a matter of values. He indicated that it was most important that we establish our concept of the ideal. What is your highest value? What is the ideal by which you wish to steer your life?

To understand Cayce's perspective on ideals, consider Plato's teaching on the subject. To Plato, ideals are the invisible templates, or patterns, that govern the visible forms of nature. Ideals are models of perfection. The visible forms can only approximate the ideals that are generating them, but can never achieve the ultimate perfection of the ideals themselves. A perfect circle is an ideal. All circles in nature approach the ideal, but none are exactly perfect. A perfectly straight line is an ideal. In nature, there are no perfectly straight lines, only approximations. In other words, the search for "the perfect ten," to use a phrase from a popular movie, is a search guided by an ideal, but a search that will find only better and better approximations to that elusive ideal of perfection. The *perfect* "perfect ten," in other words, exists only as an idealized, spirit form in the superconscious region of the mind. We can conceive of some of its qualities, but we can never find it perfectly realized in physical form.

When Cayce asks us to develop a concept of our ideal, he means to formulate our highest value in its most perfect form. It's an exercise in raising your consciousness to the superconscious mind. An ideal is meant to stimulate emulation and guide our actions, but not to hold out hope of perfect success. Navajo rug weavers, for example, although guided by an ideal of perfection in their painstaking work, nevertheless purposefully introduce a flaw into their weavings. They realize that perfection is something that belongs to the gods, not to humans.

Ideals are the parents of ideas. Ideals are unreachable patterns of superconscious perfection. As an ideal filters down into more tangible patterns of the subconscious regions of the mind, it loses some of its ideal qualities in the specifics of the ideas it generates.

Cayce warns us not to confuse ideals with their offspring, ideas. You can tell if you're dealing with an ideal or an idea by whether or not what you're considering is capable of fulfillment. If your highest value can be achieved, it's only an idea and not really an ideal. Some people, for example, have wealth as their highest value. We can achieve wealth. It's not an ideal. Wealth is a specific idea generated by the ideal of infinite resources and the lack of any limitation. Some people have happiness as their highest value. We can achieve happiness, so it's not an ideal. Happiness is a specific idea generated by the ideal of a spiritual paradise, a state of unlimited joy or bliss. On the other hand, perfect love, harmony, or peace are closer to being ideals. They represent ideas of perfection that can provide continual inspiration toward evermore perfect realization.

Wealth and happiness are wonderful. So what if they're not ideals? What difference does it make whether your values pertain to ideas or ideals?

Once they materialize, Cayce remarked, ideas die. They

no longer motivate. How many people have achieved wealth only to wonder, "What next?" Once we obtain the valued ideas we're striving for, there's a letdown feeling. Anticipation is part of the excitement, it motivates us and provides enthusiasm. Only values that are truly based on an ideal can keep us going, only ideals can continue to provide inspiration.

It's worth investing the time to decide upon your current ideal and develop a feeling for it. What's your highest value? What's the spirit in which you would like to live? Perhaps a single word, or an image, can express it. Later chapters will provide you with additional methods of expressing your ideal. Learning to express your ideal, in fact, is one way to channel your higher self.

The Ideal of the Christ Consciousness

The choice of ideal is up to us. Cayce doesn't hesitate, however, to make a suggestion. He indicates that the ideal choice of an ideal is the Christ Consciousness.

The Christ Consciousness is that awareness held in the mind of Jesus and expressed in that life. Jesus said, "My Father and I are One." It's an awareness of the One God and an awareness of the Oneness of all life. It's a life that expresses the fundamental commandment to love God and to love one's neighbor as oneself. Your neighbor and you are one. We're all one in God. Jesus was aware that God was living as a man, incarnated in his body. He was also aware that it's the same for all of us. God incarnates in each of us.

According to the perspective of the Cayce readings, what makes Jesus special is his total awareness of divinity within, his willingness to accept it, and to live it. That awareness filled every cell of his body. He lived it in every act of his life. He showed that it's possible for a human being to live the Christ Consciousness.

To sin is to "miss the mark." When we turn our backs on our awareness of oneness and take our physical being, our existence in the material world, as the prime reality, we miss the mark. When we place more emphasis upon what's *created* rather than upon the *creator*, we miss the mark. When we insist that our own egos be the principle rulers of our lives, we miss the mark.

Cayce often defined sin as *self*, meaning to focus on our separateness rather than on our oneness. Sin creates its own punishment. No one else need punish us. The focus of separateness creates fear. Fear creates defensiveness. Defensiveness builds further separation.

The antidote to fear is love and the antidote to the experience of separateness is to focus on oneness. If you feel lonely, forget yourself and reach out to someone in love. That is the spirit of the Christ Consciousness.

The Christ Consciousness is an ideal that can provide continuous inspiration for a lifetime. It's less a religion than a perspective on life. As Joseph Campbell points out in his survey of mythology, *The Masks of God*, the ideal of the Christ is a universal symbolic motif. It's best symbolized by the cross. It's the cross on which Jesus was crucified, it's the cross on which the Norse god, Odin, died, and he too was reborn. The cross represents that apparent contradiction and the real conflict of being both limited by a physical body and being infinite in spirit, of our being both human and divine, of our each being unique individuals and yet all of us being the same being—God.

Dying on the cross to be reborn means to let the ego personality resign its claim to the throne so that our true individuality may live with the ego as the servant of that life. Cayce indicates that our personality is like the mask we wear, formed to please and appease others, to look good in the eyes of others. Personalities are social creations. Our individuality, however, is who we really are underneath the personalities. Each of us is a soul, a soul of eternal life, capable of infinite creativity, each expressing the One God in a totally unique manner.

Although Cayce uses the specifically Christian terminology and symbology of the Bible, he's speaking from the perspective of a universal consciousness. Biblical terms, unfortunately, like God, Jesus, Christ, resurrection, salvation, and sin, to name a few, have developed diverse emotional meanings for many of us. To those who are fundamental in their Christian beliefs, Cayce's interpretation of the Bible is radical. To those who have been hurt, or have been made to feel guilty or ashamed because they couldn't live up to the traditional interpretation of Christianity, or couldn't "believe," as faith is so often phrased, mention of anything Christian is noxious.

Cayce is less concerned with beliefs, with what he called "isms," than he is with consciousness. He's more committed to the power of love than to the apparent power of any set of words or terms. If you find the term, Christ Consciousness, to be objectionable, search within yourself for your own sense of your ideal. What's important is that you look within and become conscious of what is there, that your own intuition guide you to the ideal that you would choose to govern the spirit by which you live.

Channeling the Ideals of the Higher Self

At this point, we can now look at Cayce's approach to channeling the higher self. It's to attune to an ideal, and then to set oneself aside so that the ideal may express itself.

Ideals are the currency of the higher self. The ideal you set for yourself, in fact, is what determines the qualities of the higher self that you will experience.

We encounter Cayce's model for channeling the higher self in many instances throughout this book. The model has two parts and they seem to run counter to one another. One is a structure, a fixed point, a standard. That's the ideal. The other is a free-flowing process, spontaneous, a willingness to let go. Hold on to an ideal and let yourself go.

Cayce isn't unique in his model of channeling the higher self. Paul, who said, "I die daily so that Christ might live in me," expresses that same model. Modeling intuitive functioning, the Zen archer taught us to become one with the target, then loose the arrow. Another counterpart to

Cayce's model is Augustine's advice, "Love and do as you will."

Set the ideal, then be spontaneous. If your ideal is set, you can trust in the flow. You begin channeling the ideal of your higher self.

Channeling Sexual Energy

All energy is from one source. There is really only one energy in creation. That energy is God, is love. It's the same energy that holds atoms together, makes lightning, creates earthquakes, rises in the body as Kundalini, or descends upon us as the Holy Spirit. It's this same energy that we experience as sexual energy. Cayce indicated, in fact, that sexual energy is the strongest physical force within the body.

Whether energy is a constructive or destructive influence, spiritual or evil in its effect, depends upon how the energy is *patterned*. Sexual energy is no different. We can channel sexual energy into constructive patterns of expression, or we can be hurtful to ourselves or others in its use.

In his book, *Sex and the Spiritual Path*, Herbert Puryear presents a comprehensive explanation of Cayce's thinking on the topic of sex. Fundamentally, Cayce made no judgment about sex. He saw it as creative energy. He neither condemned nor condoned any particular sexual relationship or activity. Instead he focused on the level of understanding and awareness the person brought to sexual expression. He asked the person to judge it for themselves. Especially, he would ask the person to examine his or her ideals and purposes. What ideal or purpose was a particular sexual behavior fulfilling? He was both realistic about this human urge—it was one he had dealt with himself in his past lives—as well as idealistic, for he considered it as a beautiful expression of human love and creativity.

What seemed to be most hurtful to a person was to turn God's creation, the human being, away from awareness of its origins and oneness with God and to focus on self alone. The same was true for sex. It's perhaps the closest we come to being creators ourselves, where we channel the creative force itself. No sex act or sexual relation is necessarily bad in and of itself. Rather, it's the purpose or the desire that the sexual event is expressing that determines its value. We recognize this truth by the fact that we have two vocabularies for sex, on the one hand referring to it as *making love* and, on the other hand, describing it in more physical terms. Sexuality for the sake of one's own self-gratification is, in the perspective of the Cayce readings, destructive and confusing, leading to attachment to appetites rather than a guide to an awareness of God and the divinity of another person.

This same principle applies to other forms of channeling. If going into a trance and uttering profound wisdom is performed for the purpose of self-achievement, for self-gratification, it likely will lead to confusion. Going into a trance state to channel something of value that can be used, whether it's for oneself to grow, or for someone else to use, then it will more likely be of value.

For Parents Only: Channeling New Life

For many people, their most cherished experience as channels comes as being parents of children. The birth of a child is a marvelous event. Even though we understand the facts of life, it still seems like a miracle that people can bring new life, a new *person*, into the world.

The conceiving of a child doesn't begin, according to the Cayce readings, when the sperm and the egg meet. It begins much sooner even than "the gleam in the father's eye." It begins as the mother and father begin to join forces, cooperate, and make a life together. What the parents think about, what's on their minds, their ideals, what's in their hearts, is of essential importance in what soul they will attract to incarnate in the physical embryo.

Cayce stresses the importance of the spiritual and mental preparation of the parents, besides the physical preparation of the mother, prior to physical conception. Coming to an agreement about an ideal is important, and sharpens the combined focus of the parents. Praying together about their purposes in bringing a child into the world also focuses their channeling efforts.

We might ordinarily assume that the personality of the child, what genes it takes from each parent to form its hereditary endowment, or its particular soul identity, is outside the scope of our control. Cayce indicates, however, that we have a great influence on shaping what enters through the combined parental channel. The law governing parental channeling—and it governs channeling spirit entities as well (see Chapter Nine)—is "like attracts like." What the parents love, the mental and spiritual environment they create, and their degree of consciousness of purpose, will attract a like-minded soul. Drs. William and Gladys McGarey, in their book, *There Will Your Heart Be Also: Edgar Cayce's Readings about Home and Marriage* provide many examples of this effect. The Cayce readings call for conscious parenting, the parents needing to take an active, responsible role in preparing to become the channels of a soul coming into physical form.

The Heavenly Home

What better way to be a channel than to provide the means where heaven can exist on earth. According to Edgar Cayce, creating a home is doing just that. Home is the model, and our closest experience on earth, of the heavenly home. Home is where the heart is, home is where we return after our long journeys, home is where we're truly ourselves. Making one's home like heaven on earth is a rewarding experience in channeling.

What is an ideal home? Cayce indicates that it's a home with an ideal. From there, the home itself becomes ideal in the help it provides. Discussing their experiences struggling to work with an ideal in a home with six children, the McGareys write, "We start where we are, with all our confusion, all our problems, all those material situations calling for solution, and into that complex combination we instill an ideal chosen as we move not toward self, but toward God.'' Edgar Cayce's grandson, Charles Thomas Cayce, and his wife, Leslie, also discuss their experiences of working to become channels of an ideal home and family in their book, *Building Healthy Relationships*. What their accounts have in common is an appreciation for *the little things*.

Take companionship, for example. A desire for companionship was God's motivation for creating souls and companionship is an essential quality in the ideal home environment. If you think about what are your favorite moments of companionship in your home situation, perhaps you will agree that it consists more in the little things of everyday life, such as sharing meals, than in intense, special events.

It's easy to take for granted the pleasures of companionship in home and family until one becomes homeless or loses one's family. It's easy to equate channeling with spectacular spirit oracles. To remind ourselves of the heavenly delight of home companionship is to remember that some of our most precious moments of channeling are the simple, subtle pleasures of making room for someone else to share our life.

Love: A Channel of Miracles

Of the many wonderful things that can be said, that have been said, about love, perhaps it's sufficient to say that when you forget about yourself and reach out to someone in need you're a channel of love. Cayce defined love as the ''giving out of that within self.''

To experience love is to experience a giving from within. That experience is something that we recognize and can easily distinguish it from taking, and from wanting. Given freely, love is a testimony to the fact that we're not hollow, or empty inside, but contain a spark of creative spirit.

As do many great teachers on the human condition,

Cayce has much to say about love. In his waking life, Cayce was a devoted student of the Bible and his trance readings on love reflect that tradition. Among his channeled teachings about love is the insight that love motivates every soul, although it may be the love of money or the love of fame. He notes that some of the attributes of love are patience, kindness, gentleness, and forgiveness. He reveals that love displaces fear, a theme that has become popular among New Age teachings today. God created us out of love and God's love guides us. Where we create our own obstacles in life, God's love provides the way for us to learn from them and grow out of them. Where we have created our own ways to separate ourselves and hide from God, God's love has provided a way for us to return to our awareness of Oneness with God. There's only one commandment, to love God and to love one's neighbor as oneself. As long as there's life there's hope, if there's hope there's possibility, and if possibility exists, love directs it better than hate.

Beyond these familiar concepts about love, however, Cayce also reminded us of something about love that we don't often consider. Love is a law unto itself. Love is a channel of miracles because it can transcend the law of cause and effect. It can break the rules!

We often read, or see on TV, inspiring stories about the power of love. The enduring love of one individual can overcome insurmountable odds in saving a life, or make an impossible change in a hopeless situation. You can probably think of your own example. Recently, the award-winning movie, *Stand and Deliver*, was a testimony to the power of one teacher's love. Jaime Escalante, by believing in his students, by loving them, was able to help them not only raise their self-esteem but also their academic achievement, and thus gain a new lease on life.

Yet we don't need to look to such heroic expressions of love to see its power to break the bonds of cause and effect. Each of us, in countless ways, find ourselves violated in some manner by someone else's inexcusable action. Their insensitive or hurtful act causes us to become angry. There's cause and effect, and it may continue, like a row of falling dominoes, toward an inevitable conclusion. By an act of forgiveness, however, by accepting what happened and forgiving the person, you can break the chain. Forgiveness isn't always easy. Some things are hard to accept. Yet we know inside that it's true that forgiveness heals. It brings change. It's one of love's creative powers to perform miracles. We have an opportunity to perform such a miracle almost every day of our lives.

Every day, every moment of our lives, we give of ourselves toward one goal or another. With every heartbeat, we channel love. And what our heart dwells upon, what our minds think about, we become or experience in our lives. We continually channel our energy, our love, our ideas, our ideals, our actions into creating life as we would have it. It's the most everyday, both ordinary and miraculous, channeling we do.

PART II

Basic Channeling Skills

CHAPTER FIVE

Meditation:
Channel of the Spirit

"Meditation is listening to the Divine within."
　　　　　　　　　—Edgar Cayce, 1861–19

"Meditation is *emptying* self of all that hinders
the creative forces from rising along the
natural channels of the physical man to be
disseminated through those centers and sources
that create the activities of the physical, the
mental, the spiritual man."
　　　　　　　　　—Edgar Cayce, 281–13

"In deep meditation there descends the influence
to open the channels along those vistas, as
has been given, to inmost recesses of the Creative
Forces in body, that arise then to the varied
centers and find expression either through the
movements of the body, in the hearing of
sound, in the consciousness of odors, in the
activity of the vision, or there's just the
presence that may be read as the open book. Or,
to put in other terms, as has been given, the
records of time and space—present and future—
are upon those films that lie between time
and space, and they become attuned to those

forces of the Infinite as the cells of the body
become attuned to the music of the realms of
light and space and time.''
                              —Edgar Cayce, 275–39

''If ye will study to *understand* the opening of
the channels or the centers for the deeper
meditation, then the spiritual and psychic
awakening may be brought forth. But do not
allow self to be overcome with this until ye
understand how and why centers are opened
in meditation.''
                              —Edgar Cayce, 1552–1

Jack Pursel was a salesman with no background in
metaphysics when he decided to take up meditation. He didn't
know much about it but tried to sit still and quiet his mind.
He usually fell asleep but kept practicing. One day when he
woke up from his meditation, his wife had some surprising
news. He had been talking during his meditation. He wasn't
aware of it at all. She had taken notes and showed him what
he had said. That began his experiences being a channel for
Lazaris.

Pat Rodergast was sitting in meditation when a vision
began to disturb her. She resisted seeing it for some time,
but then finally decided to allow it to be there. She then saw
someone surrounded in golden light. When she asked who it
was, the reply was, ''I am Emmanuel.'' For some time she
would simply sit in meditation and be with Emmanuel.
Gradually, she allowed Emmanuel to speak to her, and then
she repeated to others what Emmanuel told her. Thus Pat
become a channel for *Emmanuel's Book*.

These two well-known channelers credit meditation as the
womb that spontaneously gave birth to their channeling
practice. Many other channelers have a similar meditation
story. Their experience proves Cayce's contention that to
intentionally make conscious contact with the higher dimensions, begin with meditation.

Meditation on the Breath: A Channel of Inspiration

I'd like to describe for you an approach to meditation that goes right to the heart of becoming a channel. To begin, simply focus on your breathing and study it for a moment. Note the obvious: Breathing has two parts. There's an inhalation and an exhalation. During inhalation the chest and abdomen extend as the lungs fill with air. During exhalation the chest and abdomen relax.

The exhalations can be very relaxing. As you observe your breathing, allow yourself to follow your exhalations into relaxation. Every time your breath goes out, you can relax a little bit more. The more you relax, the easier it will be to do the next step.

What I'd like you to try next is to pay attention to your breathing without changing it in any way. Sneak up on your breathing so it doesn't know you're watching it. Observe it in its natural flow without influencing it by your presence. Make sure you're not touching it in any way.

If you're like most of us, as soon as you watch your breathing you'll feel that you're influencing or controlling it in some way. Maybe you'll help an exhalation complete itself and get the next inhalation going. Maybe you'll touch it ever so gently, to adjust it, or simply because you can't help yourself. It's hard to watch your breathing without feeling that you're influencing it.

Stop for a moment. Assure yourself that you *can* control your breathing. Take a slow, deep breath. Set the pace yourself. Decide how long you want to hold it. Now force the air out at your own pace. Decide when you wish to take in the next breath and make your breathing obey. Decide when you wish to stop this exercise in proving your control and let your breathing return to normal.

Think for a moment: If you're not controlling your breath now, who is? Most of the day, and all night while you sleep, your body naturally regulates your breathing without your help. Does your body need your help now as you sit there watching your breath? No, of course not. Keep that in mind and use it to reassure yourself while you try once again to watch your breathing without effecting it.

Here's a hint. As the breathing goes out, let it go while you relax. Then let the next breath happen of itself, in its own way. Try it. Let the breathing happen to you. Think to yourself, "It breathes me."

Perhaps I can motivate you to persist in this practice by revealing that what you're doing is a form of meditation. The Zen Buddhism tradition calls it meditating on the breath. The instructions for this form of meditation are quite simple. Focus on your breathing, watch it, let it be.

Not only is watching the breath an ancient form of meditation, but also it's an important and meaningful way to be a channel—a channel of inspiration. You're learning to allow the breath of life—the spirit—to flow through you.

All religious traditions have linked the breath with spirit. The Cayce readings are no exception. We all depend upon this invisible mover, the air, for our life—it touches all that lives. The word, *inspiration*, reflects an understanding of this relationship. There's a link between the process of breathing and being quickened by spirit, animated by genius, or aroused by creative intelligence from a source beyond our individual will. In meditation we can experience breathing as a similarly wondrous channel of inspiration.

If you relax, you begin feeling the breath coming to you on its own. If you can get out of your own way and trust in the coming of inspiration, it happens. Each inspiration feels like a gift—it comes from within, yet the spontaneity suggests that it's not your doing. There's a feeling of grace, ease, peacefulness, and gratitude. The thought, "It breathes me," can be very soothing.

When you're calm, you can be a channel of inspiration simply by allowing yourself to be so. You don't have to think about when to breathe or worry whether or not you will breathe. You simply accept, experience, and allow the inspiration to happen. To get out of your own way, to step aside and watch your breathing go by is to become a channel of inspiration. As much knowledge or wisdom can come through this channel as through any other. Practice it as we continue our studies and you'll better appreciate its value.

Becoming a Channel of Awareness

Sometimes we get so upset, we can hardly think straight. If a crisis situation catches us by surprise, our mind races with worry. Hundreds of different possibilities, things we might do, things that might happen, appear all at once. It's hard to gather our thoughts and make a plan.

At such times, to get a hold on myself, and to calm down, I know I need to relax and clear my head, so that in a few minutes it's easier to gain perspective on the situation. As I quiet down I can think more clearly and see things in a different light. What at first had been an upsetting trauma overwhelming my mind now simply is a set of factors to consider in developing a solution. I can begin prioritizing my values or needs. I'm sure you've had the same experience. You recognize that when you calm down you gain perspective and can think more clearly.

Extend that calm further, and the perspective becomes still clearer. Achieve an absolute calm and we might expect to achieve an absolute perspective. "On a clear day, you can see forever." As Zen teachers say, "When the waters become still and quiet you can see clear to the bottom." In the language of the new science of holography, it's the *coherence* of the laser beam, the uniformity of its wave patterns, that gives the laser its magical powers.

In meditation, as we quiet ourselves and calm down our thoughts, we too become more coherent and tap into a more powerful intelligence. It's like rising above the fray to become silent birds floating high in the sky. We access a greater awareness, a larger perspective, with all of the wisdom that we might expect.

With a simple exercise I can put you in touch with your channel of greater awareness. Afterward, it'll be up to you to keep that channel open.

Pick a word or a simple image that you feel comfortable

with having in mind. When you've decided upon this *focus*, I want you to concentrate on it, and nothing else. If you picked the word, "happy," simply think of that word, over and over again. If you picked the image of a balloon, simply picture that in your mind, keep looking at it, and nothing else.

After you've done this for a few moments, you'll realize that it's not that easy. Other thoughts and pictures come to you. Your mind distracts easily. That's okay, keep trying. Whenever you find yourself thinking of something else, simply return your attention to your focus. Try it again for about a minute to get the feel of what it's like to keep returning to your focus.

Now reflect upon what happened. You repeated your focus in your mind. From time to time, you would be aware of other thoughts and images. They seemed to spring from a mind of their own, regardless of your desire to keep focused. You'd return your attention to your focus and the renegade thoughts would pull you away again. It was almost like a tug of war.

As I describe the process, you can recognize what I'm saying. You were aware of your efforts to keep focused, the persistence of stray thoughts, and the frustration you felt. You may have also noticed the mental commentary about the process that ran through your mind.

Now that you reflect upon those moments, realize that you were aware of it all as it happened. Note, then, that somewhere in the back of your mind there was a witness. It was a silent witness. It simply observed. Although your inability to keep your mind focused may have frustrated you, the witness experienced no such emotion; it simply observed everything. It took no sides in the struggle, made no commentary; it simply was aware.

Does that awareness feel somehow familiar? Isn't it that same awareness that's always with you in the backgound? Isn't it that same awareness that has been with you since you've been a child? We usually don't pay much attention to its presence in the background. We're busy with our experiences, doing this, thinking that. Our sense of "I," of who we are, is created from our experiences of thinking and doing. Yet it's really only a little *i* compared to the silent *I am* in the background. In fact, this silent witness is often called the awareness of the *I am*, or the *I am awareness*. It's the first level of consciousness of the higher self. It's the doorway to experiencing the truth of the mysterious biblical statement, "Be still and *know, I am, God.*"

Meditation is the gateway to this knowledge, the path to this channel of awareness. The exercise you just did was, in fact, a basic process of meditation. In meditation there's a focus. It can be a sound, a word, a sentence, an image, the breath, or even simply the flow of thoughts themselves. You concentrate on your focus and whenever your attention strays, you return it to your focus. You place your intention to stay focused in gentle opposition to your mind's natural tendency to amuse itself with spontaneous activity. These two forces meet and gradually cancel each other out, leaving the presence of the *I am* awareness to reveal itself in the background. That awareness is itself a channel of far greater awareness.

The Higher Consciousness Within Is Not Above You

A woman once asked Cayce about an upsetting experience she had while meditating upon a point of light just above her head. In her meditation, she had something like an out-of-body experience where she found herself suspended at a great height up in the sky. The experience frightened her and she was hesitant to meditate again.

Why do you suppose that she would meditate by focusing on a point above her head? It seems natural for us, when thinking about sources of higher consciousness, to visualize these sources as existing *above* us.

Slightly above and behind the head is where many people experience the voice of inspiration, where they sense their guardian angel, or feel the presence of their higher self, like a hood of hallowed energy. I certainly have had these experiences myself. Meditating upon the Divine, or opening to the higher self, it might be a natural tendency to focus on a spot above the head.

In response to the person's question, however, Cayce answered that the experience arose from her intention to focus on something beyond or outside of herself. He reminded her that God isn't above us, but within us. Meditation is a process of seeking an attunement, but with an awareness that's within us.

He advises us to *raise* the consciousness to that *within* self and then the higher self or God meets us there. It's fascinating to grapple with the apparent contradiction. Try to imagine both *raising* your awareness as you also direct it *within*. Don't go *outside* of yourself, stay *within*, but *raise* your consciousness.

What does it mean to go within? The first thing is that rather than having your eyes look outward, turn them inward. You can't actually reverse the eyeballs in their sockets, but you can close your eyes and turn your attention inward, to thoughts and feelings. As you do so, notice that there's a natural tendency to be still, to be quiet. Now you seem to be *listening* within. You're *feeling* your way within, and awareness is no longer focused in your head, but all through the upper torso. Some people describe it as seeing with the heart.

Now what about *raising* your consciousness? You can sense the immediate tendency to move right up to the very top of your skull, but if you do, you'll find it's not long before you're rising up, outside your head. You're no longer within yourself.

Returning within, try another approach. Becoming silent again, you'll find that being quiet feels *lighter* than thinking about worries, which feel *heavier.* Such terms are the language of psychic awareness, in which *vibrations* are described as higher/lower, light/denser, subtle/coarse. Following the path of calmness in search of higher vibrations, therefore, is a more fruitful approach.

As you ease back behind your thoughts in search of further silence, begin to sense the presence of that background awareness, the silent witness. It feels very, very light. Sense the subtle levels of awareness within it. It's an intuitive space, a very enormous universe within. Within this spacious awareness, there arises the possibility for *raising* your consciousness without going outside of yourself.

Within this universe search for the feeling of the ideal, "The Peace that surpasses all understanding." It's a particularly fine vibration. Immediately there's a feeling of moving *higher within*. Clearly, higher refers to a state of consciousness, not to a place.

This brief tour inside your mind may help you get started finding your own way of *raising* your consciousness *within* yourself.

Seeking Answers From Within

During meditation we can seek answers from within ourselves. This ability is simply an extension of the fact that when we're calm, we can think more clearly. As we move more deeply into meditative awareness, that clarity becomes a source of greater intelligence.

Cayce assures us we can contact an awareness that knows answers to the questions that confront us. We can find, in fact, that all knowledge is within. To discover this resource of infinite wisdom, there are but a few requirements. We learned most of them when studying how to develop intuition.

We learned Cayce's suggestion on how to obtain our intuitive response to a decision we have to make. First determine the best possible solution you can and make an inner commitment to it. Then enter meditation and wait for a feeling of "yes" or "no" to comment upon your plan.

This same approach can be extended to receiving guidance and insights in meditation. Having a need to know and the intention to apply the knowledge helps draw the guidance to you. It also helps to follow the adage, "The Lord helps those who help themselves." In other words, do your best to work out a solution yourself. Channeling guidance during meditation will then be easier because you're already drawing upon your natural resources to their fullest extent.

It's hard sometimes to work through those first steps. Sometimes we want a shortcut or we might distrust in advance what our own solution or answer might be. I know from personal experience, however, that if I'll commit myself to an initial answer, perhaps on paper, or maybe just saying something out loud, I've actually begun the channeling process. It clears my mind of any preconceived thoughts. It also pulls the plug on my blocks to knowledge, starting a flow. Having made my initial statement, I can enter meditation in a more receptive mood.

Today, for example, before beginning work, I am concerned about planning my day. I especially want to ensure a period of quality time for writing. I make a list of things I need to do today, and organize a tentative schedule. I try to make an honest self-study of my attitude toward today's work. I feel tired. I advise myself to focus, not on how much work there's to do, but on what I like about doing the work. Enjoy the process is the advice I give myself for today.

Now I enter meditation. As I start to quiet my mind, I'm aware of many levels of thought. At first there are the thoughts I can almost hear spoken. They're already in verbal form. Behind them are more implicit thoughts that don't have words until I begin to focus on them. And deeper still, far in the back of my mind, I can sense an awareness whose silence suggests superior knowledge. I want to seek guidance from as deep a source as possible. I want it to express my current ideal, *Love*.

I rest the focus of my attention on the feeling of love. My mind wanders, of course, and I gently return to focusing on love. It becomes less an idea, more a feeling, then more of a total experience. I absorb it into my body and relax.

Twenty minutes later, a little beeper sounds a reminder that it's time to return. I return in my quiet, loving mood, and ask myself, "What about my day today?" Out of the calm mood of love arise ripples from a distance source. I await their arrival and soon I feel a soft voice speaking to me. It's like thoughts, but with feelings that remind me of a tone of voice. It says that I need to rearrange my plans so that I do my exercising first, that I go for a walk before anything else. I sense knowing that something is coming today that will divert me from my walk if I wait until this afternoon.

Then I find myself imagining, or seeing, someone approaching me. I see myself shaking somebody's hand. The person is requesting something. I see myself pulling a hand out of my pocket and I send this hand out to someplace in this person's life and suggest that the person follow. The understanding comes that I'll do them a better favor by showing them how they can provide it for themselves. I thank my inner guidance for this image and return to meditating on love, to see if there's any further information for me.

I see my writing work ahead of me. I focus on loving the process of the work and suddenly I find myself thinking a new thought about the topic I'm to write about next. I realize that it fills me with enthusiasm. It's just the inspiration I need to get started again. Again I thank my inner guidance.

I get up, go for a walk, and ponder my inspiration. By the time I return, I have the first few sentences ready to write down. I am soon engrossed in my work. Then I'm interrupted by a phone call from someone wanting my help with a project. While discussing it, I suggest an alternative approach, for which the person already has the needed solution. I thank my inner guidance for having prepared me. Later in the day, a family emergency requires an unexpected trip away from home, and I'm thankful that I had my walk early in the day. There would have been no time for it that afternoon. My meditative guidance certainly proved helpful.

Receiving such guidance in meditation takes practice. Putting the guidance into application, and trying to follow through on it is also important in developing this channel. The chapters that follow, on inspirational writing and the imagination, will provide further tools to use for developing the ability to channel guidance through meditation. Working with those alternatives will help the meditative channel become more available to you.

Meditation is a very portable guide that travels within you everywhere. With experience, you'll find that you can get quick guidance simply by taking a moment to attune to the feeling of your ideal.

Meditation on an Ideal

People asked Cayce questions about many different experiences that they had in meditation. Some people heard sounds, others saw visions, smelled odors, or felt coolness or cold air pass by. Other people experienced pain, tingling, and other sensations in the body—shaking, vibrations, and emotions. He explained that a lot more goes on in meditation than you might suspect.

Meditation isn't a period of doing nothing or where nothing happens. It's a time where other dimensions, other levels of reality, or vibrations, become an influence on the person. During meditation a person becomes a channel that is receptive to the energy of many invisible influences.

In our normal walking state, Cayce explains, we're susceptible to subliminal psychic influence. Research has certainly confirmed that claim. During meditation, Cayce warns, we become even more susceptible to that influence. Again, research has confirmed that meditation improves psychic sensitivity.

To explain certain people's experiences in meditation, Cayce explained that other minds, including those of the dead, as well as other forms of spirit energy, have much easier access to us when we meditate. Unlike in sleep and the dream state, when we automatically have protection, in meditation our protection isn't automatic. That's because in meditation we're voluntarily opening ourselves by our intentions.

Approaching meditation in the spirit of curiosity, in the spirit of letting go of one's defenses to what may come, isn't particularly advisable. Instead approach meditation in the spirit of *attuning* yourself to the *highest* within.

Recall the two symbols from the dream incubation tradition. There was a protected sanctuary and there was the coming of the benefactor. Cayce's teachings on meditation involve a similar approach.

Perhaps you have heard people say that when they meditate, they "surround themselves with light." Some people actually imagine a circular, egg-shaped bubble of white light surrounding them as they begin to meditate. Such an image is a way of expressing one's intentions for meditating.

It's like dressing up when we go out to a special occasion. Our special attire enhances our frame of mind and casts off our normal cares or worries. It's also like creating a boundary that separates and protects us from everything else that wouldn't be in accord with our intentions.

Within the protected sanctuary of our purpose for meditating, we can now open up to what we might receive. Waiting within this sanctified mental space, we meditate, whatever our method, upon a focus.

Cayce would have us make our focus our ideal. Meditating upon the breath, for example, can be focusing upon the ideal of the free flow of the spirit within. Cayce would have us choose our ideal carefully, something that's at least as universal as the Christ Consciousness. That's because whatever your focus in meditation, it's like tuning your mind into that particular channel. You receive the energies of that wavelength in a pure, concentrated form.

The clarity of mind we achieve in meditation Cayce compares to the attunement to a single vibration. Others have called it *coherence*, to mean when a wave pattern shows only one, single frequency, like a laser beam focused by a ruby crystal. As we attune ourselves to our ideal, we and the ideal merge into a single, coherent channel of energy. When we meditate on our ideal, the pattern of energy contained in that ideal actually affects us. The more perfect the attunement, the greater this effect.

When we meditate, more so than at any other time, we become a channel for spiritual energy to influence our being in the pattern of our ideal. It's like arranging a house to become a channel of solar energy, so that when the sun shines it warms the home. Meditation is a way of aligning our mind so that we're completely receptive to the energy of our ideal.

Cayce reveals that during meditation we're actually focusing the energy of creation and shaping its influence upon us. Every cell of our body begins to align itself with that pattern. Spiritual energy, patterned by the ideal held in the mind, comes through us and changes into physical intelligence within the body. How this energy becomes encoded into the cellular awareness of our body takes us onto another very amazing chapter in Cayce's teachings on meditation and channeling.

Meditation and The Book of Revelation

While giving a reading concerning a person's physical problem, Cayce noted that the Bible's Book of Revelation contained important information about the human body. At a later time, Cayce's colleagues pursued this intriguing comment and asked for clarification. What resulted was an important series of psychic readings interpreting the symbology of this enigmatic biblical text. You can find these readings in Volume 2 of the Edgar Cayce readings, *Meditation, Part 1: Healing, Prayer and The Revelation*. In his book, *Interpreting the Revelation with Edgar Cayce*, J. Everett Irion provides a comprehensive commentary and explanation of what is perhaps the most scientifically validated of all Cayce's prophetic insights.

The Book of Revelation, according to Cayce, is a symbolic description of what happens in the body of a meditator. Specifically, it describes what happens in the *endocrine system*, the network of our body's glands. Through his interpretation of the symbology of John's vision, Cayce explained how the endocrine system is like a brain unto itself. The various glands are interconnected via the nervous system and the bloodstream, as well as through means science has yet to discover.

What science *has* discovered is that Cayce anticipated, in great detail, the modern field of *psychoneuroimmunology*. In his description of how attitudes and emotions affect the body's immune system, Cayce functioned as a genuine prophet. He explained how the endocrine system functions as a *transducer* of energy, something that changes energy from one form to another. The endocrine system operates to change patterns of *psychic and mental* energy into *physical* patterns within the body, and vice versa. It's in the endocrine system, not the brain, that mind and body merge.

Cayce explains that what happened to John during his revelation experience is a prophecy of what will happen to any meditator. Specifically, as John held in meditation the ideal of the Christ Consciousness, the pattern of psychic energy in that ideal began operating on John's endocrine system to create a certain pattern of physical effects.

One effect is the stimulating of the *Kundalini* energy. The term, Kundalini, is an ancient Hindu word for the body's psychic energy. A coiled snake at the base of the spine has often been its symbol. The Christian concept of the Holy Spirit, symbolized by the dove, is the Western equivalent of Kundalini. In *Kundalini for the New Age*, Gopi Krishna explains that originally, Kundalini was *the deity of speech*. It gave the gift of inspired speaking and is thus comparable to speaking in tongues during the Pentecostal experience of the Holy Spirit. The difference between the two symbols concerns the traditional pattern in which the practitioner encourages this energy to awaken in the body.

In Eastern traditions, the Kundalini energy is active within a series of seven psychic centers, or *chakras* (meaning wheels). Eastern tradition has always pointed to the endocrine glands as somehow being the physical counterpart to these psychic centers. Different psychic centers control different psychic abilities. The pineal gland, corresponding to the *third eye*, gives clairvoyant vision. The adrenals activate mediumship, or channeling the spirits of the dead.

Revelation and the Seven Centers
The Seven-Headed Beast: Kundalini as Envisioned in Revelation

Figure 9

Eastern tradition warns about opening any one of these centers in isolation. Instead, the most common approach is to *allow*, not *force*, the center at the base of the spine, where the snake is coiled, to awaken. The snake then rises, works its way up through the centers, finally reaching the crown center, associated with the pituitary, the master gland.

In his interpretation of the Revelation, Cayce showed that

Christianity has had a secret tradition all its own concerning the psychic centers. In the symbology of the Revelation, the psychic centers are the *seven* churches, the *seven*-headed dragon, etc., depending upon the condition of the centers. The events in Revelation, however, tell of a particular pattern of awakening these energies. It's a pattern set in the ideal of the Christ Consciousness.

Recall from Chapter Four that this ideal involves the conscious awareness of the presence of God residing in the body. The birth of this awareness necessitates a death for the ego and a rebirth into a new spirit of being. For such a profound transition to occur in a graceful manner, it's important that the psychic centers be activated in a particular pattern. Cayce reveals that the Lord's Prayer, taught by Jesus, is actually a formula for patterning the opening of the

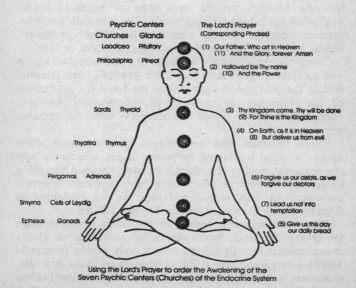

Psychic Centers		The Lord's Prayer
Churches	Glands	(Corresponding Phrases)
Laodicea	Pituitary	(1) Our Father, Who art in Heaven
		(11) And the Glory, forever Amen
Philadelphia	Pineal	(2) Hallowed be Thy name
		(10) And the Power
Sardis	Thyroid	(3) Thy Kingdom come, Thy will be done
		(9) For Thine is the Kingdom
		(4) On Earth, as it is in Heaven
Thyatira	Thymus	(8) But deliver us from evil
Pergamos	Adrenals	(6) Forgive us our debts, as we forgive our debtors
Smyrna	Cells of Leydig	(7) Lead us not into temptation
Ephesus	Gonads	(5) Give us this day our daily bread

Using the Lord's Prayer to order the Awakening of the
Seven Psychic Centers (Churches) of the Endocrine System

Figure 10

psychic centers. Figure 10 shows how the Lord's Prayer directs attention to the psychic centers in a particular pattern.

The pattern is more like a top to bottom approach, rather than from the bottom up. Invoking, in the Lord's Prayer, the "Our Father," we invite the opening of the crown chakra first. The prayer then takes us downward through the other centers. Yet Cayce doesn't describe a simple downward progression. Cayce indicates that it's how the endocrine glands function and interact that determines the sequence. In particular, as you can see from the diagram, after moving down through the upper four centers, the progression jumps directly down to the lowest center. It then proceeds in a seemingly jumbled fashion before moving back up again. The apparent jumble corresponds to critical effects occuring in the adrenals, the Leyden, and the pineal glands.

The adrenals serve as a broadcaster, amplifying the exchange of signals among the other glands. It's important that the adrenals not be in a state of agitation before beginning their broadcasting work. The adrenals are what science recognize as the center of the "fight or flight" reflex, a stress response corresponding to anger or fear.

Cayce noted that there's a special link between the Leyden and the pineal. We know today, for example, that stimulation of the pineal with light affects the Leyden's production of sex hormones. In terms of psychic activity, this link connects the inner vision of imagery with the creative principle.

Cayce indicates that the opening of the centers when upset, or when motivated by power urges, affects the way the adrenals amplify the signals passing between the other centers. Thus fear or anger have more potential negative consequences than sexual activities, as we explained in Chapter Four. Here's the reason for the difference.

When John's centers opened in the pattern just described, the endocrine glands functioned in harmony to allow God's consciousness to fully inhabit John's body and be present in John's awareness. The Book of Revelation does describe, therefore, a "second coming" of Christ. It's the birth of the Christ Consciousness in John. God's incarnation in John's body, as was the case with Jesus, becomes a totally conscious experience.

It's a physical event, grounded in the body. It's by meditating on the ideal of the Christ Consciousness that the body is prepared to become a channel of such an experience.

The Body Is the Temple

Even though mind the builder sets the ideal and tunes the channel of our inspirations and spiritual experiences, the body nevertheless participates in the channeling process. A radio that's in need of repairs has difficulty tuning in the stations. Cayce repeatedly reminds us that the body is the temple; it's where we meet with God. Cayce follows a long line of tradition that appreciates the value of purifying the body, as well as the mind, in preparation for channeling experiences.

A healthy body is important, of course, in all our endeavors. Books such as Dr. Harold Reilly's *The Edgar Cayce Handbook for Health* provide the details of Cayce's advice concerning caring for the body with proper nutrition, exercise, and rest.

Cayce wouldn't have us become health nuts, or fanatical. He cautions us to remember that it's not what we put into our body that defiles us, but what comes out of it, by way of our thoughts, speech, and actions. He also notes that it's not the substance itself that causes harm, but what we *digest* of it. In other words, we're not what we eat, but what we digest of what we eat. This principle is part of something we have already learned with regard to dreams: It's not what we learn that changes us, but what we apply of what we learn.

Cayce's approach to purification can best be summarized in his thoughts on fasting. The essence of fasting, he noted, isn't the abstinence from any particular substance or activity. Instead it's the setting aside of what *we think* we should be doing at any particular moment and *letting the spirit dictate*. In other words, he looked at fasting as another way of becoming a channel of the spirit.

I have found his advice helpful when participating in sweat or steam baths, another purification practice he advocated. The hot steam attacks the surface of my body like a thousand sharp pins. Its easy to fight the heat by tightening my body in defense. A natural instinct for self-preservation makes it tempting to try to *endure* the heat until my time is up. On the other hand, if I can set aside that attitude and relax my body, I can openly *embrace* the heat. My pores open in surrender while my mind surrenders its worries. It becomes a genuinely purifying experience for *mind and body*.

Cayce's attitude is similar toward other physical preparations for meditation. He recommended, for example, the use of scent, chanting, music, and breathing exercises before meditation. Yet we should treat none of these preparations mechanically, leaving them to do the work. They're but aids to help us remind our body of its potential for attunement. They can only evoke what is within us. We can prepare our bodies only for what we're ready to express in consciousness.

Meditation as Channeling

In meditation, we set aside our normal thoughts and focus on an ideal. In doing so, we become a channel for the spirit of that ideal to pattern our experience, to pattern the energy that flows through our body. In meditation we channel the life energy, the creative forces themselves, as they quicken our awareness of our Higher Self. Whether we think of it in terms of Kundalini energy, the Holy Spirit, or the spirit of Love, all spirit, all energy, is of God. Meditation is a process of channeling God's energy through us in a pattern that's most in tune with our consciousness of that Higher Self. Each time we turn within and open ourselves to become a channel of that consciousness, we take another step forward in being able to express that awareness in our lives.

CHAPTER SIX

Inspirational Writing

"As to the activities of what may be termed the
channels through which individuals may
receive inspirational or automatic writings, the
inspirational is the greater of the activities—
yet may partake of both the earth-earthly things
and the heaven-heavenly things, while the
automatic may partake only of that source or force
which is impelling, guiding or directing.
The inspirational may develop the soul of the
individual, while the automatic may rarely
reach beyond the force that is guiding or
directing."

—Edgar Cayce, 5752–4

"The real inspiration is the arousing of the
consciousness of that *within*!"

—Edgar Cayce, 1597–1

"As I surround myself with the consciousness of
the Christ-Mind, may I—in body, in purpose,
in desire—be purified to become the channel
through which He may direct me in that He,
the Christ, would have me do"; as respecting

> an individual, a condition, an experience. And
> as ye wait on Him, the answer will come."
>   **—Edgar Cayce, 1947–3**

An inner voice said to Helen Schucman, "This is a course in miracles—please take notes." She found the thought disturbing and ignored it as best she could, for as long as she could. At the time, Dr. Schucman was a psychologist working at the Presbyterian Hospital in New York City. Robert Skutch's book, *Journey Without Distance,* gives the historical account of Schucman's experiences. A trip to A.R.E. in Virginia Beach to investigate Edgar Cayce's perspective on psychic phenomena provided the needed encouragement. She discovered that in some of his readings Cayce had described a method he called *inspirational writing.* He indicated there was no limit to the type of inspiration, knowledge, or wisdom that could come through such a channel. After much hesitation, she finally decided that she would follow the advice of her inner voice and begin to take notes. She set her pencil to paper and began to write.

She didn't lose awareness; she always knew who she was and what she was doing. She was writing down the thoughts that were coming to her. What resulted has become a highly influential masterpiece of inspirational literature, *A Course in Miracles.* It's a three-volume work channeled completely through inspirational writing.

A Course in Miracles certainly isn't the only work of inspirational writing that has made headlines. Another bestseller was *Jonathan Livingston Seagull.* The author, Richard Bach, was on a walk one day when he heard an inner voice declare, "Jonathan Livingston Seagull." There was more. He went home and began writing immediately, furiously, trying to keep up with the flow of words that were coming spontaneously to mind. In one sitting he provided the world with one of its most uplifting stories. It's an allegorical story of a seagull that learns to fly beyond the flock's limited assumptions and who shares this secret with others. It's also a story that suggests its own source, the potential for being a channel of inspiration. When you ride the spirit on a mission to bring the truth of that spirit to others, you've begun quite an adventure.

It's not uncommon to hear authors describe moments in their work when they ride a creative impulse. The words flow effortlessly from an invisible source through the author's hands and onto the page. At those times, they rarely take credit for what they write. To them it's a gift and their role is simply as a channel.

Though perhaps few of us would claim to be inspired writers, most of us can relate to what these authors are describing. We all know what it feels like to struggle over the words when trying to write something. Some of us have also had the opposite experience, perhaps when charged up while writing a letter to a friend, where the words just poured out onto the page. If you've had such an experience, you've tasted a hint of inspirational writing.

From the description people give of their experience with channeled writing, however, it might seem like *ghost writing*. The person hears a voice, an invisible source, dictating the material. Is this voice the intuitive channel of one's higher self, speaking from the source of universal intelligence? Might it instead be coming through the subconscious, a channel not only of the author's own submerged thoughts, but also perhaps of the thoughts of other people, living, dead, and otherwise?

Being spontaneous, going with the flow—these are qualities of being a channel. Yet to be a *constructive channel*, to grow in spiritual awareness through channeling, we need other qualities beyond simple spontaneity. In stream of consciousness writing, for example, there is no special attunement, except to allow whatever comes to mind to flow out onto the paper. If we first attune ourselves to an ideal, however, as in meditation, we allow our whole being, mind and body, to resonate with the spiritual energy of the ideal. Then when we let our thoughts flow directly onto paper they will reflect and express that spirit. Here we have inspired writing, a channel of the higher self.

Learn From Your Breathing

In the previous chapter, by focusing on our breathing, we learned how to be a channel of inspiration. Our meditation on the breath can become a basis for learning inspirational writing.

Consider the three modes of breathing: controlled, automatic, and inspired. Each of these modes of breathing corresponds to a method of writing.

We observed how, when we focused on the breath, we tended to control it. We can also exert full control over our breathing, determining when to take a breath, how fast to breathe, how deeply. Much of our writing is that way. We decide what and when to write. We control the entire process. We mull over our thoughts, and when we arrive at a satisfactory thought, we write it down. In both cases, in controlled breathing and intentional breathing, it requires attention and effort.

Much of the time, our breathing proceeds automatically and we pay no attention to it. The subconscious mind controls our breathing and it transpires outside of our awareness. When our breathing is on automatic, it expresses our emotions. We may breathe shallowly when we are upset, or we may even momentarily hold our breath. We may feel tired, or sad, and heave a deep sigh. All these things happen outside of our awareness.

In a similar fashion, automatic writing is writing without awareness of the act. Not only is the writer unaware of what is being written, but also unaware, or in control, of the hand movements that are producing the writing. The handwriting happens by itself, controlled by the subconscious mind. Sometimes the handwriting is very different from the person's ordinary penmanship. How this is possible will become easier to understand a bit later when we examine the phenomenon of *dissociation*.

In contrast to automatic breathing, in meditation breathing we are aware of the breathing process. Like automatic breathing, the flow of the breath happens by itself. Yet we don't feel out of control. We have voluntarily suspended our own interference with the breathing, yet we could assume control at any moment. We are consciously allowing our breathing to express itself naturally while we watch. By becoming very calm and relaxed, by trusting in our breath, we allow ourselves to be inspired.

The process of inspirational writing involves our maintaining an awareness of what we are writing. We allow the writing to proceed on its own. We put our pen or pencil to the paper, or our fingers on the keyboard, and allow writing to happen. We are aware of what we are writing, but we aren't intentionally writing anything. We don't decide upon thoughts to record. Instead, we simply allow ourselves to begin writing, watching our thoughts reveal themselves as we write.

Learning to meditate on the breath helps us channel inspirational writing. To allow writing to happen by itself, we must relax and trust in the spontaneity of the writing process. If we are nervous about what we might write, we hold back, we choke up. A willingness to trust in inspirational writing without first knowing what you will write requires a meditative frame of mind.

Meditation, in fact, is what Cayce prescribes as the first step in beginning a session of inspirational writing. We meditate to attune our consciousness to our ideal, to the highest within us. At the end of the meditation, we simply continue our attunement by expressing it in writing.

Cayce's formula for developing the channel of inspirational writing is similar to our general formula for channeling. First we tune ourselves to our ideal, and then we step aside to allow spontaneous expression.

Inspirational writing makes a perfect case study to understand Cayce's approach to channeling the higher self. It's different from the popular stereotype of channeling another *being*. Automatic writing, in fact, a technique Cayce discouraged, is a prime example of this stereotyped form of channeling. Inspirational writing is a way to channel higher consciousness, but automatic writing is "trick shooting."

Dissociation and Automatisms:
A Channel of the Subconscious Mind

To explain the difference between automatic and inspirational writing, I'm going to introduce a couple of five-dollar words: *dissociation* and *automatism*. They are terms from the psychology of the subconscious mind and altered states of consciousness. They relate to phenomena that have both abnormal, or mind disturbing, and parapsychological, or psychic, possibilities. Like the *voice* of intuition, it's another example of the "good news, bad news" aspect of the subconscious mind.

We usually think of the subconscious mind as simply a storehouse of memories and feelings. It's actually more than a box, or container. It's a subsystem of the mind. It has intelligence, it perceives, and it thinks. Cayce noted that the subconscious mind manages the workings of the body and the habitual aspects of our lives. That's a big job, but an important one.

If the conscious mind had to run everything, we would have to move very slowly. We would have to think about every step that we take, every action, every word, every breath, every heartbeat. It would drive us crazy. Fortunately, we naturally delegate these responsibilities to the subconscious mind. It functions as our servant.

Our conscious mind wakes up in the morning, for example, and says, "I must get up now and get dressed for work." While we busy ourselves thinking about the day, the subconscious mind takes over and follows our instructions. It lifts our legs out of the bed, it takes us into the bathroom and brushes our teeth, it gets us dressed. We don't pay much attention to these actions. The process of getting up and getting dressed is mildly *dissociated* from our conscious mind. All the little details of our actions occur as *automatisms*—reflex actions directed by the subconscious.

Driving a car is another activity that is largely automatic. Our conscious mind is free to daydream while the subconscious mind manages the car. It takes charge of the gas pedal, the brakes, the steering wheel, watching the road, and it gets us to work. We barely pay attention to the trip unless the subconscious alerts us to something out of the ordinary, such as an accident. We can trust the subconscious mind, as a rule, to follow our orders and discharge our intentions. Sometimes, however, it surprises us with its faithfulness.

Suppose our spouse asks us to be sure to remember to pick up something on the way home from work. Outwardly, we agree to remember. Under the surface, however, we may feel, for any number of reasons, annoyed by the request. Later, as we drive home, the conscious mind daydreams, leaving the trip to the subconscious mind to administer. As the car passes the turnoff for the errand, the subconscious mind says, "Well, let the captain keep daydreaming . . . we know he doesn't really want to do that errand anyway." On returning home, the spouse asks about the errand. We suddenly realize and confess in all innocence, "Oh, I *forgot*!"

This example shows how the subconscious can express itself when the conscious mind is dissociated from the action. The forgetting was an automatism, controlled by the subconscious mind. The forgetting wasn't consciously on purpose, but it did express a genuine feeling within the subconscious.

The subconscious mind also manages the mechanics of speech, the process of forming words in our mouths to express our thoughts. Like driving a car, the act of speaking is often dissociated from awareness. This situation may allow for an automatism, the leaking of a subconscious feeling. Perhaps you've heard, for example, of the "Freudian slip."

John is out with his wife when they run into her old boy-friend. When she makes the introductions, John blurts out a greeting, "I'm very mad to meet . . . I mean *glad* to meet you!" In this Freudian slip, John's spontaneous greeting happened so fast that the production of the words was dissociated from awareness. That lapse of awareness allowed John's subconscious feeling of jealousy to express itself. The subconscious mind slips in the sound-alike word "mad" and gets to express its true feeling. The uttering of the word, mad, is an *automatism*. It didn't happen voluntarily, but involuntarily, like an automatic, knee-jerk reaction of the subconscious mind. Expressing a greeting is so habitual, not paying any attention to it (dissociation) provided the opportunity for the slip (the automatism). When the cat's away, the mice will play.

The cat is the conscious mind and the mice are inhabitants of the subconscious mind. If you recall from Chapter Two, we briefly mentioned that Cayce taught that all subconscious minds are in contact with one another. As shown in Figure 11, the subconscious mind isn't only a channel of information about the unconscious feelings, it's also a channel of telepathy.

Automatisms can do more than express your unconscious feelings. They can also express subliminally perceived telepathic information, from the living and the dead alike.

Automatic Writing vs. Inspirational Writing

Handwriting is another activity to which we give little attention. As we focus on our thoughts, our subconscious mind manages the hand movements necessary to form the letters on the paper. Handwriting can thus also be a source of automatisms. Have you ever made a Freudian slip of the *pen*?

Psychotherapists find automatisms useful ways to learn what is troubling a patient. They listen for slips of the tongue and analyze "forgotten" appointments. They also sometimes purposefully induce dissociations in order to encourage automatisms to reveal the contents of the subconscious mind. For example, Dr. Anita Muhl describes in her book, *Automatic Writing: An Approach to the Unconscious*, how she uncovers the source of patients' difficulties by inducing automatic writing.

One induction method is to hypnotize the person and give suggestions that the hand will soon begin writing. Meanwhile, the person's attention is dissociated from the writing

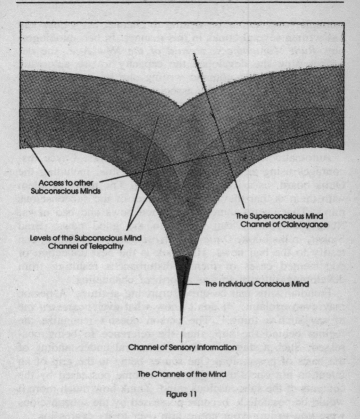

Access to other
Subconscious Minds

The Superconscious Mind
Channel of Clairvoyance

Levels of the Subconscious Mind
Channel of Telepathy

The Individual Conscious Mind

Channel of Sensory Information

The Channels of the Mind

Figure 11

process by being engaged in conversation. Dr. Muhl cautions that it's important to approach the automatic writing carefully. She and the patient examine each piece of writing together. They digest what the subconscious has revealed before proceeding further.

Psychics have induced automatic writing in themselves as a means of channeling information. Ruth Montgomery, for example, uses automatic writing to channel her *guides* and has written several books in this manner. In her autobiography, *Ruth Montgomery: Herald of the New Age*, she describes how she developed the capacity to use automatic writing. Through automatic writing she has demonstrated most of the skills normally associated with trance channels. She can perform psychic diagnostics, see into the future, as well as contact spirit guides and extraterrestrial beings. Clearly, automatic writing can be a productive form of channeling.

Automatic writing does have its drawbacks. Cayce discourages using any dissociated automatisms, including the Ouija board, as a form of channeling. The major problem with them is that they form a channel of the subconscious mind. That means there's both good news and bad news. Ruth Montgomery can testify to the good news. Brad Stoker, in his book, *Ouija: The Most Dangerous Game*, can testify to the bad news. His book is the best collection of documented cases of mental disturbances resulting from developing automatisms as a form of channeling.

Freudian slips can be quite surprising at times. A person may even exclaim, ''I don't know what ever *possessed* me to say such a thing!'' The person doesn't recognize the feeling behind the slip, thus the reference to being possessed. Such a statement shows a natural understanding of the basis of possession. One senses being in the grip of an intention not one's own. We can become possessed by the contents of the subconscious mind. Think how much more it would be possible to become possessed by the subconscious were you to turn your entire arm over to its expression.

Although Cayce does warn about possession and the drawbacks of dealing with discarnate spirits (which we will discuss more in Chapter Nine), his major concern lies elsewhere. Cayce notes that writing automatically, with the subconscious mind as the source of the material, results primarily simply in the production of channeled material. What comes through may affect the person (it is hoped not in a detrimental way), but there's no growth in the process itself. It's more like learning a trick than learning to grow in consciousness.

You can teach your conscious mind to dissociate itself. You can distract the conscious mind, not requiring anything on its part. Whatever the subconscious mind wishes to express can then come through as automatisms. What you've learned is a sleight of hand trick.

Alternatively, you can learn to still the conscious mind, teaching it to quiet itself. You can learn to attune yourself to the spirit of an ideal. You thus learn to make your conscious mind a channel of the superconscious mind. Inspirational writing promotes growth in consciousness.

Inspirational writing is more valuable than automatic writing, therefore, because it helps you grow in your awareness. Recall when practicing meditating on the breath, the conscious mind grows in its ability to trust. It witnesses the miracle of inspiration. It becomes a part of that process. It learns not to fear letting go. In automatic breathing, however, the conscious mind learns nothing except to witness the expression of the subconscious. Without scrupulous study of what emerges, as in Dr. Muhl's approach, the conscious mind remains a cork bobbing on the sea of the emotions, unmindful, even, of its plight. Cayce remarked that through automatic writing you can be a channel of the most profound material, yet have your own life be in shambles. There are many cases to attest to this fact.

As the diagram shows, in inspirational writing the conscious and the subconscious mind work together as a channel for the superconscious mind. The superconscious mind is invoked through the use of the ideal. The meditative state attunes the person to the ideal, to a particular pattern of activity of the superconscious mind. The superconscious can use material from the subconscious, if needed and appropriate to its purpose. The ideal serves as both a magnet and a filter for what will pass through the channel (see Figure 12). Otherwise, as in automatic writing, whatever is in the subconscious mind that desires expression can come through. Expression is the subconscious mind's only desire. The

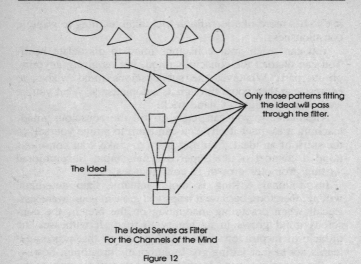

Only those patterns fitting the ideal will pass through the filter.

The Ideal

The Ideal Serves as Filter
For the Channels of the Mind

Figure 12

superconscious mind, however, focuses expression toward a purpose in harmony with an ideal.

Are you seeking a shortcut, Cayce asks us, or are you seeking that which will bring truth into your life? Seek what brings the spirit of the truth, that which brings life itself, something that will help you grow. Bringing forth a "wonderment," as he called it, is of limited value, except to perhaps satisfy a desire to learn the trick or to distinguish oneself among others. Bringing forth life, on the other hand, is something of true value.

Experiment With Inspirational Writing

Begin your experiment with inspirational writing by a period of meditation. When you feel you have entered into the spirit of your ideal, then begin your writing. Don't concern yourself about what you will write, simply write.

One way to get started the first time is simply to write out your ideal. Perhaps you begin with a single word or a phrase. Maybe you'll find yourself just writing that again and again. Whatever you write, it doesn't matter.

For example, perhaps my ideal is to *be the best I can*. So I write that down: "to be the best I can." I want to keep the writing going so what happens next is that I find myself just repeating the phrase, "to be the best I can, can, can, the best is the best, I will be the best I can be my best." I am aware of what I am writing, I'm aware that I'm repeating myself, but I don't judge it. I don't do anything that will interfere with what my hand might feel inclined to write. And then I find that it's changing, evolving some more meaning: "I can be my best, the best in me can come through me when I am me to be myself the best I can be." I'm starting to warm up and it's getting a little easier to trust in the process. "I'm best at me when I'm just me, being me, that's the best I can be, not trying to be anyone else. Trying takes trying but just being me comes natural. The best in me comes from being me. When I let me be I sometimes surprise me. There's more to me than I can see." I'm still just playing around, but it's starting to be less trivial.

It helps to take a playful approach, especially in the beginning. Being playful can be freeing. Don't take it too seriously. Being self-conscious, concerned about doing something wrong, or feeling a need to write something important, can get in the way. Being a channel of inspirational writing, like most channeling methods, requires that you be willing to let go of any demands upon yourself for performance. You certainly need to forget about grammar and punctuation! You need to forget about whether or not you're doing it "right."

In training inspirational writing to others, I have found that most people have a tendency to hesitate before they write. They may wait for a "voice" or for a really inspiring thought to arise that they can write down. Asking yourself if your thoughts are important enough to record can be paralyzing. Evaluating, censoring, or filtering your thoughts before you write them will keep you from writing in an inspirational flow.

It's deadly to insist that you won't put anything down unless you know it's profound. It makes you feel like you have a chisel in your hand and you're going to carve these words into stone. Meanwhile, television cameras tune in on what you're about to write and satellite transmission stations are ready to broadcast it live around the world on the evening news. You feel such a sense of stage fright you can't write anything.

I've found it easier to begin by just writing anything. Writing anything and nothing in particular, just playing with the words, is a good way to get started.

What you learn about channeling from inspirational writing is that it is a lot easier to receive ideas while writing than while sitting there waiting for the ideas to arrive. People who've practiced any of the channeling methods will confirm that starting the flow is the hardest part. You can verify this principle for yourself. Each time you sit down for a session of inspirational writing, the first words will take the longest. You'll also find that your most inspired writing won't be these first words, even though you may have spent five minutes selecting them. Your best work will appear while you're writing and will be material you didn't have even a second to think about first. You'll learn not to let getting started hold you back. Beginning to write is the beginning of wisdom.

You'll soon get used to writing without knowing in advance of each word what you'll write. As you feel more comfortable with this process, you'll concentrate less on the mechanics and more on staying in touch with the spirit of your ideal. As you pay more attention to your meditative frame of mind, and less to what you're writing, your writing will become less contrived and more inspired.

Rather than focus on how you're doing, *focus on your feeling of attunement and let it express itself* in your writing. It may start as a trickle. How much, how fast, or what you write, doesn't matter while you're writing. Cayce's advice on this matter is similar to most professional writers. While writing, don't evaluate what you're writing. Save judgment for later. Cayce recommends, in fact, that you don't read your inspirational writing for thirty days. Just keep having writing sessions. A good session is one where you write freely, not where you write well.

When you're first learning inspirational writing, don't worry too much about an ideal preparation method. It'll only add to the burden of getting started. After you feel comfortable with the process of inspirational writing, however, you can experiment with perfecting the preparation period. Inspirational writing is really an extension of meditation, so all of Cayce's advice on preparing for meditation applies here as well. In addition, the creative arts can be a useful method for developing attunement. I've found that listening to music, and even dancing to it, are great ways to get in tune for a period of inspirational writing.

Do feel free to use your favored writing medium. Some people like the feel of moving a soft lead pencil across the paper. Others appreciate the ritualistic quality of using a fountain pen and ink. People who do a lot of typing or word processing prefer to use a keyboard.

Answers From the Higher Self

One of the principles of channeling Cayce taught was that a genuine need is the greatest stimulant to the flow. Meditation, or an attunement to an ideal, shapes the flow. Need, and the opportunity to apply the channeled material into application, stimulates the flow. Responding to a need can be a powerful approach to inspirational writing.

Cayce often reminded us of the biblical promise that if we ask, and turn within, we will find an answer. We can test that promise through inspirational writing just as we learned to do in meditation. One of the special values of inspirational writing is that we can use a form of role playing to get answers from our higher self.

When sharing his approaching to channeling, Ron Carey

teaches to first imagine what it would be like to be God. Then pose a question to yourself. Imagine God hearing that question. Allow yourself to answer the question as God might.

In the dream incubation ritual described in Chapter Three, the seeker played the role of a higher self figure. It proved to be a valuable tool for gaining insight. You can use this same scenario as a structure for inspirational writing.

Here's what you do. First imagine some person who's the personification of your highest ideal. It could be a real person you respect very much. It could be a religious figure, an imaginary person, or someone you encountered in a dream.

Second, for your meditative attunement, allow yourself to imagine what it feels like to be this person. Then begin writing down those feelings. Use inspirational writing to express what it feels like to be your higher self figure.

Now you can pose questions to that person. Use inspirational writing to obtain the answer from your higher self.

I imagine, for example, that wise old man from my dream. I feel his simplicity and his compassion. I imagine what it must be like to see into the depths of things. I begin writing and express more of this person's consciousness. "I see with my heart and feel with my eyes. I touch with my ears and listen with my hands."

Then, as myself, I pose a question, "What is the best way for me to explain the concept of inspirational writing?"

I shift gears, once again becoming the old man. "How has this writing been for you? What has been your experiences with it? How do you work with it? How do you struggle with it? Speak simply from the heart. Tell them of your own experience."

There's my answer.

You don't have to accept the answer you get. In fact, it's worthwhile to ask follow-up questions. Perhaps the answer you get is too simple, like "be yourself." You might point out to your higher self that it's not that easy. Ask it for more specific advice, pin it down. Wrestle with the angel and it will bless you.

The Inspired Word and Creativity

One of the things I value most about teaching inspirational writing to live audiences is to see the look on people's faces as the process begins to flow. I enjoy hearing their exclamations of surprise and their expressions of gratitude and satisfaction. It's hard, when you don't know what's going to come out, to let go and begin writing. Looking through the material afterward, people find that perhaps half of it's either nonsense or old, familiar thoughts. Then they discover here and there real gems! People find phrases and sentences that are truly new thoughts, or bold or challenging notions. They sometimes channel downright inspired words of wisdom and beauty.

I can't count the times I've heard someone say, "Gosh, I didn't know this was inside of me! I never would've believed that I could've written something like this!" Because they weren't dissociated from the experience, because they were present at the birth of the inspiration, they can feel it as indeed coming from within themselves, from their attunement, their state of mind. They can reflect upon how it felt to be in the mood of their ideal and how the words came from that state of mind. They can feel that love, that peace, that stillness, or that joy, of their ideal. They can feel it in their bodies, in their minds, and their writing reflects their state of consciousness. It's a wonderful experience. Inspirational writing can be a profound experience in channeling.

When the emphasis is on the process of tuning into your feelings, not on being inspired with holiness or wisdom, the pleasure of inspirational writing is available to all of us. Even people who feel they're not very verbal or good with words can enjoy it. Teachers of creative writing who work with the culturally handicapped or the illiterate often use an approach similar to inspirational writing. They teach these people to focus on their feelings and encourage them to play with the sounds of words. They suggest letting words just pop into mind, in any order, revealing creative word strings that surprise their authors at how well they express their feelings.

Such experiences testify to what Cayce taught as truly the important value and power of words—to create consciousness. Words bring our awareness into the consciousness of being. In this respect, Cayce often reminded us of the biblical statements concerning the creative power of God's *Words*: First, there was the Word! The ancient Mexican cultures echoed this awareness. The thought that the only way the finite human being had a chance to touch the infinite was through what they called "hearts and flowers." By this phrase they meant words of *feeling*—inspired words. Special words allow a transmission from the source to the audience. Attuning to the source, allowing your words to be guided by that source, you offer your audience a chance to resonate themselves with that source.

I have deep respect for inspirational writing and for speaking as well. When I lecture, I first prepare notes as a preliminary attunement to the material. Then I meditate before my talk to attune myself to the spirit in which I wish to address the audience. Once I begin the lecture I find myself speaking extemporaneously, saying many unplanned things. Often I find myself mentally standing beside myself, listening to what I'm saying, picking up new ideas. Someone may come to me afterward to thank me because my lecture met a personal need. If so, it was when I was speaking inspirationally, and not while delivering any of my prepared remarks, that I touched that person. Cayce would explain this phenomenon by reminding me that my subconscious mind is in contact with the subconscious minds of the people in the audience. Having set my ideal to meet people's needs, my spontaneous remarks were not randomly telepathic, but guided by the ideal set in the governing superconscious mind.

In order to write or speak inspirationally, I have to set aside my desire for a noble accomplishment and simply join in the fun of the process. A sense of fun and playfulness often allows the inspirational mode to come to you. Don't let your seriousness of purpose dictate a seriousness of style. Playfulness adds another link between inspirational writing and creativity. Play, letting yourself go into the fun of the process, is an important factor in both inspiration and creativity.

As a form of channeling, inspirational writing teaches us what Cayce wanted us to learn. It's not necessary to go into a deep trance or be a psychic clairvoyant to experience channeling something profoundly moving for yourself and others. He would have us develop our channeling ability in the conscious state as much as possible. The more we can accept ourselves as a channel while in the awake state, the more we realize a simple, yet profound, truth. Being ourselves, being who we really are, is an ideal and perfectly valid means of channeling our higher selves.

CHAPTER SEVEN

Artistic Channels
of Creativity

"In music, or the art forces, may the greater
expression of the abilities or the emotions.
of self be given,—in its ability to help or aid
others to find themselves. This may be the
channel of service through which greater joy may
be a part of the present experience."
—Edgar Cayce, 1921–1

"The lifting of the emotions for creative influences
in the affairs of individuals, whether in song,
in dance, in art, or in music . . . have been the
channels through which the entity has given
expressions of the emotions of body, the emotions
of soul. When these are of the constructive
nature, no greater channel is open for the material
manifestations of spiritual truths; yet no
channel may be made lower in bringing self-
indulgences than in the expressions of same."
—Edgar Cayce, 871–1

"When the real music comes to me—the music
of the spheres, the music that surpasseth
understanding—that has nothing to do with me
'cause I'm just the channel. The only joy

for me is for it to be given to me and transcribe
it. Like a medium. Those moments are what
I live for.''

—**John Lennon**

I like to play in the dirt. Today I garden, but when I was a
child I created miniature city landscapes. With rocks and
sticks, I built little dwellings, surrounded by hills and
valleys carved in the dirt. Facedown, close to the ground, I
imagined being very small and walking among the places
that I created. Those were magical moments.

Yet it's easy to lose the magic of creativity. The day I
looked at a neighbor child's dirt roads and towns, and
compared his skillful creations with my own crude construc-
tions, the magic was gone. With that one glance, that one act
of comparison, I changed creativity from a process of
self-expression to a contest for recognition and approval.
Experiences in school only confirmed this mistaken notion.

Many years later, in a brief dream while napping, an old
friend from college announced, ''You have thrown away
your creativity by comparing yourself with others!'' This
fellow had become a prize-winning artist, his works in
collections around the world. In college I envied his creativity, which was evident in everything he undertook. It was
this same person who introduced me to dreams, to the
spiritual basis of the arts, and to the work of Edgar Cayce.
The dream made me reflect long and hard upon my attitude
toward creativity. I began a long journey to reclaim my
birthright.

Since then I've learned that I wasn't particularly unique in
my understanding of creativity. Most people evaluate their
creativity by comparing themselves to people who have
worked hard in developing their talents. They then conclude
that in comparison, they themselves are not very creative.
For many of us, creativity tends to become the ability to
make an applaudable or marketable product, not a process
of self-expression.

The Cayce readings perspective on creativity and the arts
contains some important lessons about our being channels.

Although these days trance channeling may appear to be the height of channeling achievement, Cayce indicates that it is the arts that provide the channeling opportunities for the greatest expression of spiritual truths. Our inherent creativity is thus both a powerful and fun way to explore and develop our ability in channeling our higher self.

The Spirit of Creativity in the Arts

Artists of all types, whether musical composers, painters, sculptors, poets, dancers, playwrights, comedians, or chefs, pay allegiance and give credit to inspiration. Although they've worked hard to make their inspirations come to life, all give credit to flashes of insight—the spontaneous flow of the imagination—when they are channels of creativity.

Their statements aren't surprising. We're willing to grant that artists have inspiration. We assume that artists are more creative than we are, that they have some special, secret connection to the process of channeling. Yet the essential secret of creativity that artists apply is the same secret that lies within the being of every one of us.

Just for a moment, imagine being a flower seed buried in the earth. Gradually you break open and sprout above the ground into the sunlight. Imagine the feeling of your cells multiplying and shaping your form to become a mature plant. You produce a bud and it opens into a beautiful flower. Imagine absorbing water through your roots and nutrients from the soil, transforming sunlight into food within your body. As a flowering plant, you channel the energy of the sun, of the earth, and of the air into a beautiful flower for all to enjoy. What a creative thing to do!

How does a plant know how to be such a magnificent channel of creativity? A plant is just being itself, it's expressing its nature. It doesn't have to learn how to grow, it doesn't have to learn how to work with sunlight. It does it naturally, yet it is no less a channel of creativity.

Are we, as human beings, less gifted than plants? Can we be less blessed than the plants and animals? Can we be less creative than these creatures, less capable of creating the means of our livelihood, of expressing the beauty of our nature?

Recall Cayce's view of creation that we explored in Chapter Four. God is the Supreme Creator. As souls, we are miniature replicas of God. Like God's own creativity, we channel energy by patterning it with the mind to create our material form. The pattern of our thoughts govern our actions and our life experiences. We already are channels of creative energy. The challenge seems to be for us to accept that gift and develop its expression.

How can we go wrong? Well, it's easy for us to focus on the end product—does it win us money or praise? A concern for material rewards is too often top priority. Less often do we focus on the *spirit* in which we do something. Think again about the plants. What is the spirit in which a plant flowers? Do plants look over their shoulders at other kinds of plants, and wonder why they aren't as good? No, of course not. Yet we tend to look at other people and their productions and make a comparison. When we compare ourselves with others we sell ourselves short. And we lose sight of our own creativity.

Creativity flourishes with self-esteem and self-confidence. It requires a willingness to express ourselves. New Age composer and pianist George Winston has remarked, "Art is the way we can manifest our spirit in the material world." When our self-expressions have this as their ideal, to express the spirit, as it appears uniquely to each of us, whether through art, or in our daily lives, we have touched the true purpose and essence of creativity and channeling. Diego Rivera, the successful and influential Mexican public muralist, once said, "An artist is above all a human being, profoundly human. . . . If the artist can't feel everything that humanity feels, if the artist isn't capable of loving until he forgets himself . . . then he isn't a great artist. The great artist loves his fellow man, he works to contribute whatever he can to bring harmony between men and the earth, and among all men."

The Temple Beautiful

In his psychic readings, Cayce gave some fascinating accounts of a period in Egypt, approximately 10,500 B.C., that are very important in understanding Cayce's perspective on the arts as a reflection of the general task of being channels of creativity. These readings concerned the Temple Beautiful and the Temple of Sacrifice. They were what we would consider today comparable to a combination hospital, church, school, and theater. The purpose of these temples was to either purify people of disease or initiate them into the mysteries by raising their consciousness through the arts. The continuation of the culture depended upon the work of these temples because it was there that citizens learned to exercise their talents in the service of others by assuming control over the creative forces themselves. It was a time where the arts were actively employed as a holistic mode of education and transformation.

In the Temple Beautiful there were a series of special preparations to the physical body that began with meditation and bathing. Afterward, an artist gifted in the use of odors would mix a unique combination of scented oils to elicit an elevation of consciousness. Cayce indicated that of all sensory effects, odor has the most powerful influence on the body. An artist gifted in the use of color and design would then dress the person in clothing and adornments to bring awareness of the sanctity of the body.

Architects designed the temple space to evoke the awareness of spirit. Moreover, artists of interior decoration created furniture arrangements, using color and symbolic insignias, that evoked the feeling of heaven itself. More than simply elevating the mood, the interior was designed to *instruct* the emotions and senses in how the patterning of spirit manifests the forms of the earth.

When an initiate entered the temple, musicians began to create sound vibrations to affect the body as well as consciousness. These musicians were trained therapists who could tune into a personality and improvise music to bring into awareness troublesome emotional patterns, purge them, and then begin to raise the person's consciousness. Other artists showered the initiate with colored lights that also work on emotional vibrations. Still other therapists led the person in bodily movements, dancing, chanting, and singing to cooperate and become one with the music.

Cayce indicated in these readings that through chanting and dancing with the proper music, one's conception of one's body in the material world can change to the point that one becomes aware that everything consists of vibration. One's body appears full of light and color. In such an experience the initiate was introduced to the mystery of creation. The person thereby learned how energy is the basic reality, and learned how to pattern it toward desired manifestations.

Cayce's description sounds almost like science fiction. He asserted, however, that there is no more powerful method for revealing spiritual truths than the arts. Some of you may intuitively feel the truth of that idea. If so, you can appreciate the power of having artists of many different media working in concert to operate on all levels of a person's being.

In today's world of art therapy, there isn't the same degree of integration of the arts as in Cayce's description of the Temple Beautiful. There is an appreciation, however, and some substantiating research, for the healing effect of the various individual art forms. California State University psychologist Janet Lapp, for example, has verified that listening to music can alleviate migraine headaches. Yale University psychologist Gary Schwartz has verified that the aroma of spiced apples can lower blood pressure, and the aroma of peaches can reduce pain.

Clearly, art can affect consciousness. It can inspire us, evoke emotions, or create higher emotions. Cayce suggested that we cultivate both our ability to respond to the fine art of the masters as well as taking the time to learn to be active ourselves in the creative process of art. Once we establish a relationship between creativity and our ideals, we can use both methods, appreciation and participation, to improve our ability to channel our higher selves.

Ideals, Art, and Creativity

The genius of a Van Gogh painting amazes us. That he cut off his own ear seems insane. But then we remind ourselves of the close association in our folklore, and somewhat confirmed by research, between genius and madness. Those who have an inner genie, who listen to inspired voices, sometimes seem touched with a bit of madness.

It's not true, however, that in order to be creative it helps to be a bit mad. Mental disturbances interfere with creativity; they don't add to it. A person who has learned to work constructively with the creative forces will be a greater artist than one who is at the mercy of such forces.

The tension between profound creativity and madness provides another lesson about channeling. Cayce indicates that although the arts are the greatest channel for the realization of spiritual truths, he also warns that no other channel can unleash such destructive influences. Anything with the power to elevate our consciousness must also contain the power to destroy it. Here's another example of the good news/bad news brought by the subconscious mind.

It depends, Cayce says, upon what the arts excite in those who are involved in their creation and what it evokes in those who are exposed to the arts. Certain kinds of music can elevate our emotions to sublime levels, giving us a feeling for realms of the superconscious mind. The goose bumps we feel hearing the Hallelujah chorus from Handel's "Messiah" makes us aware of how music can touch us. Other types of music, however, can excite our emotions, arouse our anger and other passions. Without thinking about it, we tap our feet to the rhythm of the music, and without thinking, we can parade off to war to the beat of a patriotic march. Today we have become more sensitized to music and have witnessed many a national debate over whether or not certain types of music are even safe to listen to.

If Cayce were alive today, I'm sure some of his psychic readings would make reference to television and the movies. No doubt he would comment on the controversy concerning sex and violence. Examining the effect of these two influences on the hormonal system (as we explored in explaining his insights on meditation and the Book of Revelation), Cayce indicated that opening the channel when the adrenals are overstimulated, as in fear and anger, is much more hazardous to an individual than an overstimulated sex center. Although we might be at risk, in our involvements with creativity and the arts, to fall under the sway of sexual appetites, it would be far more dangerous to have our fears and angers stimulated. Such stimulation is much more provocative of mental disturbances and the anguish of obsessive, compulsive states of mind than sexual stimulation.

In one very interesting experiment on the effect of cinematic art on people, Harvard psychologist David McClelland studied the effect of two movies on viewers' immune systems. Watching a movie about Nazi concentration camp atrocities weakened viewers' immune systems, leaving them more vulnerable to disease. Watching a movie about Mother Teresa's charitable work, however, strengthened their immunity to disease. The ideals expressed in the movies affect our bodies in subtle but profound ways.

As in any form of expression, Cayce would have us consider our ideals. When it comes to the matter of the influence of the creative arts, his concern is more than simply choosing one value over another. When opening ourselves to the channel of creative influence, ideals also serve as a safety anchor.

The ancient Greek poet, Homer, appreciated the stabilizing effect of ideals in helping us remain open to the inspiration of the gods without exposing ourselves to their dangers. In the *Odyssey*, the hero's famous journey takes him past the island of the Sirens—bewitching women whose enchanting songs lured countless sailors to their deaths on the shoals. Odysseus wanted very much to hear their music but could not risk his ship and men. At the suggestion of a helpful goddess, he stuffed his men's ears with wax so they could not hear the enchanting music. He ordered his men to tie him to the mast and, should he ask to be set free, to bind him more tightly. As their boat sailed past the island, Odysseus appreciated the Sirens' power. With sweet voices, their songs offered him all knowledge and prophecy. It was so tempting that he had the urge to throw himself in the water and swim to shore. Being tied to the mast saved him from destruction. Fortunately, he was able to get the positive benefits of the Sirens' song without having to pay for the experience with his life.

In Odysseus's bold strategy we can see a parallel to Cayce's insights on ideals. We may interpret the sailors as lower parts of the personality or the workhorses of the subconscious mind. When opening to a powerful channel—such as the creative energies—it's important not to let the lower personality be touched by these energies, or interact with it. In order for Odysseus himself—who we can see as wishing to evoke the higher aspects of the personality, the superconscious mind, or the higher self—to not be hurt he must bind himself to an ideal. The mast of the ship provided the firm grounding of an ideal, functioning as the centerpoint of leverage through which the power of the winds and the call of the spirits exert their force. Their force is channeled through the mast to drive the ship.

Just as Odysseus can surrender his consciousness to the spirits only after he has firmly bound himself to the mast, to safely follow the formula, "Love, and do as you will," we must first be certain that we are firmly anchored in love.

A Spiritual Appreciation for Art

Cayce suggested that we take the time to appreciate great works of art. In an age of technology, the world's art is available to us everywhere: inexpensive reproductions, paperback books, the movies, music cassettes, television, and videocassettes. We can use the artist's perception of the world as a stimulant to our own perception.

Look at a Van Gogh painting of a sunflower. In a real flower you'll now be able to see its glowing colors and its expressive poise in a new way. Tune into ballet on television and watch the dancers who have perfected their bodies to be able to move so gracefully to music. As you watch them, empathically unite with them as if it is *your* body moving and feel the freedom, the sense of being uplifted, the excitement and the joy that such emotion brings to the soul. We can all dance in our imagination. Empathic exercises like this can open us to contact soul forces within.

Most of all, Cayce recommended listening to music. He notes that music, of all the art forms, can help us bridge the gap between the physical body and the infinite reaches of consciousness. Music also serves as a bridge between changes in activities, to help change our mood when we need to relax, or when we need to get up and work.

When describing the Temple Beautiful, I indicated how music was used to cleanse people of any troublesome emotions and elevate them to higher states of mind. As suggested in these song lyrics, "Whenever I feel afraid, I whistle a happy tune," Cayce advises that we can use music to transform our emotions. For example, Pir Vilayat Inayat Khan, the head of the Sufi Order in America, confided in an interview that he dealt with his intense grief after the accidental death of his wife by listening to Brahms's Requiem every night for several days. He said the music absorbed his grief and reoriented him back into his love of life. I'm sure you have found yourself quite spontaneously drawn to listening to certain kinds of music when you have been under the sway of emotions. Listening to the right music not only helps you experience your feelings more clearly, but also it helps you deal with them, and helps change your mood.

New Age music, fast becoming a popular musical category, isn't new in its intent. Many classical composers were also interested in affecting the listeners' consciousness. As Helen Bonny and Louis Savary demonstrate in their book, *Music and Your Mind*, listening to music is a natural way to enter an altered state of consciousness. I find that listening to music, in combination with relaxation, is a wonderful way to open the channel to inspiration and visions.

This use of music shows another way in which fine art can be of use to us in developing our channeling abilities. Formulating our ideals in words alone can be a very abstract star to guide by. Finding art and music that express the feeling of our ideal can help us in our attunement. Such art can be used like Odysseus's mast. While playing fine music that we trust, we can allow our imagination to float as it pleases, knowing that it is being guided by something of value. We can meditate on a work of art and again allow our mind to wander on its own, knowing that we are being guided by our ideal.

Nature as Master Teacher of Creativity

Most artists credit nature as the master teacher. Looking at nature's interlocking forms and colors provides them continual inspiration. Cayce once remarked that no one is so wise as to have nothing more to learn from nature. When discussing intuition, Cayce recommended spending time with nature to learn to realize the reality of oneness. With regard to becoming a channel of creativity, Cayce again pointed to nature as a teacher.

Listen to the sounds of nature. Cayce indicates that if we can attune ourselves to those sounds we will be getting close to hearing the music of the spheres, that celestial music played by the angels.

To increase the power of this experience, Cayce recommends imitating with your own voice the sounds that you hear in nature. I've found this suggestion leads to very interesting experiences. When you're in a nature setting, perhaps listening to the waves upon the shore or the winds in the trees, find your own way to hum or make sounds that blend in with nature's sounds. In this way you further attune yourself in an active way with nature's vibrations. In Chapter Thirteen, where we consider the creative forces from the standpoint of healing, we'll get more in touch with nature using this method.

It's important to remember that nature is everywhere. Although it's wonderful when we can get away from the city and go out to wilderness areas, don't think that's the only place that nature exists. As our teacher, all aspects of nature everywhere reflects something about the human soul. You can learn something about channeling from examining and reflecting upon any aspect of nature you meet.

I see a weed coming up through a crack in the cement. It shows me the power and persistence of nature. The weed reminds me that even though I can't (usually) escape my need to structure my life, there nevertheless remains in me a natural instinct for a more spontaneous life. Just like the weeds, sometimes my creativity will also break through and sprout in the midst of my structured activities. There are so many different pressures on our time, and we've become so hemmed in by our structures, that we feel there is no time or place for our creativity. The weed says otherwise. We have opportunities for creativity every day of our lives.

Now I see a bird flying in the air. I join it in my imagination and fly along. What does this bird teach me about channeling creativity? As I soar with the bird along the currents of air, I recognize that going with a feeling, being able to surrender to an activity and coast along with its energy is part of the channeling experience, too.

Finally, I look at a little ant carrying a bread crumb four times its own size. I recognize that channeling creativity is not simply a matter of inspiration, but also of perspiration. I see that persistence, the willingness to make enduring efforts, is often required to manifest goals that feel so much larger than my own abilities.

Participate in the Arts in the Spirit of Play

Cayce stressed the importance for us all to find some way to actively participate in the arts, especially music. He suggested that it would be of benefit to everyone to find some way to express oneself in music. Of all the arts, we carry the ability for musical expression with us at all times.

It's easy to have fun with music and Cayce suggested that even learning to play a kazoo, or humming music on a piece of paper placed on a comb is worthwhile. Do you remember playing on such a homemade toy from your childhood?

We need to remind ourselves from personal experience how naturally uplifting it is to *make* music. We've become very shy about this form of expression, but making music is such an easy way to recapture some lost channels of creative expression.

A wonderful channeling exercise is to sing to yourself in the shower or while driving to work. You can sing along to the tunes on the radio. Even better, you can make up your own melodies and sounds to express your feelings. Cayce suggested simply using play words like "la de da" is a fine way to sing. Let yourself go! Playing with sounds, if you'll approach it playfully, is a wonderful way to recapture the spirit of childhood innocence.

Exploring the sounds you can make with your voice has another important dimension. Cayce indicated that our voice is the highest vibration we can achieve with the physical body! No wonder that of all religious music, choral pieces are the most uplifting. What's the sound that most resembles the feeling of your ideal? Let's hear it! Louder, and with more feeling—don't hold back!

Cayce also suggests practicing chanting sounds, like *Om* (Ahh . . . Ohh . . . Mmm) to experience the vibratory effect in your body as well as the effect on your mental state. Make the sound in different ways, in different pitches, until you find the way that makes your whole body resonate with feeling. When you're willing to set aside self-consciousness, you can channel with your voice a surprising amount of expression from your higher self. An amazing experience awaits you.

On a more mundane plane, another of Cayce's suggestions was to hum to yourself, even silently. None of these sound exercises are for an audience, just for yourself. As Snow White's dwarves suggested, "Whistle while you work," so Cayce suggests adding silent humming to your daily chores and activities to invoke an awareness of the invisible forces available to aid and guide you during the day. It also grooms your mood and helps the work along.

Quiet or silent humming can also be a form of prayer, a source of comfort, or an expression of love. If you practice silent humming enough, you'll soon discover that you are channeling tunes you've never heard before. It's great practice for cultivating the willingness to flow with your spontaneous, improvised self-expression. You may find yourself even becoming a channel of creativity for the work at hand.

When you are alone, dancing adds another vital channel of expression to the music. Dancing out your feelings, to the accompaniment of music, is one of the methods used in the Temple Beautiful to transform emotions. Dancing out our dark moods can inform us of our values, of what we might be longing for, or missing in our lives at the moment. Then, on the positive side, inventing a dance to express the feelings of our higher self can be a very enriching experience as we help that state of consciousness incarnate in our physical body.

In workshops, I often invite people to call upon dream images, of problem areas as well as of higher states of mind, and ask these symbols to reveal their "song and dance." By allowing a dream image to express itself in sounds and in movement, we can begin to channel the energy of that symbol, as well as any message it may bring. This approach is quite reminiscent of the approach of Native Americans as well as other indigenous people. It's also an ancient form of channeling.

Creating Life Seals

Cayce gave us a way to experience another aspect of the Temple Beautiful—the evocative power of symbols. He suggested that we create for ourselves what he called a Life Seal. It is something like a personal poster displaying various symbols related to your ideal, your feeling for your higher self, and of your soul's purpose for this life.

You can construct a life seal by either drawing it yourself or by making a collage from pictures cut out from magazines and other sources. A collage can be a very effective approach and may appeal to those people who don't feel they can draw. In either case, choosing the symbols and designing the layout is the most important part of the life seal, requiring you to familiarize yourself enough with your ideal to decide how to express it in pictures.

To begin, ask yourself, "What is my highest ideal?" If, for example, the answer is *love*, then what images or symbols come to mind that evoke your feeling for that love? Perhaps it is a rose, a mother and child, or the sun shining upon the earth. If you have trouble thinking of images, try looking through magazines and books of artwork for pictures that remind you of the feeling of your ideal.

Other questions to ask yourself might be, "What are the most important qualities of my higher self?" "What do I consider to be my purpose in life?" "What talents do I have?" Consider what images or symbols best express the answers to such questions.

Your dreams are a wonderful source of symbols to include in your life seal. Look through your dreams for particular images that are especially meaningful to you. Look also for images that relate to the questions mentioned above, such as symbols of your higher self, images related to your ideal, or symbols that reflect special talents or qualities that you admire.

The next step is to place these symbols into some arrangement. Placing them within a circular format suggests that all of these images are aspects of a whole. Other formats might be an oval, a square or a rectangle, or even a cross or some other shape. When placing the symbols within the desired format, the upper/lower, left/right, and center positions can be meaningful in themselves. For example, one way to think about your soul is as a journey in growth. The left refers to where we have come from and what we are bringing with us. To the right can suggest where we are headed. The center can suggest the essential focus of this life. The top area can suggest ideals, values, or a guiding wisdom. The bottom area can suggest raw energies or other natural resources to develop, or our foundation. Use an arrangement that makes the most sense to you, that feels right. Move your symbols around on the page until you find the most satisfying picture.

Life Seal Made from Dream Symbols
Janet Smith

Figure 13

The most important thing about a life seal is how it affects you, not other people. The purpose of the life seal is not for show, or to impress others, but rather to stimulate yourself. Its purpose is to evoke in you, the person who made it, a sense of higher purpose, a sense of higher consciousness. It's to serve as a reminder to you during the day of your higher self. It is like a commercial for your spiritual life. In conjunction with music you have found that evokes your ideal, it can be a wonderful aid to attunement, as a preparation for channeling through inspirational writing or other methods. Your life seal can be a growing expression. Feel free to continue to work on it, to change it, or even to create a different one entirely. As your awareness develops of your higher self, allow your life seal to reflect that growth in consciousness.

Creativity and Channeling

Psychologist Teresa Amabile at Brandeis University presented students with the task of creating a poem. She wanted to test the effect of attitude upon creativity. Dr. Amabile asked one group of students, before beginning the writing task, to imagine what fun it is to play with the sounds of words and how satisfying it feels to be able to express oneself clearly. She asked the other group of students to imagine how good it feels to be praised for good work and to be admired as creative. After these brief imagination exercises, the students had a few minutes to compose a brief poem. Dr. Amabile gave all the poems to a panel of poets to evaluate for creative merit. The judges' ratings indicated that the students who first imagined the joy of writing produced much better poems than did the students who began by imagining the joy of praise. Clearly, students who were motivated by the *internal* pleasure of the *process* of writing proved to be more open channels of creativity than those students who were motivated by the *external* factor of admiration for their *product*.

This experiment confirms what teachers and philosophers

of creativity have known for some time. Focusing on the end product, and how it might be judged, blocks creativity. Creativity flowers when you lose self-consciousness by becoming absorbed in the process of working with the materials. Cayce gives the same advice for learning to develop your channeling ability. Don't develop it out of a desire to perform a spectacle that wins admiration, but out of a love for the process of giving expression to your ideals.

Watercolor painting taught me this same lesson. Trying to paint *pretty pictures* proved difficult. When trying to tame the watercolors to perform what I had in mind, I usually ended up with a mud puddle. When I set aside my demands and expectations, and began to learn how to interact with the materials themselves, discovering how the paints wanted to be washed across the velvet surface of the paper, and how the different colors played with one another, the watercolors themselves became my partner in creating surprising effects. Furthermore, as I explain in *Getting Help From Your Dreams*, my dreams then joined in the play, revealing unexpected ways for me to interact with the watercolor materials, leading to more creative cooperation and still more satisfying experiences. Within a year I was painting with watercolors in a most beautiful manner, in a style uniquely my own, with no need or desire to compare myself with others!

The practice of a creative art involves an attunement to the materials at hand, becoming one with the paint, becoming one with the sounds, becoming one with nature. When we allow ourselves to improvise, whether in the doodlings that have no purpose, or the humming of the melodies that come to us, we open a channel of creativity. Being creative demands that you set aside your expectations, get out of your own way, and let the activity happen. Creativity happens in action, not while you sit idly waiting for inspiration.

Inspiration is a word that touches both upon a source of intelligence as well as creativity. Cayce stated that psychic and creative ability were essentially the same. They both originate and owe their existence to the nature of the soul's superconscious awareness and its inherent creativity. When we attune ourselves to the ideals of our higher self, we open a channel not just to knowledge and wisdom, but also to inspiration and creativity.

Practicing being in the *spirit* of creativity, owning our birthright of unique self-expression, is very important in developing the awareness of channeling ability. It doesn't take any more effort to act inspirationally than it does to act out of habit. Each can be a form of spontaneous expression. Acting out of habit requires no awareness, however, though acting inspirationally requires the presence of awareness. Yet you allow yourself to be as you are, to do as the spirit moves you. The presence of awareness offers the possibility of making choices, but habits exclude choice and keep us in our routine ruts. Breaking the expected routine is an essential ingredient in creativity.

It isn't a matter of not having enough time to be creative, but a matter of keeping one's awareness open to the possibility. Everything we do during the day can be done in a variety of attitudes. No task is too small to warrant your loving attention. Who knows what might happen if you hummed to yourself while you attended to that task? Work can be transformed to play. The word, *recreation*, means rest and renewal, play and creation. Although creative play challenges most of us where we are overly serious about how well we can *perform*, its essential value is in teaching us the joy of being a channel of expression, a channel that can express in a manner like no other—the living, felt presence of the higher self.

CHAPTER EIGHT

The Visionary Channel of the Imagination

"The visualizing of any desire as may be held by an individual *will* come to pass, with the individual *acting* in the manner as the desire is held."

—Edgar Cayce, 311–6

"For anyone with great imagination, of course, is intuitive; though oft may be called by others only imagination—when it is the movement of influences upon the very active forces of the individual entity."

—Edgar Cayce, 1744–1

"Oft is the entity capable of seeing, hearing, that which to others does not appear to exist. Do not attempt to belittle or dissuade the entity from those impressions that are coming through from that called imaginative or subconscious force in self. Rather reason with, counsel with, as to the proper application of the *source* of that felt, heard, seen, experienced, and its *usefulness* as to conditions that arise in the experience of a body."

—Edgar Cayce, 1911–1
(about a seven-year-old girl)

Thundering horsemen, angels, a black sun and a moon of blood, creatures with six wings, seven-headed dragons, all these and more dramatic images came to John the Beloved as he sat in meditation. There's perhaps no more startling example of channeling in the Bible than John's Revelation. As if the heavens opened to him, John was given a vision of things to come.

Cayce interpreted the Revelation as an accurate portrayal of what happens in the endocrine system as every cell in the body develops awareness of the Christ Consciousness. Although John's vision is full of imaginative, symbolic imagery, it's nevertheless accurate and educational. The images reveal an important truth. The imagination proves itself to be a very important channel of revelation.

It's easy to equate the imagination with imaginary. By imaginary we usually mean *not real*. Often we say, "I'm just imagining it" when we mean, "It's not true! I'm just making it up!" To realize the full potential of our channeling ability, however, we must discover that the imagination is a very important connection to a dimension of life that's *very real*. Through the imagination we can perceive what's otherwise unseen, what Cayce calls the *invisible forces* of creation. The imagination is a channel of not only psychic sensitivity, but also of inspiration and visionary perception.

Understanding the reality of the imagination may require some imaginative effort on your part. What Cayce revealed about the imagination contradicts our usual way of imagining the difference between what's real and what's "only imaginary." This chapter may require extra study.

The Boy Who Saw True

When Edgar Cayce was a young child, he had many invisible playmates to keep him company during his time out in nature. He learned that no one else could see these little people, except his mother and one neighbor girl. In addition to these ethereal inhabitants of the flowers and streams, the young Cayce once met another visionary companion.

According to the account given in Thomas Sugrue's biography, *There is a River,* Cayce was thirteen years old at the time. We know about the encounter because he discussed it with his mother afterward. He was out in his lean-to retreat, where he read the Bible. He looked up and thought his mother had come to bring him home. But as she began to speak, the music of her voice and the wings on her back told him she was someone he didn't know. She said she had come in answer to his prayers and would grant his most favored wish. Thinking of Jesus' disciples, he said that he wanted to be able to help people, especially sick children. Later events proved that his wish had been granted.

Although we usually think of Cayce as operating as a trance psychic, his ability to see presences that were invisible to others indicated that he had psychic vision in his waking state as well. Just how powerful a channel visionary perception can be became evident in 1952, when the metaphysical writer Cyril Scott presented to the public a most unusual book. It's the private journal of a young British boy, who kept a diary from the time he could write until he was about twenty years old. In the boy's later years, his wife urged him to publish it as a book. He agreed on the condition that it be published anonymously several years after his death under the title, *The Boy Who Saw True*. What this boy saw with his visionary imagination, in fact, echoes much of what we learn in this book about the perspective of the Cayce readings.

The boy's journal is full of both the ridiculous and the sublime, written with the kind of innocent candor that children can express so well. Sightings of Jesus are mixed in with childish discussions of such topics as moles and passing gas in church.

Without realizing it, he has psychic eyes. He sees gnomes playing in trees that make him laugh. He cries over the death of a loved one, yet he sees the dead as alive. He wonders about this paradox himself and figures it's because of the crying that goes with saying good-bye. He complains

The Visionary Imagination

Figure 14

about grown-ups who tell him not to lie, but get angry and deny it when he sees the truth and says it.

This boy had the ability to see people's thoughts. They appeared to him as images surrounding the person. For some time, he thought this was a normal ability that everyone had. He tells the story of a woman who visited his house. He saw a strange-looking man above her shoulder. He asked her, "Why have you got an old gentleman sticking to you?" She jumped in astonishment at the remark. He described him for her, and when he mentioned a red mark (a scar) on his cheek, she involuntarily replied, "Why that was Mr.——" and looked at him uncomfortably. A few days later she questioned him about it, and that was when he discovered that not everyone saw these visions. He was also able to tell her about her past based on the images he saw around her.

Cayce would have us understand that *thoughts are things*. They're alive, they affect those around us. Thoughts are one element of the unseen forces and can be seen through the imagination. We're connected to one another through the subconscious mind. This particular boy—and he's certainly not unique in this capacity—experienced this connection through the imagination. His imagination saw true.

The boy was perpetually sick as a child, had to drop out of school, and had a home tutor. His tutor took an interest in what the boy saw after the boy told him what he saw about the tutor's past. From then on, when the tutor would visit, the boy would tell the tutor what the spirits he saw were saying. The tutor would write down these remarks, then go over them with the boy for his lesson that day.

On several occasions, the boy saw Jesus standing at the foot of his bed. On one evening he wrote, "His lights were so lovely, all gold and pink and blue and green and yellow like the rainbow we saw through the window that time. He looked as if he wanted to comfort me for the horrid day I had. . . . This is the third time I've seen him, but I wish he'd come oftener."

On one of these visits, Jesus promised to visit the boy one day when the tutor was present because he wanted to tell the boy some things that the tutor would have to explain to him. The first time the three of them met, Jesus explained to the boy that he wasn't really Jesus, but was someone who had been the boy's teacher through many lives, that he was called an *Elder Brother*. The tutor had a background in Eastern philosophy and was able to explain to the boy what the teacher had meant. The boy remarked that the voice of this spirit teacher was certainly more gentle than the preacher in church.

Once while listening to music the boy had a very realistic daydream of himself sitting in a cave, being attended to by a servant, or a student. He writes that his Elder Brother explained to him that these were memories. On other occasions, a student of the Elder Brother appeared to him. He explained that he was asleep in another part of the world, thousands of miles away, coming to visit in his astral body. This student explained that the boy also traveled in sleep and sometimes they met.

The Cayce readings describe exactly the same type of communication between people while they sleep. Many of our dreams are actual visits with others.

On occasion, the boy would see his dead grandfather. Sometimes his grandfather provided helpful advice. The boy asked his Elder Brother why his grandfather didn't know, however, about living many lifetimes. The Elder Brother replied, "Imagine not that those who shed the mortal body become possessed of all knowledge. If you go to a strange country and dwell in a town, do you on that account acquire knowledge of and belief in all the religions and philosophies of that country?"

Cayce often remarked that people don't become any smarter after they die, except to discover that there is life after death.

The Elder Brother had many other teachings. Considering the complexity of the topics, they were remarkable for their simplicity. His explanation of karma is similar to the nonjudgmental approach given in the Cayce readings. The Elder Brother said, "The ordinary man on earth usually saddles himself with business ties, social ties, family ties, and a thousand duties and responsibilities which he can't get out of, and which tie him to a given place. He may take a yearly holiday, but sooner or later he has to return to resume his business activities, pay and collect his debts, and fulfill all his other obligations. Having in the first place created all those responsibilities, he has to go through with them whether he likes it or not." He explained that the soul has to return to teach itself wisdom through having experiences.

The boy asked how a soul might come to not have to return for another life. The Elder Brother explained that besides paying off debts and not doing anymore evil, one needed to learn to do good *for its own sake*, like the way an artist labors in love at his work, with no expectation for reward.

Echoing Cayce, he told the boy, "Strong desires act somewhat like a boomerang; you hurl them forth into time in the shape of desires, and they come back to you in the shape of fulfillments." He explained that incompleted strong desires bring you back to the planet to fulfill them. Fame, for example, isn't in itself bad, but the attachment to fame, or what we might call dependency, creates bondage. True happiness is found within, he said.

The Elder Brother introduced the boy to another teacher, who was called a Lama. The Lama's teachings were also quite similar to what we have learned from Cayce: "No matter the color of the light shining through the colored glass, the sun is the same . . . and so it is with the one SELF shining through a myriad individual selves, which are as but the colored windows through which the sun of the SELF doth shine."

The boy grew up to become a successful businessman and had continued contact with the Elder Brother for the duration of his life. In his afterword to the book, the editor notes that people who have studied the boy's account have speculated that the Elder Brother, the boy's "imaginary" teacher, spoke like an evolved master.

The important thing to note, however, is that the boy didn't channel this wisdom by going into trance. In a normal state of consciousness, through the powers of imaginative vision, the boy experienced his lessons like normal conversations with a teacher.

How can the imagination be such a channel of psychic sensitivity? As we attempt to understand this apparent paradox, we will see that the imagination is our one organ of perception that does tune to the infinite. It's the aspect of our mind that is itself most closely akin to the invisible forces of creation.

Creation in the Imagination of God

To understand the relationship between the imagination and the creative forces, Cayce would have us first reflect upon the biblical statement that we're created in the image of God. One way to interpret this statement is to say that we look like God. Cayce explains that our being like God doesn't mean that our body has a physical appearance that resembles God. Instead it means that, as souls, we're functioning models of God. One basic way we function like God is that, like God, we create through our imagination.

In fact, that it is God's imagination that's the source of Creation is another interpretation to being created in the image of God. It is an interpretation that Cayce would have us ponder. Out of the mind of God came images. Those images are us, the souls that we are. Can you imagine it?

Tune up your own imaginative powers and try to get a feeling for what it might be like to be a figment in the imagination of God—a figment to which God gives free rein—free will.

It might help if you were to contemplate for a moment what it's like to have something in your imagination. Imagine an animal, a dog, for example, standing in front of you. Give the animal free will to do as it pleases. Don't control it. Giving it life without controlling it is not that easy. Try it. It will give you more respect for God's channeling ability.

As you watch the dog in your imagination, notice if it knows that it's a figment, a creation, of your imagination. Try to make mental contact with the dog. Can the dog become aware of you? Can it become aware of the fact that you're creating it? How might this come about without your forcing the issue, without your taking away the dog's free will?

To make it more interesting, allow this dog to continue to exist in your imagination for the next week. Let it do as it pleases. See what it does. Perhaps it will discover something that you find interesting, perhaps it will alert you to danger that you were unaware of. If you can give the dog free will to explore as it chooses, chances are that it will do something that will surprise you, that will extend the range of your awareness. Believe it or not, Cayce indicates that we can play a similar role for God. Our conscious minds, and their inquisitive contact with the sensory world of materiality, function as an organ of God's perception and self-discovery.

In his later years, Carl Jung had a dream that gave him a feeling for what it was like to be created in the imagination of God. He tells the dream in his autobiography, *Memories, Dreams, Reflections*. In his dream he enters a temple where he discovers an ancient man who's meditating. And he realizes in the dream that as this ancient one meditates images are arising in the man's imagination. Jung himself is a dream of this ancient one.

The Creative Power of Visualization

We use the word, "imagination," as we do the word, "dream," in several different ways. Besides meaning a region of inner experience, to think new thoughts or sense the realms of possibility, it also refers to inventing and creating. When Martin Luther King, Jr., announced, "I have a dream!" he meant dream in the visionary sense of being able to imagine a possibility so vividly that he felt called to help it achieve realization in the physical world.

People of such imagination are no idle daydreamers. They are active channels for their visions. Their innovative images come to life in new products and services as well as revolutionary theories and social structures. Where would we be without the active imagination of Thomas Jefferson, the Wright Brothers, Thomas Edison, Einstein, Gandhi, and countless others? Although the activity of the imagination often upsets the social order of the status quo, it's a powerful force in shaping the world.

Without imagination, we are lost. Confronting insurmountable national or world problems, we seek leaders with vision, not only to invent solutions, but also to guide us in their implementation. In our personal lives, we use our own imagination in no less an actively creative way.

We have already studied the power of the mind to create reality. In Chapter Four we learned that "Mind is the Builder," that what we think, we become. Through its pattern-making ability, the mind channels spiritual energy into physical manifestation. Cayce sometimes used the term, "imaginative forces" to describe the power of the mind's patterning process. If you look at the circumstances of your life today, notice how much you can recognize as being the product of something you previously had held in your imagination.

The act of visualization—*holding* the product of the imagination firmly in mind and *acting* as if it will materialize— harnesses and shapes the imaginative forces to create in physical reality. Through visionary daydreaming, the imagination seeks out new, creative patterns of possibility. Through visualization, the imagination acts as a channel for their creation in fact.

In the years since Cayce revealed to us this possibility, social scientists have confirmed the importance of a person's self-image in shaping behavior and the self-fulfilling influence of expectations in shaping the outcome of one's efforts. Medical science has now confirmed that we can, indeed, use mental imagery to control the workings of the body. Experiments have shown that the power of visualization extends down to even the level of the single, individual cell!

What is this active power of the visualized image? Cayce tells us that imagery is the language of the subconscious mind, that portion of the mind that rules the body and steers most of our actions. Imagery is the process of experiencing in *patterns* rather than in linear, logical thought. Mental images, whether felt, seen, or thought, exert their power through their holistic pattern of meaning. Logical thought has the power to refine our awareness in a sharply focused manner. Images have the power to *move* us, their patterns working on us in many ways simultaneously.

Try, for example, to tell your mouth to become wet. Say

to yourself, "Salivate!" over and over. See how much response you get. Now try using an image. Imagine holding half a lemon in your hand. Imagine squeezing it until beads of juice appear on its surface. Bring that lemon to your mouth and suck the juice. If you can imagine it, you'll see what I mean. Your mouth gets very wet! Although a thought only makes you think, an image touches and affects our whole being.

Today, every teacher of some system for "how to be a success" preaches the power of positive imagery. Respected corporate advisers, such as Dr. Charles Garfield, author of *Peak Performers: The New Heroes of American Business,* echo Cayce's advice about setting an ideal, visualizing a goal, then acting as if it were coming to pass. Imagination creates reality.

The boy who saw true could predict people's future simply by examining the forms and figures hovering around the person's head. He was seeing their thought forms, etheric patterns of activity in the imaginative forces that were at work creating the person's future. It's in this realm of etheric forces that the imagination is a channel of creation.

The Etheric Field of the Imaginative Forces

"There's nothing as powerful as an idea whose time has come." "Thoughts are things." "Imagination is reality." Such statements turn our world inside out. They suggest that the world of the mind is more real than the world of physical objects. In Cayce's view of the world—and most spiritual traditions share this view—the physical world is but a fleeting shadow, an effect, an end product, of the mind's patterned projection of spiritual energy. Recall Cayce's formula for channeling creation, "Spirit is the Life, Mind is the Builder, the Physical is the Result."

In Chapter Four we saw how Cayce, Plato, Carl Jung, and Rupert Sheldrake, each in different terminology, envisioned a fourth dimension, the realm of the Mind "at large," as governing the visible realm, or the physical world. Patterns in the Mind—images—exert a shaping influence upon energy as energy precipitates into physical form. The process by which a pattern precipitates an idea into the brain of the conscious mind is the same process that precipitates an idea into the manifest forms of nature. Cayce called this influence, this force exerted by patterning, the "etheric" force or the "imaginative force." The reason the imagination is able to *see* these invisible forces is because the imagination *is* the activity of those patterning forces. It's because, as Cayce explains, *the perceiver and the perceived have the same ONE source*: the imagination!

This connection, by the way, between imaginative *seeing* and imaginative *creating* also exists within the endocrine system of the body. Recall from Chapter Five that these glands govern the transformational bridge between mind and matter, between energy as spirit and energy as physical events. We actually experience this bridge, Cayce points out, through our *feelings*. Feelings are sensitive to the spirit as well as being physical sensations. Cayce further notes that images in the imagination arise first from feelings. If you don't think you imagine well, begin with sensing feelings! Recall also from Chapter Five that Cayce revealed that there was a connection between the activity of the light-sensitive pineal gland and the Leyden gland. This hormonal connection reflects the link between the third eye of visionary seeing and the reproductive creativity of manifestation. Times of heightened visionary imagination correspond to times of intensified creative feelings.

We can now explain how the boy who saw true used the psychic sensitivity of the imagination to see what he saw in the etheric realm. Figures 15 and 16 are diagrams of the spiritual, mental, and physical realm, and their corresponding superconscious, subconscious, and conscious levels of the mind.

In Figure 15 we see the situation of the boy seeing gnomes or fairies. These so-called beings are the activities, at the etheric level, of the imaginative forces patterning the forms in nature. The domain of these forces is the subconscious mind. The subconscious mind of plant life connects

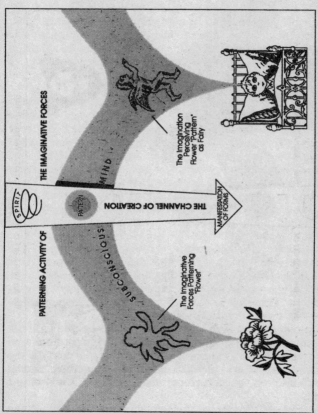

The Boy Who Saw True Envisions a Fairy in the Flowers
Figure 15

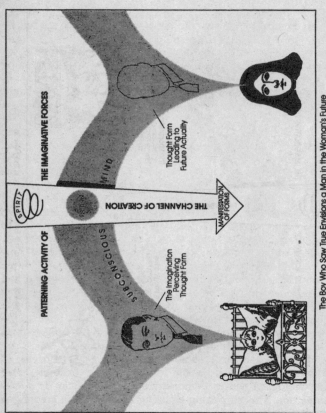

THE IMAGINATIVE FORCES

PATTERNING ACTIVITY OF

SPIRIT

THE CHANNEL OF CREATION

PATTERN

MIND

SUBCONSCIOUS

MANIFESTATION OF FORMS

Thought Form Leading to Future Actuality

The Imagination Perceiving Thought Form

The Boy Who Saw True Envisions a Man in the Woman's Future
Figure 16

with the subconscious mind of the boy. With his imagination, the boy sees, through the channel of the subconscious mind, the imaginative forces shaping the plants. His imagination experiences these in the pattern of gnome activity, a personalization of the patterning of the imaginative forces.

In Figure 16 we see the situation of the boy seeing the thought forms "sticking to" his visitor. These thought forms are etheric patterns of the imaginative forces in the visitor's subconscious mind. These patterns are about to be manifested in the visitor's physical life, in events that will soon come to pass. With his imagination, the boy sees, through the channel of the subconscious mind, these thought forms and is able to predict the visitor's future.

If the imagination sees the etheric forces, what do the eyes see? The imagination isn't an alternative to seeing physical reality with the eyes. Instead it's actually the psychic, intuitive foundation, the receptive and formative background of the ability of the physical eyes to see. We do our seeing with the *mind's eye*, not the eyeballs. We cannot see what we cannot first imagine. Imagination is more basic than seeing. What our eyes see adds but physical detail to what our imagination has already grasped through intuition.

Perceptual illusions are good places to experience how our mind affects what we see more than the eyes do. In the example shown in Figure 17, what you *imagine* seeing will determine the *pattern* of information gathering your eyes will follow in perceiving the pen lines. Where your eye focuses depends upon whether you pattern that information search by imagining that you're looking at a young woman or an old hag. Which do you imagine seeing?

This illusion, developed by Professor E. G. Boring, of Harvard University, is but one of many examples that psychologists use to demonstrate that *perceiving is a creative act*. This surprising equating of seeing and creating is what Cayce means when he says that it's the same source that creates manifestations that also experiences them. It's why the word *visionary* means both perceptive and creative. Perceiving and creating reality are soul mates!

I know it's hard to understand. By the time you finish this

Which Woman Do You Imagine Seeing?

Figure 17

chapter and the next, however, you may appreciate more why it's worth the effort to try to understand this puzzling relationship between perceiving and creating. It's this equation of the imagination with reality that explains why, as we'll see, there's so much overlap between someone channeling a spirit and someone pretending to do so. Acting as if something were true has the effect of making it true!

The Psychic, Inspired Imagination

Sometimes, when you give the imagination free reign, it proves to be inspired, or psychic. You may feel like you're "just making it up," creating it yourself. Yet you may later discover that your imagination was being receptive to patterns outside your personal storehouse of knowledge. The creativity of the imagination can be shaped by psychic influences. Whether you look at it as inspired or psychic, in both cases the imagination can be a channel of patterns originating outside the boundaries of your own experience. As Cayce pointed out, creativity, psychic, and inspiration have the same source—the soul.

As you lie next to a tree daydreaming, you assume your thoughts are your own. Your imagination spins images and stories based on your past experiences and your hopes and fears for the future. It's your own private world, right? Not exactly. While daydreaming, your imaginative illusions may often reflect a psychic influence. Patterns from someone else's thoughts and feelings could well be patterning your own daydream. ESP researchers have found that one person's thoughts can exert a subliminal influence upon the daydream patterns of another person. The daydreamer doesn't even suspect it! Subconscious minds are connected.

Sometimes, the superconscious mind exerts an inspirational, psychic influence on the imagination. It happened for me when I was preparing the dream tent for the incubation ceremonies I described in Chapter Three. As I set out to erect the tent, it suddenly occurred to me that I had assigned myself the task of creating a shrine. Out of a simple cloth tent I was to create the vibrations of a sacred sanctuary for people to decorate as their own special place. How could I expect people to imagine that the tent could be special if I didn't erect it myself in a sacred manner? I couldn't even imagine how to do that, but somehow I had to make it up.

I decided that my only option was to enter meditation and attune to the ideal of *the holy, sacred shrine*. After coming out of meditation, I engaged in the action equivalent of inspirational writing. By acting as if my intuitive responses were the actions of an experienced holy person, I allowed myself to channel sacred tent-erecting behaviors. I didn't know what I was doing, but I had to ignore that fact. I allowed myself to improvise as my imagination dictated. As evidenced by the special dreams that people had while sleeping in this tent, it seemed that my tent-erecting process was truly inspired by the archetypal ideal of the shrine I had hoped to channel.

A couple of years later, I found other, corroborating evidence of the inspirational dimension to what I had done. Studying the accounts of Native American rituals involving sacred spaces, I discovered that many of the experiences I had while erecting the tent were extremely similar to traditional rites. I had enacted, in many details, an archetypal pattern of behavior having to do with sanctification and purification of a ritual location. My imagination had proved to be a channel of patterns in the universal mind. Through a process of pretending and role playing in a meditative frame of mind, my imagination channeled something from beyond my conscious knowledge.

Developing Imagination Through Pretending

Many readers may fear that they can't use the channel of the imagination because they can't visualize. It's a natural concern, but unfounded. We all visualize. We can't see without imagery. What most people mean when they say that they can't visualize is that their images aren't as clear or visual as what they see with their eyes. The solution is easy, if you're willing to accept it: Simply pretend!

Here's how it works. Instead of trying to *visualize* your arm immersed in warm water, for example, *pretend* that your arm is immersed in warm water. Take a moment and put your arm on the table, or on the side of the chair. Then *pretend* that your arm is resting in a dish of warm water. What does it feel like to pretend that your arm is in warm water?

If you study what happens, what mental processes you perform, you will probably be able to confirm what I'm about to describe. Perhaps you feel that your pretending isn't a very vivid experience. If so, what is it that you're paying attention to that helps you feel that your pretending isn't vivid?

Children pretend all the time. Kids don't concern themselves with how vivid their pretending is, or whether it's occurring through images or thoughts, or even that their pretending is different from reality. They're too busy playing in their pretend world to notice any of that. They become absorbed in their pretending. It becomes real.

Is it possible that you aren't allowing yourself to become absorbed in your pretending, but are holding some part of yourself in reserve? If you devote more of your attention to comparing the quality of your pretending to what you think it should be like, or to how you experience external reality, then you can't expect your pretending to be very vivid.

Learn a lesson from children and the secret of creativity discussed in the previous chapter. Focus less on the product and more on enjoying the process. Allow yourself to become absorbed in your pretending and your imaginative channel will grow in vividness and vitality.

You don't have to be a professional debunker of claims of the paranormal, like the Amazing Randi, to have a laugh over what I'm suggesting. I can hear such a skeptic's sarcastic remark: "First you suggest that imagination is the same as reality. Now you're saying that if you can't imagine the reality you want, just pretend that you are!"

I can't expect a materialist perspective to accept the primacy of the mind over physical reality. Yet there's something in that criticism that does need to be examined. That is, how can we distinguish between imagination in the service of wish fulfillment and imagination as a psychic channel of inspiration? It's the role of ideals to help us invoke imagination in the service of truth rather than our desires.

Role Playing

Here's some pretending we've all done. Pretend that you're asking your boss for a raise, or you're asking a friend for a favor. This kind of daydreaming is quite common. When you have such a daydream, how do you get the other person in your imagination to act? In our daydreams, we play the role of all the people involved. In playing a role, we enter through our imagination into the character of another person. We set ourselves aside and channel the spirit of that character.

Roles themselves are something we naturally adopt. We play the role of friend, worker, spouse, or parent. When we play such a role, we're the channel of that relationship. We give of ourselves in the spirit of the relationship defined by the role. Sometimes we can be possessed by our roles. Perhaps you've met a schoolteacher who treats everyone like a student, or a lawyer who deals with every situation like a courtroom contest.

Other roles allow us to express things that we didn't even know we had in us. Have you ever put on a Halloween costume and found yourself getting caught up in the spirit of your character? Have you ever had the opportunity to put on a Santa Claus costume to discover just how wonderful you can be with children? In *Miracle on Thirty-fourth Street*, the man who claimed to be Santa Claus was so convincing in that role that he actually manifested the spirit of Christmas! Actors find that they sometimes play roles that become very inspiring for themselves as well as their audience. What started as pretending and acting became a channel of a quality of spirit. Imagination becomes real.

The Role of the Higher Self

Roles can be tools to use to enter certain states of awareness. What would it be like to play the role of your higher self? Cayce's formula for being a channel of our higher selves is to attune to our ideal, set self aside, and let the ideal express itself. Imagine what it might be like, then, to have the opportunity to play the role of someone who personified the ideals of your higher self.

The use of masks and costumes among aboriginal peoples around the world testifies to the power of roles as a channel of the spirit of higher values. When we put on the mask, we hide our own face. It allows us to get out of the way, to forget about our own personality. When we put on the costume, it allows us to attune to the spirit of the role. It's like stepping inside of the ideal itself and becoming it.

In aboriginal rituals, the people might dance while wearing the skins of animals. They believe that the spirit of that animal descends upon them and takes over the body. They say that the spirit *mounts* the dancer. The use of the word mount has two meanings. There's the sexual connotation, of the union of energies. There's also the channeling connotation, that the person's body has become a vehicle for the spirit to ride. The two connotations both reveal that the essence of channeling the spirit of a role is to become *one with* that role. It's the same principle we learned in studying intuition. It applies equally well to the use of the imagination as a channel.

In the dream incubation ceremony described in Chapter Five, I asked the dreamers to make masks to represent their higher self figures. When they wore their masks, they attuned to the spirit of the ideal their higher self role represented, and enacted it. It proved to be an inspiring form of channeling.

Playing the role of a higher self figure inspires a more superconscious mentality than the person's ordinary thought processes. When in the service of an ideal, the imagination serves as a channel of inspiration.

Channelers who ask their spirit guides whether or not they're really spirits or a product of the person's imagination often receive the reply that it doesn't matter. The two alternatives, the spirit guide explains, are the same.

Cayce would have us understand that when you attune to a certain frame of mind, you draw information from the subconscious and the superconscious that corresponds to that frame of mind. Whether you're channeling wish fulfill-ments or inspiration depends upon whether or not the frame of mind corresponds to an ideal or simply a desire. Role playing your higher self, an ideal frame of mind, can be a valid form of channeling.

Channeling Visionary Guidance From the Higher Self

What do you suppose happened when Cayce went into his psychic trance? On a couple of occasions he described what he experienced while entering that special state of con-sciousness. His description contained the two types of symbols that formed the scenario of the dream incubation ceremony. He said that he had visions of going to a special place, the Hall of the Akashic Records. There he met an old man who handed him a book containing the needed infor-mation about the person seeking the reading.

In one of his psychic readings he described this special place. He said:

> "The walls are jasper, the ceilings are beryl, the
> doors are beryl, the floors are pure gold, the
> light is the Lamb. The shape is not square, not
> perpendicular. . . . Much is here that may be
> given to those that seek to know the mysteries
> of those influences that go to make up that
> which impels man in his activity in the earth."
>
> **(5756–12)**

Clearly, it was a very special place. In contrast to this beautiful description of the Hall of Records, Cayce didn't describe the person who brought him the records beyond calling him an "old man." We may assume that the old man was one of Cayce's symbols for his higher self. Although in the trance state, Cayce described his journey as an elevation of consciousness, Cayce's conscious personality experienced it as a symbolic journey to a special place to meet an esteemed benefactor, the Keeper of the Records.

Having an imaginary journey that proves to be of value wasn't an experience unique to Cayce. The boy who saw true experienced similar adventures in his daydreams. You too can learn to receive guidance from such an inspirational daydream.

You know what it's like to have imaginary conversations with your friends, spouse, or boss at work. Why not have one with an inspiring teacher? In exploring inspirational writing, we discussed how you can have question and answer sessions with your higher self. You can engage this same process in a daydream.

Think of a special place where you'd like to meet with your higher self figure. Imagining being in that place will put you in the mood of your ideal. While you're there, basking in the wonderful vibrations of your power spot, imagine seeing your higher self figure approach you. Experience the person's special qualities and what it's like to be in that person's presence. Pour your heart out to your higher self, expressing what's on your mind. Then simply listen as your higher self responds.

If you practice this method, you'll find that your imagination will provide you a very convenient channel of guidance. You can experiment with endless variations of this basic approach. An excellent resource for imagination techniques is Dr. Mike Samuels's book, *Seeing with the Mind's Eye*.

You can intensify the process by playing music to accompany your daydream. As we've learned earlier, music can create a bridge to connect you with the infinite reaches of the imagination and the superconscious mind. To learn more about the use of music with the imagination, you'll want to read *Traveler in Inner Space*. Written by music therapist Carol Bush, it describes what can happen when you add music to your daydreaming and gives many suggestions about particular musical pieces to evoke specific mood states. What could be more natural than curling up on the couch while your favorite symphony is playing and becoming absorbed in an uplifting daydream?

Learn to trust in your imagination. If you can give your

imaginal dog a long leash, you'll find, like the boy who saw true, that the imagination is a channel of wondrous teachings and guidance.

Meditation teaches you to become a channel of the spirit, of inspiration. Through inspirational writing, you learn how to express yourself while in a meditative state of mind. Working with the creative arts, especially music, you can attune yourself even more gracefully to the superconscious realm. With your imagination, you have a vehicle that knows no limits. To intensify your channeling experiences even further, you can learn to use self-hypnosis to become totally absorbed in your ideal state of consciousness. Now we enter the domain of trance channeling and you're well prepared for this next stage of your adventure in learning to channel your higher self.

PART III

Adventures in Trance Channeling

CHAPTER NINE

Who's There?
Identifying the Spirit Who Speaks

"Changes in the dimensional conditions [of a person upon death] does not alter that which is known in the earth plane as desire. If the desire is in that direction that there may be an association with, an aid to, a seeking of such associations, then only the means, the channel, the way, the course, is necessary to complete the communication."
—**Edgar Cayce, 5756–8**

"Anyone may speak who may seek, if the entity or the soul's activity will allow same; or if the desire of the individuals seeking so over commands as to make for a set channel."
—**Edgar Cayce, 507–1**

"There is being awakened within self a power, an influence. *Do not* allow this to be directed by an entity that does proclaim himself or herself as *being* the guide. Why? For, as indicated, the abilities have been such in self—and the soul development—that to call upon the Infinite is much greater, much more satisfying, much more worthwhile in the experience of an individual

> soul than being guided or directed merely by an
> entity outside of self that—*as* self—*is* being
> in a state of transition *or* development.''
> —**Edgar Cayce, 338–2**

In his book, *Trances*, the journalist Stewart Wavell tells us of his travels to Malaysia to observe the Semai's trance dancing. The tribe's medicine man begins the dance himself, with some slow, swaying motions and a bit of singing. Women pounding on the ground with bamboo stompers or hitting gongs provide an accompanying large rhythm section. Soon the men join the medicine man in song and, one by one, get up and begin dancing.

The women quicken the rhythm and the men begin to surrender to the music. The women beat out a still faster rhythm and the men enter a dancing trance state. They whirl their arms and spin about. Some fall down to peals of laughter from the women.

Some of the men begin talking in voices. These speeches elicit even more laughter from the women. Wavell learns that the entranced men leave their bodies and rise up into the sky to join the birds in flight. Spirits of the dead take the opportunity to enter those unused bodies and share their thoughts with the crowd.

Eager to speak, these spirits have much to say to their waiting audience. Mainly they scold the tribespeople for their misdeeds. The living can keep no secrets from these spirits. They reveal illicit flirtations and other choice pieces of gossip for all to hear. The women laugh heartily. They find the statements amusing and a great source of entertainment. It's the tribe's equivalent of "Saturday Night Live."

Clearly, the Semai don't put the spirits on pedestals. They don't worship them. On the contrary, they consider the spirits mischievous and untrustworthy. The Semai know that the spirits can often lead a person astray or into danger. When Wavell inquired why the spirits acted that way, the answer he received was somewhat surprising. It's because the spirits are jealous—they're dead while the people are alive!

The activities of aboriginal groups around the world suggests that some form of communications with spirits, however we might understand that term, has been with us since the beginning of time. The Semai's tongue-in-cheek perspective indicates a casual wisdom born of countless centuries of experience.

In our modern culture, however, we're not casual about spirit contacts. We find it a bizarre form of occult activity or perhaps a deceptive fraud. National polls, however, indicate that the majority of Americans believe there is some kind of life after death. And many more than you might suspect have had what they feel are encounters with the dead. Yet our lack of understanding of the nonmaterial world makes it difficult to have any meaningful perspective on spirit communication.

Popular channeling celebrities give voice to some puzzling identities. Kevin Ryerson's Tom McPherson claims to be the spirit of a Shakespearean pickpocket. J. Z. Knight's Ramtha claims he is a 25,000-year-old warrior. Jack Pursel's Lazaris explains that he is simply a spirit, one who never has been alive in a body. Pat Rodergast's Emmanuel claims to be part of us all. The various possibilities are confusing.

Who speaks through a trance channel? What sort of visitation might you be inviting should you decide to experiment with trance channeling? As we'll see, not all spirits are what they seem.

The History of Spiritualism

Sir Arthur Conan Doyle, the creator of Sherlock Holmes, wrote the story of how spirits came to the modern world. Reading his two-volume work, *The History of Spiritualism,* you get the impression that the channeling craze of the 1980s is a rerun of events during the 1850s in America.

Spiritualism began on March 31, 1848. There had been mysterious rapping sounds in the home of the Fox family in Hydesville, New York for several weeks. On that particular evening, in desperate response to these sounds, Kate Fox, the youngest child in the family, snapped her fingers. A rap replied. Kate snapped twice and got two raps back. However she snapped, the raps echoed her faithfully.

Conan Doyle pointed out that when the telephone was invented, or the transatlantic cable, very mundane messages were first transmitted, but communication over those channels soon became much more sophisticated. The same was true for the invention of Spiritualism.

Witnessing her daughter's discovery, Mrs. Fox gave the raps a code—one rap for *yes*, two raps for *no*, and the dialogue began. Soon neighbors, then townspeople, and finally investigators came to the Fox home to interrogate the rapper. Someone taught it the use of the alphabet, and the channel of communication further improved. The rapper claimed to have been murdered, identified the name of the murderer, and indicated that it had been buried in the cellar. Next day the cellar was dug up and human remains were found.

Within two years, a new religion—"Spiritualism"—had a well-established membership. A technological explosion provided new and different means of contacting the spirit realm. Coded raps gave way to providing spirits with trumpets to sound their voices, then people learned how to offer their own voice boxes as a channel for spirits to speak. The word, *medium*, meaning somebody through whom the spirits of the dead communicate, had become a household term.

It was the publicity that helped sprout this new religion so fast. When word traveled of the rappings at the Fox household, rappings quickly spread to other locations. Hundreds of people were showing evidence of mediumship. Prominent people, public leaders, and celebrities reported their conversations with the dead and helped establish credibility. Converts to Spiritualism claimed that it gave tangible proof of a life hereafter, what the afterlife was like, and helped the living understand how to live better lives. Church groups and scientific organizations joined forces in ridiculing and denouncing the phenomenon. The extensive press coverage magnified public awareness, but added nothing to public understanding.

Parapsychology Tests the Spirits

Writing in 1926, Conan Doyle noted that in the seventy years since the beginning of Spiritualism, understanding made little progress. Confronting the enigma of spirit communication did, at least, give birth to parapsychology, the scientific study of paranormal events. Sixty years since Holmes's book, however, parapsychology may have developed more sophisticated ways of testing mediums, but has determined that such research will never be able to prove or disprove the reality of life after death. Instead, it led to some convincing demonstrations of the telepathic ability of the medium's spirit guides.

Eileen Garrett, for example, was a well-respected medium. Author of several books on the subject, including *Many Voices: The Autobiography of a Medium*, she also founded the Parapsychology Foundation to promote scientific research. The noted parapsychologist, J. Gaither Pratt, describes in his book, *The Psychic Realm: What Can You Believe,* an experiment involving Mrs. Garrett's mediumship.

While Mrs. Garrett was in trance, researchers presented her spirit guide, Ouvani, with the names of twelve different people, unknown to all involved, and requested detailed information about each of these people. Afterward, researchers cut up copies of the transcripts to create several hundred separate sentences. They randomly shuffled these statements and created a true/false questionnaire. All twelve people examined the questionnaire and indicated, for each separate statement, whether or not it was personally true. The results proved that the people judged as true those statements that Ouvani had actually made about them much more often than they did so for statements made about the other participants. The odds of this particular result were quoted as being "one million, seven hundred thousand to one." The experiment proved that Mrs. Garrett and her Ouvani voice at least had ESP ability, but it didn't prove whether or not Ouvani was in fact who he claimed to be—a spirit from the dead.

Was Edgar Cayce a Medium?

Cayce's trance channeling seems quite similar to mediumship. He entered an altered state of consciousness and delivered information about the afterlife and the conditions of those deceased. He seemed to be in communication with spirits.

Sometimes those sitting in attendance could overhear Cayce's side of the conversation, but they couldn't hear what the spirits themselves were saying. In one instance, for example, the record indicated Cayce as saying, "Don't all speak at once. . . . All together then now, huh? Uncle Porter, too?. . . . Oh, he is *grown* now, huh?. . . . Uhhuh. All right. . . . Yes, I still play baseball. . . . Sure! Yes ma'am!. . . ."

During many of his readings he would comment about the presence of some entity. Sometimes he would relay information to one of the sitters, "Your mother wants you to know that she is okay."

On many occasions, therefore, Cayce appears to be in communication with the spirits of the dead, having a normal conversation. On other occasions, however, he evidenced mediumship in the traditional sense, where a spirit spoke through Cayce's mouth to address the audience directly.

On at least seventy-five separate occasions did Cayce function as a medium. The record of many of these instances appears in *Psychic Awareness*, Volume 9 of *The Edgar Cayce Readings*, under the heading, "Spirit Communication."

Cayce's mother came through on occasion, for example, and would talk to Cayce's wife, calling her "Sister." Cayce's old physician from Hopkinsville came sometimes to give advice to Cayce's son Hugh Lynn, identifying himself at the end by saying, "This is Hill." A man who used to be associated with Cayce's work came through on a reading for his wife and talked considerably about his existence after death. He encouraged his wife to come to see Cayce for advice, and referred to Cayce as "your friend, my friend." In one reading concerning a business project, three different individuals, identifying themselves by name, came through and gave their input.

Besides the spirits of relatives and acquaintances of the people present, entities from the distant past also spoke through Cayce. In one instance, when the sitters asked the source to identify itself, the reply was, "Zorain, a student of Zoroaster." In another reading, the reply was, "Joseph—I, Joseph, would counsel you," meaning the husband of Mary, Jesus' mother.

In all these cases, which are indistinguishable from typical mediumship, there are a number of factors that distinguish them from Cayce's usual style of speech when giving a reading. As in the final example, where Joseph supposedly identifies himself, the word, "I," is used. Cayce never said "me" or "I" in readings, except in these instances where another identity was claiming to speak. Cayce always said, "we are through," "as we find," or "through these channels." In a number of instances, the entity speaking addresses the sitter in a personal, or familiar way, unlike Cayce's normal mode of referring to the person asking for the reading. In other cases, the tone of voice, or feeling of the person speaking, was unlike Cayce's own presence. In one reading, for example, Gladys Davis Turner, Cayce's lifelong stenographer, heard her dead brother speak directly to her. She confided to a friend that she just *knew* it was him.

This intuitive, feeling response on the part of the people present was sometimes a very dramatic indicator of the profundity of what was happening, regardless of how you might interpret it. Perhaps the most dramatic instance involved the appearance of the individual who identified itself as Michael, the Archangel.

According to the records, Michael interrupted a reading, coming through in a thunderous voice that rattled the windows: "BOW THINE HEADS, I MICHAEL, LORD OF THE WAY!" Depending upon the occasion, Michael would encourage the sitters or rebuke them, concerning their work. The effect on the audience was to create a profound, stunned silence, tears, and a heightened sense of spiritual attunement. These occasions had the revelatory effect of an oracle, a contact with a divine presence. For a more detailed, first-hand, eyewitness account of these appearances by a professional psychologist, read Harmon Bro's *A Seer Out of Season: The Life of Edgar Cayce*.

All these examples show clearly that at times Cayce did perform as a medium and channeled an astounding range of entities. All of these occasions, however, add up to *less than 1 percent* of the times that Cayce went into a trance. More than 99 percent of the time he functioned, not as a medium, but as a channel of his higher consciousness, as we'll appreciate more later.

Cayce's Perspective on Mediumship and the Subconscious Mind

In a reading that Cayce gave immediately after an instance of spirit communication with his mother, he indicated that such communication has little value for proving life after death. He encouraged that we can, however, learn much from it to gain a better understanding of the subconscious mind. Such study can stimulate one's personal awareness, he indicated, leading to the direct experience of oneself as a being of spirit.

The subconscious mind, unlike the conscious mind of our sensory-based egos, is a stratum of the mind that extends beyond the boundaries of any individual body. When a person dies the personal conscious mind dies with the body, but the subconscious mind remains unaffected. There is life after death, but it's the life of the subconscious mind. Like the Tibetan tradition, Cayce asserts that our dream images, or subconscious desires and fears, continue their existence after the death of the body.

Cayce makes an important distinction about this continued life. There are the continued *effects*, which arise from the permanent records of all thoughts and experiences—the Akashic Record. Thoughts are things, Cayce repeated often, and those thoughts live on in eternity. There is also the continued *activity*, which is the soul's spirit journey in other dimensions of being. Much of what passes for contact with the activity of that spirit, however, is actually contact with the *effects of the records* of the entity's experience patterns in the subconscious regions. That confusion is one reason that spirit communication is of no use as proof of life after death.

Here's an example to illustrate how a person might interact with an independent thought form, experience it as the activity of an independent spirit, yet where no spirit is actually present. Human beings create programs that run computers. Once programmed, the computer will run by itself. There is no longer any human being present, just the person's recorded thought patterns.

There exists a notorious computer program called "Eliza." Researchers created her to perform like a sympathetic counselor. Make a statement about how you feel and she will respond with a question to help you clarify your feelings. She is programmed to identify the crucial words in your statement, choose from a pool of her own caring words, and then reply with an appropriately counselorlike probing question: You say, "I'm feeling low today." She replies, "Tell me more about how you're feeling low today." As you interact with Eliza, you get the impression that she is listening very attentively and cares about you. Eliza feels real. Yet you're interacting with no one, only the implications of a thought pattern left behind by a computer programmer years ago.

If you continue to interact with Eliza, you note a certain tiring repetitiveness in her responses. It's also frustrating when you can't get any further clarification on something beyond how she has already responded. Such limitations are exactly the same type of frustrations experienced in some instances of spirit communication. In these instances, we're not communicating with an active spirit, but the *traces of the deceased's thought patterns*.

It's also possible for several people to simultaneously have contact with such thought patterns. At the same time, therefore, and in far corners of the world, different people can claim to be channeling the same historical person from the past. The same holds true for past life memories.

Different people can pick up the recorded impressions of the life of Attila the Hun.

In such cases, they may not remember the same details, or channel the same information. Why is that? Isn't a computer programmed to always perform the same way? It is , but it depends upon how it's questioned. Communication across the channel of the subconscious mind, according to Cayce, operates on the principle of *affinity*. In the popular jargon, that translates as "like attracts like." When we channel the thought patterns of the deceased, or recall their past life memories, we do so in a selective manner that most resonates with our own subconscious feelings, motivations, and needs.

The same principle of affinity applies to communication with the active spirit of the dead. People's interests and desires don't stop when they die; they continue to be active within the subconscious regions. When there is a bond of love, or a common concern, such as a shared intense interest in a business activity, there is the needed affinity between the living and the dead. There can then be created channels not only of communication, but also of obsession, or possession.

When a person dies with unfulfilled desires, or compelling interests, those needs serve as attachments, keeping the active spirit searching for a means of expression. Chemical addictions, sexual cravings, overeating, gambling, and other compulsions with an intense emotional component, create specific and strong magnets, attracting them to similarly inclined people among the living, who can provide channels of vicarious satisfaction.

Cayce indicated that a living person can call upon the active spirits of the dead, and, depending upon their availability and the affinity of mind, they will come. It's not, however, to either party's benefit to have such contact, beyond a brief reassurance of the continuation of love. The deceased need to develop their awareness of higher realms of existence, to go to the light, as it were. The living have very little to do by way of helping the dead in this process except to pray for them to awaken to the light. We don't help by communicating with them except perhaps to say, "What are you doing listening to me instead of focusing on the light and going on?"

On the flip side of the coin, the dead have little to teach the living. Cayce notes that the dead don't gain wisdom from the death experience except for the realization that life goes on. Sometimes they aren't even aware that they have passed on because their awareness continues via the channel of the subconscious mind. That gives them a heightened telepathic sensitivity, however; a sense of continued contact with the living. A spirit of the dead can therefore demonstrate impressive ESP powers. The living, who can contact the subconscious only indirectly, easily mistake such ESP as greater wisdom and become fascinated with the spirit's revelations. Pursuing such phenomena distracts all concerned from their own inner development. It's for that reason that Cayce had reservations about the practice of mediumship.

Edgar Cayce and Eileen Garrett Channel for Each Other

In 1934, Edgar Cayce and Eileen Garrett met for an unusual experiment. They gave a psychic reading for each other to exchange viewpoints on the source of each other's channeling ability. The two sets of readings confirm Cayce's description of the difference between channeling one's higher self and channeling a spirit guide. The only difference was one of personal perspective, reflecting Cayce's religious orientation toward union with God and Mrs. Garrett's philosophical orientation toward understanding.

When Eileen Garrett went into trace, her spirit guide, Ouvani, confirmed that Cayce made use of "his own light," the clairvoyant understanding of his higher self, to get his information. Ouvani indicated that although Cayce was making a very generous gift of himself to the person seeking the reading, this approach to channeling was harder to do than making use of a spirit guide as an intermediary. In fact, Ouvani indicated that the procedure was taking a physical toll on Cayce. Ouvani suggested that there was at least one spirit guide that would be perfectly happy to help Cayce obtain the needed information. It had already covertly done so in the past when Cayce's own energy level was too low. When asked, Ouvani wouldn't name this spirit but suggested it was up to Cayce to decide whether to cultivate that contact. At the conclusion of this chapter, we will learn how Cayce responded to Ouvani's advice.

When Cayce read for Mrs. Garrett, he described her psychic ability as a talent developed in past lives through a sincere desire to teach others about metaphysical principles. He indicated that her mediumship today was motivated in that same spirit of promoting understanding. Her channeling ability, he said, was a combination of her own soul awareness as well as assistance provided by "influences" that, like her, had an attitude and desire to teach others. When asked more about her spirit guides, he suggested that it wasn't for him to say, but something that she needed to become more aware of through her own seeking from within.

The Psychoanalysis of Spirit Guides

Some thirty years after the Cayce–Garrett readings, Eileen Garrett asked Ira Progoff, an expert in Jung's psychoanalysis, to interview her spirit guides. She wanted to learn more about their true nature. Were they actually, as they claimed, people who had lived before; or were they, as many psychologists believed, a part of her own personality? She had serious doubts about either of these standard interpretations and wanted a deeper understanding of the meaning of her mediumship.

Progoff presents his interviews with Mrs. Garrett's spirit guides in his unusual book, *Image of an Oracle*. He asked them probing questions about the nature of their being, stimulating them to clarify their own self-concepts. In return, they probed Progoff's own understanding and evoked developments in his self-awareness. He was deeply touched by this work.

He interviewed four different entities. The first, Ouvani, identified himself as a young Arab soldier in the 1200s who had died in battle. Ouvani was the entity who interacted with Cayce during the Cayce–Garrett readings. The second, Abduhl Latif, said he was a Persian physician who lived in the 1600s. The third, Tahoteh, named "The Giver of the Word," described himself as a god who was with Moses when he received the Law. The fourth, Ramah, also a god, referred to himself as "The Giver of Life."

Progoff learns that questioning them about their *identity* is inappropriate. They cannot give a meaningful answer to an inappropriate question without falsifying the whole topic. Asked if he had lived before, for example, Abduhl Latif answers yes, but tries to get Progoff to understand that he is talking more about the continuity of human experience rather than the continuity of individual human beings. Furthermore, he learns that these spirits are intimately connected to Mrs. Garrett herself, and to get rid of them would be to get rid of her, and vice versa. He learns that rather than ask *who* is speaking, Ouvani or Mrs. Garrett, it would be better to ask *what quality of consciousness* or level of reality is being expressed at the moment. This conception is similar to that suggested by the source of Cayce's readings, describing it as accessing a particular state of consciousness.

On the other hand, Cayce himself, when describing what it was like to enter that state of consciousness, said he often experienced receiving his information from a person, an old man figure. Progoff concludes, however, that it's not correct to interpret such figures as subpersonalities of the channel. We're contacting a level of the mind that is transpersonal, that is impersonal, that goes far beyond the channel's own personality. Edward Edinger, another Jungian psychiatrist, once commented that our desire to expand our consciousness comes from "the innate urge of life to realize itself consciously. The transpersonal life energy, in the process of self-unfolding, uses human consciousness, a product of itself, as an instrument for its own self-realization."

Rather than thinking of these spirits as persons, or subpersonalities, therefore, Progoff concludes that it's more accurate to think of them as *personifications*. We may refer to Mother Teresa, for example, as the personification of love and charity, or Rambo as wild courage personified. Progoff reminds us of Jung's observations on the universal symbol of the Old Wise Man. This higher self symbol personifies the mind's capacity to bring knowledge and insight from its depths. The Old Wise Man is a *role* the mind plays when it creates pearls of wisdom and brings them to the surface.

Ouvani, for example, is the doorkeeper, a role that served to protect the open channel from the very many voices that would come through. As Ouvani points out, anyone— enthusiasts, foolish ones, anguished ones—can come through when the channel is open so that he needs to guard that opening for the protection of the instrument. Ouvani is therefore a personification of a protective function of the mind.

This approach to understanding of Ouvani's nature is reminiscent of Cayce's remark about Garrett's spirit guides: "Their names are rather in *her* experience, in *her* seeking." Progoff notes that we all know much more than we're able to put into words. Mrs. Garrett is particularly intuitive and senses a large body of information or knowledge or wisdom coming from within her. But it's so much that it disturbs and confuses her. It's larger than she can express. Ouvani is a personification of that level of consciousness within her that focuses the connection with the deeper level of the psyche to allow the transmission of information to flow through the channel's verbal abilities.

While in trace, for example, Cayce described his gift as the ability of his subconscious mind to interpret the impressions coming from the superconscious mind so that the objective mind could express it in words. The subconscious mind of Mrs. Garrett experiences or translates this self-regulatory aspect of the mind as the personification of a role, in the form of an Ouvani.

Progoff discovers that while Ouvani and Abduhl can answer questions about Progoff's private life, and can comment on his patients, Tahoteh and Ramah weren't able to exhibit such psychic talents. Progoff concludes that the *psychic* function (accessing information), and the function of being an *oracle* (delivering wisdom), exist at different levels of consciousness. Operating as psychics, Ouvani and Abduhl answer questions of a personal concern to those who are asking. Functioning as oracles, Tahoteh and Ramah, however, answer questions of universal concern. Cayce would refer to the difference between the subconscious and the superconscious levels of the mind to explain this distinction.

In order for the oracle level of the mind to function, the channel, and those seeking, have to be concerned for more than their own needs. Progoff learns that when human beings struggle and wrestle with the ultimate questions about nature, about life, the principle of *The Word*, or what he calls the inner principle of meaning, will be present there in the struggle. If the human being can persevere in this struggle, the principle of The Word will help bring inspirations or insights to that person. Tahoteh is Mrs. Garrett's personification of that aspect of humanity's mind that functions to bring new meaning.

Echoing Cayce's interpretation of the Word, Progoff learns from Tahoteh that it's a creative principle. Yet it can both build and destroy simultaneously. It comes at any point in a person's own life during a time of crisis. Echoing Cayce's Law, "in the application comes the awareness," the wisdom Tahoteh brings comes through the person's *living through* the crisis. Tahoteh, or the level of the human psyche that he personifies, isn't a shortcut through problems. It's not an instantaneous insight. Instead, it's something that evolves as we struggle at the conscious level to grapple with the issues and try to understand them.

When Progoff asks, "Why have you come, is there a purpose in your coming and speaking through Eileen?" Progoff learns about changes on earth and the role of prophecy throughout history in helping us deal with such changes. Some twenty years later, on the Merv Griffin show, Lazaris explained that the purpose of his coming was to instruct us of the true nature of our reality and to remind us of our talents, so that we might take a more constructive role in shaping the future of the planet. Cayce expressed similar themes in his readings. The oracular level of the mind speaks an unchanging message.

The Darker Side of Trance Channeling: Whatever Possessed Me?

When we watch J. Z. Knight go into a trance on television and then see Ramtha get up and begin to address the audience, we might well wonder, is J. Z. possessed? Is she a multiple personality? These interpretations of what happens when a person channels a spirit guide have a certain amount of validity. Not that such channelers are possessed, or are multiple personalities. We learned from Progoff's investigation not to think in such stereotyped fashion. Yet there is a good amount of overlap between all these unusual phenomena, as well as in some more common, but still puzzling events of everyday life.

What possesses us to do things we know we shouldn't? How is it that we sometimes act in ways that don't seem like ourselves? Sometimes when we're out shopping we make impulsive, expensive purchases of luxury items, or buy unnecessary items from the grocery store. Men going through a mid-life crisis can engage in bizarre behavior, leave family and career, and take off with young women. Shoplifters and people with other compulsions often wonder what possess them to do things against their will or better judgment.

What possesses people to smoke cigarettes when they know all the health consequences? Nicotine addiction, certainly, creates part of the compulsion. But that's not all of it. Advertisements from past decades suggested that cigarette smoking is good for our health, good for our image. Such advertisements are but one example of the many suggestions we receive that influence our behavior, that undermine the action of our free will. Unexamined cultural assumptions are like ideas that have a life of their own. They can possess us.

Whether it's our own repressed, unconscious impulses influencing us, cultural propaganda hypnotizing us with assumptions or values that aren't necessarily true, intuitive urges based on subliminal telepathic information, the influence of the wishes of our friends and family members, or the whispering of spirits, there are many ways we can be possessed. There are many ways automatisms from the subconscious express other dimensions to our personality. Ideas, feelings, and needs in the subconscious mind can exert irresistible influences on our behavior, regardless of how they get there.

In being possessed, we're not innocent. Though we may act in accord with society's values, we also have our rebellious side. Though we value being independent thinkers, we also appreciate the respect of our peers. Our personalities have multiple faces. Whatever the source of a possessing influence, whether it is commercial advertisers or spirit guides, there is always an *affinity* between the possessor and the possessed. We all have our darker sides, our sub-personalities that we hide as best we can. The spirit whispers in our ear something that a part of us wants to hear. We just need that extra push.

In the book, *The Unquiet Dead: A Psychologist Treats Spirit Possession,* Dr. Edith Fiore concludes, on the basis of hundreds of cases of possession, that like Cayce's affinity principle, there always was, at some level, a subconscious compliance with the possessing spirit. Sometimes it's simply a matter of not wishing to take responsibility for something, or a wish to have a power or a talent without having to work to develop it. Just as Eileen Garrett's guides had an affinity for her own seeking mind, trying to understand, trying to help others, we all have affinities for the thoughts that possess us.

The psychiatrist, M. Scott Peck, describes in his book, *People of the Lie,* cases of true possession, by the spirit of evil. He tells of his experiences participating in exorcisms to remove these influences from the victims. Yet he also describes how there is an affinity to the spirit of evil within us, in our tendencies to lie, to hurt others, to deceive ourselves. Just as deep from within the psyche there rises the spirit of wisdom, personified as the higher self, so there is a spirit of evil, sometimes personified as the devil.

Cayce indicates that evil isn't a separate force—all force is the one energy of God—but that it's a pattern of use of that one force for personal indulgence at the expense of the whole, a willful and knowing rebellion against God's will. It's a powerful transpersonal pattern, existing both within and beyond the individual personality.

Nothing is more powerful, Cayce counsels us, than our own will. Nothing can possess us against our will. If we're willing, however, to engage in self-indulgence, the subconscious mind can serve as a channel of conspiring influences. Whether or not possession, in the diabolical sense of the word, will result depends upon the integrity of the psychic centers of the body. Cayce indicated that unprotected openings in these centers can occur through a variety of causes. Besides improper meditation practices and dissociated states of mind, illness, or accident, extreme emotional states, such as rage or chemical intoxication can make a person vulnerable.

You can read a fascinating eyewitness account of disembodied spirits entering the living. George Ritchie, the psychiatrist who helped popularize the study of near-death experiences, describes such an unsettling invasion in his book, *Return from Tomorrow*. While he was out-of-body during a near fatal heart attack, he saw shadowy entities entering the bodies of drunken servicemen as they fell to the floor in alcoholic stupor. Dr. Ritchie noted that unlike most people who have a complete aura of light around their bodies, the drunken servicemen had gaping holes in their auras that opened up to admit the entities' entrance. It makes you wonder if you dare ever drink too much again. You might not arrive home alone.

Possession can also occur in cases of multiple personality. As a type of mental disorder, multiple personality is an extreme example of the dissociation process we studied earlier. Unlike a slip of the pen, where a single feeling that has been pushed into the unconscious manages to slip out, cases of multiple personality result from whole segments of a person's being having been pushed into unconsciousness. The early childhood of people who develop multiple personalities have an important factor in common with many people who spontaneously develop channeling ability—abuse, neglect, or an otherwise intolerable situation that encourages the child to develop a secret, safe hiding place in their imagination. Early on they develop the talent of dissociation to keep certain parts of their personality safe from harm by the outside world.

As D. Scott Rogo so clearly documents in his book, *The Infinite Boundary: A Psychic Look at Spirit Possession, Madness, and Multiple Personality,* cases of multiple personality mirror mediumship and possession, having attributes of both. The hidden, secondary personality may subliminally influence the feelings or actions of the primary personality, just like a spirit guide or a possessing spirit. The main personality will go unconscious and disappear, like in mediumship, and the second personality emerges. The emergence of the secondary personality is more like contemporary channeling than traditional mediumship, in that the secondary personality can now have use of the body, walk about and interact with life, becoming a member of society. It may itself feel possessed, in that it senses the presence of the main personality, and feels resentful of having to turn itself back over to its dominance.

The secondary personality can also show evidence of psychic ability, much like the control spirit of a medium. There can also be levels of secondary personalities, with a higher self figure, called an "inner self helper," who can help the therapist guide the therapy. In other cases, secondary personalities may identify themselves as spirits or angels, unrelated to the person except that they have come to help out. On the other hand, other personalities sometimes appear that identify themselves as spirits of other people entirely.

When the integrity of a person is violated, whether through the repression of powerful unconscious desires or through harm to the body's endocrine system, and the person is open to influence, a wide range of intrusions can occur. Given these potential sources of possession, from the ordinary to the demonic, it seems important that we give careful thought to how we open ourselves to the psychic, transpersonal, and potentially turbocharged energy of the psyche.

Channeling Your Higher Self

After Cayce received his reading from Eileen Garrett, he gave himself a reading concerning Ouvani's suggestion about the availability of a spirit guide to help in his work. In that reading, an entity identifying itself as Haleliel spoke through Cayce, suggesting he was the guide who wished to help. After the reading, Cayce discussed the idea of channeling Haleliel with his wife and colleagues. He decided not to invite that source of assistance, but to continue channeling from the highest state of consciousness from within himself. Not that spirits never spoke through again, for they did. Yet Cayce's attitude was that in surrendering himself to be used as a channel by the Christ Consciousness, if that highest consciousness from within chose to send an intermediary, so be it. It was not then Cayce's own will, but the will of God.

It wasn't so much out of a fear of possession that Cayce turned away from relying on a spirit guide for help. In fact, in all his readings discouraging spirit communication, automatic writing, and other forms of "trick shooting," his warnings about possession were rarely the main focus of his concern. Instead, his primary consideration was that we not be diverted from growing in our *own* awareness, of developing our *own* higher consciousness.

We all appreciate the advice against developing an unnecessary dependency on a crutch. It undermines our own growth. It shortchanges us from realizing our own potential. Cayce, both in his daily life as well as in his trance channeling, taught by example that by seeking the highest within, we provide the best possible channel available. As we now turn to the topic of evaluating channeled sources of guidance, we will see once again that all knowledge lies within.

CHAPTER TEN

Evaluating Channeled Guidance

"As to whether psychic information is from those
who have attuned themselves to the influences
that are even in the material world, or to that
force or source which has been sent or given
in Creative Forces that are constructive in the
experiences of others, may only be judged
by the application of same in the experience of
the individual."

—Edgar Cayce, 5752–5

"For truth is a growing experience in the hearts
and the minds of individuals as they apply
those tenets of the law in their individual
experience."

—Edgar Cayce, 281–27

We may be stymied by a problem or a choice confronting
us. Seeking channeled guidance, from ourselves or others,
expresses a desire for increased consciousness, or awareness.
All knowledge is within, Cayce reminds us, but it often
doesn't seem that way—we aren't aware of what to do, to
choose or to decide.

Cayce indicated that we are capable of channeling the
information ourselves if we will but make the necessary

effort. Having a genuine need to know, making the necessary attunement, and having the ability and the intention to put the guidance into service seem to be the main ingredients to receiving a helping hand through channeled sources of inspiration.

When the student is ready, the teacher—whether an inner teacher or an external one—will appear, but not before. Readiness involves both the person's ability to recognize guidance and to be able to apply it. When Cayce emphasizes that all guidance comes from within, he's not just saying that it's "best" to seek from within, but that there is no way to avoid it, ultimately.

Ultimately, we have to be our own channels of guidance, even when we seek assistance from others. As we learn to use our own channels—intuition, dreams, inspirational writing, and other means—we may nevertheless find it helpful to consult a professional intuitive, a psychic who channels guidance for others. Yet to actually gain anything from such a psychic reading requires responding to the deep resonance from within as we listen, in order to recognize what may be true. Thus we touch deeper knowledge within ourselves.

Getting guidance from someone else's psychic channeling can thus help you recognize your own psychic ability. Interacting with a trance channel can also be good preparation for doing your own trance channeling.

Whether we are dealing with psychic guidance channeled from another person, or material that we channel for ourselves, we nevertheless have to learn how to evaluate that guidance. The advice Cayce gave on this subject applies to both situations. As we'll see, learning to evaluate channeled guidance is actually part of the process of channeling.

Cayce's Guidance Heuristic

A heuristic is a method of discovery. It's based on the assumption that *there is no perfect, absolute truth*, only better and more workable approximations to it. Cayce's method of discovery, although oriented toward psychic awareness, is universal in its nature. One expression of his heuristic is, "Pray hard, as if everything depended on God, but work hard, as if everything depended on you!"

The psychiatrist Carl Jung frequently noted that the unconscious seemed to produce its best results when the person had exhausted all conscious avenues of exploration and progress. He presented cases of people whose dreams, previously full of insights and helpful hints, dried up when the person became passive, relying exclusively on the dreams for help, but without making any personal effort.

Cayce's method parallels Jung's observations. You need to do your best with what you have available, and then more will be given. *Priming the pump with your own best efforts begins the channeling cycle.*

Cayce's guidance heuristic includes a complete, full cycle of the discovery process, similar to the well-known sequence of creative problem solving: questioning, perspiration and research, incubation, inspiration, further perspiration in the testing and application; then more questioning, perspiration and research, incubation, and so on.

Getting guidance is like creative problem solving. Only a piece of the solution, a tentative or partial answer is available at first, or the details of a solution need to be ironed out. Cayce's *most important principle* is that if that little bit of guidance is *tested*, evaluated by being put into *practice*, further guidance will be forthcoming down the line. Cayce often suggested to *do what you know to do*, to do your best to apply what you do have, and *more would be given* later. It's a variation on Cayce's Law, "In the application comes the awareness." This approach, based upon successive approximations to the final solution, is the guidance heuristic that Cayce advocated, regardless of the source of guidance, whether from one's own dreams or from a psychic adviser.

What is the Question?

Identifying the appropriate question is very important, as the question will influence the answer. To stimulate your dreams to answer a question, it's important that the question be worked on. I have studied people's reactions to answers that they have received from psychics and have found a common reaction to be, "Oh, I wish I had given more thought to my question." A vague question may result in a general answer. A good question needs to be specifically addressed to what you really need to know. As Cayce repeatedly pointed out, it's the desire of the seeker, the particular quality of the vibrational pattern of the need to know, that stimulates and focuses the energy from which the guidance is created.

Sometimes you don't know what you need to know. There is no question at first, just a problem, a sense of unease, difficulty, or pain. By yourself, or with the help of a good listener, it's possible to start with the felt sense of frustration, or conflict, to determine what is needed by way of guidance. Perhaps the process would begin simply by a statement of the facts: "I'm very dissatisfied with ... and I want to know what to do about it." It helps to get more specific: What exactly is bothering you and why? What are you seeking in a solution? What are your goals, what are your constraints?

As you form a question, *try answering it yourself* to see if the question is one you really need answered. Have you first studied all the relevant information? Before seeing a psychic adviser, try using the method of inspirational writing and write out a dialogue between the questioning part of yourself and that part of yourself that has answers. It's a good way to find out what aspects of the question you already have answers to and what aspects form the real meat of the question.

Clearly, such a process of clarification implies that to get good guidance, you have to do your homework. Part of that homework entails doing one's utmost to solve the problem oneself, until one's own efforts have reached their maximum effect.

Ideals and Purposes

When it comes to evaluating guidance, especially the results of applying the guidance, the outcomes that do result will ultimately be compared with the original purpose or intention. You may come to appreciate the adage, "Be careful what you pray for, you'll probably get it."

A purpose is an intention and is something that can be fulfilled by one or many goals, or outcomes. Thinking about possibly satisfying outcomes helps clarify the purpose. It's not always possible or necessary to be able to specify, in advance, an example of an outcome that would fulfill the purpose, but trying to do so can clarify what it is that you want to accomplish.

On a number of occasions in the writing of this book, I have sought to channel guidance or inspiration. A frequent reason was feeling stuck on how to present the material. The surface feeling was frustration, not being able to proceed with my work. On the surface, what I wanted was a way to proceed, to know what to say, how to say it—on the surface that was my purpose.

It was easy to get suggestions from others on how to present the ideas. Hearing these suggestions and noticing my reactions helped me clarify in my own mind what my purpose really was. It wasn't simply to get on with the writing, for example, but to clearly express my viewpoint. As it often turned out, I had to back up from my initial question, "How shall I say it?" to consider another question, "What do I really understand? What is my viewpoint? What am I really trying to say?" Here the clarification of the purpose had an effect on the reformulation of the question.

Values are important, and need to be considered carefully in preparing for guidance. Here is where Cayce's emphasis on ideals comes into play. Ideals exert an influence on the patterning of the channeled guidance, as in the sense of a "guiding star." Giving consideration to ideals needs to be a top priority in seeking guidance, not only because of the importance of aligning our purpose with our values, but also because of the quality of the energy that's activated. The ideal determines the pattern of creative energy that gives form to the guidance obtained. We can't underplay its importance.

In my own case, following Cayce's advice, I began with a verbal statement of my ideal: "Truth is beauty." Focusing on the feeling behind this statement, I allowed an image to come to me. It was of a crystal bell that sang out clearly when struck, creating in the listener a profound experience of beautiful truth. I found some music that expressed that ideal, some Bach cello suites whose exquisite patterns had a strong emotional effect upon me. Later, as I imagined that the bell's beautiful tone arose less from its exquisite perfection than from its love—its willingness to be struck and give freely of its sound, I switched to a Mozart requiem, choral music whose emotional style more closely approximated the flowing feeling of my new image of an ideal channel.

As Cayce suggested, I contemplated these reminders of the ideal, resonating with their spirit. In such a manner, I was allowing this ideal to pattern the energy that was active behind my search for guidance on how to write about some topic within this book. Not that I should expect to write that clearly, that freely, for I would never finish, but it served as a guiding image.

You can well spend as much time contemplating the ideal you want to govern the guidance as you spend formulating the question. I've often found that simply meditating briefly on the ideal resolves my problem. That simple act of attunement, creating a resonance with the creative energies patterned by the ideal, often provides an immediate channel of inspiration. If not, when presenting the question to another psychic, the time spent contemplating the ideal has a tremendous effect on the quality of the channeling received from that person.

Consider the Source

In his psychic discourses on responding to channeled guidance, Cayce often stressed considering the possible sources of the information. He pointed to several distinct sources: desire, expectations, the subconscious, as well as universal awareness.

As a source of guidance, desire operates in wishful thinking, for example, giving us what we want to be true. Either hopes or fears can be confirmed by the operation of desire in the guidance process. Desire often affects how we interpret our dreams. It's easy to see our hopes and fears in our dreams, as they are a major basis of our dreams' vocabulary. Because desire is such a ubiquitous influence on our interpretations of any form of guidance, Cayce's last step in the process—testing an application in practice—is quite important.

Expectancy operates through the imagination, where an answer is created simply from the pattern of the question. It's like a child who, when forced to answer a question where no answer is known, will make up an answer that seems to fit what is expected by the question. Here the imagination, which otherwise can be a channel of resonance to patterns of psychic awareness, becomes a willing servant to expectations. Hypnosis, by the way, helps grease the wheels of this misleading process, as you'll see in the next chapter when you learn about the "channeling of Socrates."

Trance channels, therefore, can be quite susceptible to fulfilling your expectations. Asked a question, an answer may not be forthcoming. If the pressure is strong to perform, perhaps because their abilities are in question or the seeker is desperate, an answer may be simply unintentionally invented, based upon the expectations contained in the answer. On the other hand, if a psychic responds with a remark like, "I'm not able to get anything on this question," it's a good sign that the psychic is mindful of the psychic process and has integrity about it.

The subconscious itself is a very common source of guidance. Your personal subconscious contains a host of motivations, strivings, memories, unfinished business and seeds of possible futures. Remember that Cayce has pointed out that all subconscious minds are connected. Thus your own subconscious mind, the subconscious of another person who may be channeling psychic information for you, as well as the subconscious of others, living and dead, may contribute to answers received. Because we are often ignorant of the contents of our personal portion of the subconscious, having something from your own subconscious brought into conscious awareness can have such a quality of revelation about it that it feels like it must be true. That in itself can be deceptive.

In my first psychic reading, for example, over fifteen years ago, the psychic and I sat together in meditation and then she began speaking. It seemed as if she were speaking from within me, as if her words were coming from inside me. Today, I can recognize that experience as a telepathic link-up between people in a hypnotic state of awareness, the subconscious of each in direct contact and communication with the other. When it was over I had the impression that in her reading, she had somehow reached inside me and pulled the information out. It was both a physical and an emotional sensation, as if my entire body had been permeated with awareness, and then something had been released into consciousness. There was a feeling of familiarity to much that she said, as if I recognized the truth of it—the emotional tone of what she said rang true as it matched something within me. Clearly she wasn't simply reciting facts; she was addressing me, an innermost me, in a tone that suggested deep familiarity.

Later, in listening to the tape recording of our session, I also noted a correspondence between some of the "facts" she told me and certain of my dreams and fantasy images. The psychic said she saw me standing on a beach, wearing a flowered shirt, and surrounded by palm trees. She said I would move to Hawaii. I had recently had a dream of a scene very similar to her vision. I wondered at her prophecy. Within a couple of years, the psychic proved correct. I left the academic life of an Ivy League university and moved to Virginia Beach. What initially drew me there was the A.R.E., but what really captured my heart was the beach scene itself: the colorfully painted vans with surfboards hanging out and the people wearing T-shirts with various designs printed on the front, the recreational, outdoor atmosphere that contrasted so strongly with the intellectual atmosphere of the Ivy League scene. Although there were no palm trees in Virginia Beach, it nevertheless reminded me of my childhood home in San Diego. One day I found myself on the beach in a flowered shirt and I recalled the psychic's prediction.

Looking back at this sequence years later, however, it seems to me that the psychic had indeed "read" images that were in my subconscious, images that were influencing the shaping of my future. By treating them as objective realities, she didn't encourage me to become more understanding of these images, but indirectly enabled me to become more compelled by them. Had I interpreted my own dream to reflect a psychological atmosphere, a more casual, playful, lush, and creative tone than had been my usual mood in the Ivy League academic situation I had inhabited at the time, I might have responded differently to the psychic's "prediction." Years later I gained a better understanding of what led me to make those changes in my life. It wasn't necessarily in my best interest to make the move when I did. It was more that I was responding to an urge I could no longer resist than the call of destiny. I had come East from Southern California, and I missed the ocean scene and my pleasant memories of a social life focused on sunbathing and body surfing. I was having difficulty learning to be myself and still meet the expectations of being a university professor. Because I was unhappy and anxious to make a change, I didn't examine the urge, or question it. Had I done so, I might have also grown in awareness rather then simply changing my outer circumstances.

Today, I can also appreciate how a preferred response from the psychic might have been: "There is within you an image of standing on the beach in a flowered shirt. This image represents your desire for a freer and more creative life-style. If you look within for how you constrain yourself from the freedom you desire, you may find. . . ." I'm not saying this to be critical of the psychic. She was definitely being psychic. Yet this story illustrates the fluid boundaries between subjective truth and objective fact in the subconscious mind. Cayce described the source of his information as sometimes coming from the subconscious of the seeker, rather than universal awareness and expressed having difficulty distinguishing between thoughts and actions without making a specific effort to do so.

The subconscious mind does not, in itself, have ideals, but primarily the inclination to express itself. Our desire for psychic guidance is usually based, to some degree or other, upon some peripheral desire of ours: There is always that personal element, something less than a willingness to be in harmony with the larger whole. We wouldn't be human if it were otherwise. Although we may hope that we are seeking to have our consciousness expanded, there will always be a part of us that is looking for a simple solution, one that won't require us to grow, one that will just get us what we want. The danger of obtaining misleading information is especially great in the case of seeking guidance from discarnate entities, disembodied "beings," or even psychic subpersonalities of a channel. As Cayce explained, the vibrational pattern of our desires will attract an entity that functions out of a corresponding orientation—the operation of the affinity principle in the subconscious.

A source that seems more personally suited to you may also be lower and may reflect your own subconscious. By being empathetic and sympathetic to your concerns, it seems to be on target for you, tuned in, but it may, at the same time, be serving lesser motives. I have had several such readings. They are usually quite pleasant. Invariably I am reminded of what I care about and am assured that everything will work out for the best.

Ira Progoff noted that it was Eileen Garrett's lower order sources that functioned as the telepaths, reading the mind of the seeker and communicating with deceased beings. They also had more "personality" than the higher ones. The higher ones spoke as if they were personifications of eternal principles, and manifested as identities only for the sake of the listener.

A higher, impersonal source may pay less attention to the pain and feelings of your situation and speak in the language of higher universal truths. Higher sources present a paradoxical problem and can be controversial. Universal truth, by its very nature, ignores the uniqueness of the individual.

It's universally true that what blocks us from the awareness of all the wisdom that lies within is our sense of "self." That sense of a separate self promotes fear because we feel a need to protect that separate self. The fear promotes strivings for power. The universality of this predicament is well described by Ken Wilber in his book, *The Atman Project*. It's also true that love is the way out of the predicament. In the words of a New Age slogan based on the *Course in Miracles*, "Love is letting go of fear." I would wish to be guided by no less a truth.

On the other hand, if we would do what we know to do, if we experienced it as our choice to do so, then we would have no need for guidance. We ask for guidance, not because we don't already know that we "create our own reality," but because we experience ourselves as being compelled to create it as we do, and we want to find a way to do otherwise.

Too often, sources of guidance that deal only with universal truth become a disservice in the lives of the seeker. When we use valid spiritual truths as a means of gaining personal power, we can aggravate our sense of ultimate personal isolation. Sometimes we can use the information in a Pollyanna trip of denial. ("My anger is an illusion, my fear is an illusion, my feelings are illusion, only my love is real.") Or we can use it as a tool of further self-condemnation. ("I try to let go of my anger as illusory, but I just can't do it—what a jerk I must be.") If you find yourself later feeling unworthy after contemplating the advice from your psychic guide, or find yourself more confused than when you started, you're experiencing the essence of what is controversial about these sources of guidance. It may be true that you're partially responsible yourself for this dilemma, but some sources of universal truth set you up for it.

I've found that it's best to listen to universal truth when

you're in an exalted state of consciousness, capable of a soul response rather than an ego response. Otherwise, I'm not sure that a source of universal truth is actually what I would call the "highest" source of guidance.

One image that comes to me as analogous to the meaning of the "highest" is a group of people sitting around a circle, examining the center. Each person sees the center from a particular vantage point. Each person's perspective is shaped and limited by their position on the circumference of the circle. One person sees the center from the vantage point of desire. Another sees it from the vantage point of truth. Only the center itself, which sees all points of view simultaneously is the "highest" perspective. It can appreciate each of the perspectives of the circumferential viewpoints and is in a position to integrate them. It can integrate universal truths with human limitations. Cayce would have us seek guidance from the center, not from the periphery.

Compassion is present in the highest sources of guidance. There is still the presence of the universal truths and there is an insistence on the reality of our spiritual being and how we create our own circumstances. At the same time, there is present an understanding and appreciation for our suffering and the meaning of it, as well as a sensitivity to not want to add to it. It's also patient and forgiving. Though it recognizes that there is God in each person, it doesn't talk to each person in the same way. Though it orients each person to his or her spiritual destiny, it focuses on the here and now, with concrete suggestions for the very next step of that journey of a thousand miles. It speaks in humble tones and, if you're lucky enough, it's full of humor. Nothing is as healing as being able to see the truth about your situation in a joke! It aids self-acceptance and detachment simultaneously.

Cayce was a humorist, awake and in trance, who believed the effect of humor on the mind and body was beneficial. I have often recalled two readings I received from different psychics, both of whose sources cracked jokes; not teasing me, but helping me view myself with gentle humor. One even went so far as to tune into jokes I myself had told and explicitly remind me that I had a way of accepting truth through humor. Sometimes I wonder if I got that joke!

Evaluating the Guidance

Don't get lost in trying to pinpoint the exact source of channeled guidance. Focus instead on determining what, if any, of the guidance is valuable. Evaluating the source is less important than evaluating the guidance itself. In fact, Cayce indicated that it's not possible to determine, with certainty, the exact source of channeled guidance. The guidance must be evaluated by testing its fruits!

Cayce took a very common sense approach to the matter of evaluating guidance. Does the guidance make sense? Does it speak to the situation? Is it workable? Does it seem constructive? Do you have a positive response to it? It's difficult to imagine how often these questions, as obvious as they may be, are often overlooked.

Examine the guidance from the point of view of the ideal that you set. If it doesn't meet the standard of your ideal, either you should forget it, or else you may decide that you have some soul searching to do. For example, I once asked about the prospects for obtaining financial support for a pet research project. The answer I received didn't seem to fit with my ideal, as it seemed to stress "selling" my research idea rather then "investigating" it. Listening to the reading again, I realized the psychic was implying that my ideal was the problem, that I would have to consider the utility of the research to others and not just its theoretical importance.

Assuming the guidance passes these preliminary tests, then obtain a second opinion. Cayce advocated *never to put all your eggs in one basket*. Most emphatically, he advised to never rely upon a single external channel as a sole source of information. He didn't exclude his own readings from this admonition! His source encouraged those who received readings from Cayce to compare the material with other sources. He gave readings for himself, and worked with them with the aid of his personal spiritual program, which included meditation, dreams (his source frequently admonished him for not paying enough attention to his dreams!), prayer, and the rest of the guidance heuristic that we have been presenting in this chapter.

Seek guidance from more than one source and look for commonalities and for correlations in the information. For example, compare the results of your inspirational writing with the advice of a psychic and then turn to your dreams. Form an opinion, take it into meditation and check your intuitional response. Solving a problem by correlating the answer provided through several means is a most conscientious scientific approach.

The inherited wisdom among practitioners of the Cayce readings is that if you're going to get a psychic reading from someone, get one from *at least two* different psychics.

I once had the opportunity to get readings from twenty different psychics for comparison, posing the same four personal questions to all of them. It was preliminary work in designing a research project for the A.R.E. concerned with the process of obtaining guidance from different sources. Although otherwise an impractical approach, I learned a lot about the nature of psychic readings, how they can vary, and the value of being able to make comparisons and correlations.

With two of the questions, I found that, although it was time consuming to compare and correlate the twenty different answers, it was worth the effort. I was very fortunate to have had the experience of being able to ask so many different psychics the same question. I can't emphasize enough how differently each psychic approached formulating an answer. The personality, interests, wisdom, axes to grind, styles of caring, and so on, of each individual psychic affected the reading in a very strong manner, but the influence of the channel was only apparent because I was able to make the comparisons. Taken separately, each one, definitely tapping into me, had such a powerful hold upon my attention that I would probably have been unduly influenced by any single reading. Taken as a group, however, what was particular to each channel dropped away from view. I was left with certain common themes that emerged, not from the psychic ability of the channels, but from my own searching within myself as I contemplated their varied messages. That process of comparison provided the valid guidance.

A third question regarded the topic of "past life" relationships with two people important to me in this life. No two psychics gave the same past life account of those relationships. I have since discovered, in talking with other people who have accrued many such past life readings, that my experience was not unique. On the other hand, I found that several of the psychics described similar relationship patterns, even though the past life scenarios were different. They corresponded with one another in terms of the emotional significance of the events, although not in terms of the events themselves. I found these emotional patterns to be truly meaningful to me in terms of issues confronting me in my life. It was in these patterns, which required me to *hear several different readings* in order to perceive them, that the valid guidance was given.

At the other end of the continuum, I found that with one question, I got almost an identical answer from every psychic. It proved to be in answer to a question that I myself would have answered in the same way if someone had sent me that question in the mail. When I said earlier that it pays to do your homework on your question, to try to answer it yourself first, I spoke from personal experience.

The Final Test: Applying the Guidance

The proof is in the pudding. Judge by the fruits. Practice makes perfect. Learn by doing. Sound familiar? These phrases of garnered wisdom each express something of what Cayce meant by "in the application comes the awareness." As the final, and most important, step of his guidance heuristic, therefore, Cayce advises to test guidance by applying it in practice. Determine if the guidance works. Try it out, test it, and see. That's good common sense.

Cayce also was indicating the importance of learning by doing, by getting involved. Often the value of a piece of truth isn't limited to the light bulb that it turns on in your head, or the "aha!" reaction we have, but to what we learn in addition as we put the truth into action. By getting involved in attempting to apply a piece of guidance, not only do we test it out, and test our understanding of it, but also life itself acts upon us through our experience and creates a greater awareness. That's Cayce's Law.

Good ideas are a dime a dozen, but one idea that's put to good use is of great value. The experience gained in making an idea work is like a floodlight compared to the light bulb of the idea itself.

Learn from the experience of the people who participated in the dream research project described in Chapter Three. There we learned that people who applied an insight from one day's dream received the next day a dream of clearer guidance, whereas those who sat on their dream insights received foggier dreams. I'm sure you know people who are full of insights about themselves, but never seem to practice what they preach. They end up always spouting out the same ideas, but they never change. If they would apply but one of their insights, they might make some movement and come up with a whole new set of ideas to play with.

The practice of application is also good grounding. Jung noted that insights from the unconscious were full of energy. If these images and symbols were simply contemplated, a person could become filled with energy to the danger point. He called it "inflation." In response to his term, I imagine someone puffing up like a balloon, filled with the intoxicating gases of psychic awareness, lifting off the planet.

Cayce once gave a psychic reading for a person and indicated that she was possessed. What possessed her? Not spirits, not a hidden sub-personality, but her own thought forms! He said she had become possessed by inspirations that had been sought, had been attracted, but hadn't been applied. Entertaining such fanciful ideas, but not applying them, he explained, was sapping her energy.

Jung stressed the importance of "wrestling with the

angel,'' and he suggested trying to ground some of these insights into practical, down to earth experiments in living. Now I imagine a person, instead of being puffed up by insights, plunging his or her feet into the earth. A circuit is completed, so that the psychic energy, instead of puffing up the person, is channeled through the person and propels him or her along his or her way. That seems to be the way to be responsible for knowledge obtained, to put it to use, and to be a channel of inspiration rather than just a collector of it.

In many cases, the intention to apply guidance that will be received is a prerequisite to being able to get the guidance in the first place. In Cayce's suggestion for developing intuition, for example, we learned that an actual decision be made first, then to check the intuitive reaction. The energy pattern of a person who is asking a moot or hypothetical question is different from that of a person who is asking a question where his or her life depends upon the answer.

Imagine, for example, the classic predicament: Behind one door is the fair maiden or prince, behind the other door is a raging beast. Let's make the predicament hypothetical only—when the door of your choice is open, the object behind the door will remain behind glass, for your viewing pleasure only. Now let's make the predicament real—when the door is open, the object behind the door will rush out to greet you, or eat you. Now, in which situation do you think your powers of psychic guidance will be aroused to perform their best?

The knowledge of whether or not we'll actually put into application guidance that's being sought is often available at the time the guidance is asked for. This intriguing fact brings us back full circle to the beginning of Cayce's guidance heuristic. As Cayce often reminded, don't ask the question if you're not ready to take responsibility for the answer. Knowledge not applied, he said, was much more costly than the bliss of ignorance.

CHAPTER ELEVEN

Using Hypnosis to Become a Trance Channel

"... the study of self ... may best be done by suggestive forces to the body through hypnosis."

—Edgar Cayce, 3483–1

"Each will find a variation according to the application and the abilities of each to become less and less controlled by personality, and the more and more able to shut away the material consciousness, or the mind portion that is of the material, propagated or implied by what is termed the five senses. The more and more each is impelled by that which is intuitive, or the relying upon the soul force within, the greater, the farther, the deeper, the broader, the more constructive may be the result."

—Edgar Cayce, 792–2

"As it has been indicated from the first through *this* channel, there should ever be that ideal, 'What does such information as may come through such a channel produce in the experience of individuals, as to not their thoughts, not their relations other than does such make them better parents, better children, better husbands, better wives, better neighbors, better friends, better citizens?' And if and when it does *not*, LEAVE IT ALONE!''

—Edgar Cayce, 1135–6

"Stare at a spot high upon the wall across from you. I am going to slowly count backwards from ten to one. Each time I count, take a deep breath and very slowly blink your eyes. Ten . . . blink your eyes ever so slowly . . . nine . . . eight . . ."

We are eavesdropping on a session of hypnosis. The hypnotist is giving the person instructions that will lead into the state of hypnosis. Let's continue listening.

". . . two . . . one. And now you can just close your eyes and keep them closed. Your eyelids are now very tired. In your eyelids you find a comfortable feeling of tiredness, of relaxation, or a moving sensation. However you experience this feeling, let it magnify and multiply, let it increase until your eyelids are totally, completely, and pleasantly relaxed.

"This is something you do, no one else can do it for you. Take your time and relax your eyelids. As you relax them, you can allow that feeling of relaxation to flow outward in all directions.

"Imaginary waves or ripples of pleasant relaxation now move throughout the entire face. Allow your entire face to relax. As you do so, waves of relaxation spread over the head. . . .

". . . Welcome this wonderful feeling as it spreads throughout your entire body. Completely and pleasantly, your entire body is relaxing and you slow down just a little bit . . . you can slow down a little bit more and a little bit more. . . .

". . . More in perfect harmony now, you're at your own natural level of relaxation. It's something you want, it's happening here, it's happening now."

These particular instructions are adapted from Henry Bolduc's book, *Self-Hypnosis: Creating Your Own Destiny.* They're typical of the instructions hypnotists use in leading a person into a hypnotic state. I have experienced hypnosis under the guidance of several hypnotists and have found their procedures quite similar. All induce a state of relaxation.

You may be wondering, as I did when I first began, where the actual *hypnosis* comes into play. Doesn't the hypnotist invoke some magical words to put you into a trance and take control of your mind? No. That's a false stereotype of hypnosis. Entering hypnosis is basically a process of deep relaxation while maintaining a quiet awareness. It's much like what we experienced in the meditation on inspiration, with the possibility of adding further suggestions to open the imagination to deeper channels of the mind.

Edgar Cayce's Story of Hypnosis

Hypnotism played a significant role in Cayce's development as a psychic channel. As a child growing up in Kentucky, young Edgar had a strong interest in religion, a tendency toward mystical experiences, and showed evidence of psychic abilities. The concept of a mystic or a psychic being a *channel*, however, didn't even exist until several years after Cayce began his psychic work under hypnosis.

The first time Edgar Cayce functioned as a trance psychic, there was a great personal need. According to the account given by Thomas Sugrue, in his biography of Cayce, *There Is a River*, it began with a strange event:

In the spring of 1900, at age twenty-three, Cayce began work as a traveling salesman. One night, in Elkton, a town about forty miles from his home in Hopkinsville, he stopped at a doctor's office to get some powder for a headache he had been experiencing for the past several weeks. The next thing he knew he was home in bed. A friend of the family had recognized him in Elkton, walking about disheveled and disoriented and took him home. The family doctor suspected that the headache sedative had been too strong. When he recovered he had lost his voice and was quite hoarse.

The hoarseness didn't go away and remained that way through the summer. Several doctors diagnosed and attempted to treat the malady, but without success. Cayce decided his throat was incurable, gave up sales work, and began working in photography, which was to become his career.

Hypnotism was a fad in America at the time, much like channeling was for a while in the 1980s. One of hypnosis' more dramatic aspects was the psychic powers it often revealed.

At that time, a traveling stage hypnotist, by the name of Hart, came to perform in Hopkinsville. He had a trick of inviting someone to hide an object anywhere in town, then he would ride through town blindfolded and direct the carriage to the hidden object. Hypnosis was also claimed by some—not incorrectly, although prematurely—to be the medicine of the future.

Hart learned of Cayce's problem and bet he could solve it for two hundred dollars, nothing if he failed. Under hypnosis, Cayce talked normally, but when he came out, his voice was hoarse as usual.

A physician from New York heard of Cayce's case and traveled south to try his hand with a hypnotic cure. He, too, was a failure. In a letter to the Cayce family he noted, however, that Cayce seemed to resist accepting the posthypnotic suggestions about his throat, as if wanting to take charge himself. The doctor suggested that someone hypnotize Cayce and then give him the suggestion to talk about his illness. A local hypnotist, Al C. Layne, wanted to try and Edgar was willing to undergo one final experiment.

A year since the problem had first begun, the fateful experiment in hypnosis was attempted. Layne gave Cayce the suggestion that Cayce would put himself to sleep. When Cayce was breathing deeply, the hypnotist suggested that Cayce would "see his body and describe the trouble in his throat."

Cayce then spoke in a clear voice, stating what would become his trademark of an opening line: "Yes, we have the body." Cayce went on to describe the problem in the throat as due to poor circulation. He indicated that the circulation could be improved by the use of suggestion while he was in this unconscious state. Layne gave the suggestion and Cayce's throat turned bright red. After about twenty minutes, Cayce said the condition was removed, and asked that it be suggested that his condition return to normal, and then awaken. The suggestion was given, and it did and he did. His voice was restored.

Within a few days, however, Cayce's voice was weak again. Using the same procedure as before, Layne was able to help Cayce regain his voice. For almost a year, Cayce needed these periodic hypnotic sessions to keep his voice functioning.

Layne immediately saw the potential value of Cayce's trance. Hypnotists in Europe had demonstrated that while in trance, the hypnotized person often evidenced the psychic ability to diagnose another person's illness. Cayce had been able to diagnose his own problem and effect a treatment. He might well diagnose someone else's condition. Layne decided to use Cayce's trance to build his own medical practice. Soon Layne—a self-taught, non-licensed osteopath—had opened an office and was using Cayce to secretly diagnose and prescribe treatments for patients' conditions. In this way, Cayce began giving what Layne called ''readings'' without Cayce knowing about it.

When Cayce learned what was going on, he was quite upset and made Layne promise to stop. But Cayce was dependent upon Layne for the hypnotic treatments, and they continued their work. Cayce later learned that Layne had also continued with the readings. Layne insisted that the readings were definitely on target, the diagnoses given to the patients were accurate, and the remedies suggested were working well. Nevertheless, the practice bothered Cayce and he broke their relationship. Difficulties with his voice forced Cayce to return to Layne, once more, however, and Cayce reluctantly agreed to giving readings for Layne's patients. Word of Cayce's and Layne's work finally leaked to the press and Layne, who was practicing without a license, left town.

Cayce found another hypnotist for his treatments, and gave readings for other people only occasionally as the need warranted. It took many years before Cayce finally accepted that his psychic readings were beneficial to those in need. Only then did he accept his role as a psychic.

When given the name of a person, Cayce would often describe the person's environment. On one occasion, he described the room perfectly, but noted that the person wasn't there, as he was supposed to be. Moments later, he indicated that the person had just arrived. It was as if he had traveling vision, as well as a sixth sense of knowing where to look. With his psychic X-ray eyes, he could look within the body and describe internal conditions that doctors would then verify with their own examinations.

It was the accuracy of his psychic perception and the fact that doctors who followed Cayce's prescriptions with their patients had success that convinced Cayce. His clairvoyant power was phenomenal. He once prescribed a medicine that couldn't be found anywhere. It was no longer made. Cayce then gave the formula for making it. Soon after, a letter came from a doctor who had located the formula for the treatment and it was exactly as Cayce had formulated it. On another occasion, Cayce prescribed a remedy that no one could find. Cayce then identified a particular pharmacy, described a shelf in the stockroom, and indicated to look in the rear, behind more currently used medicines. The pharmacist was located, asked to check out the directions, and found an old bottle of the remedy.

As the father of holistic medicine, he described the interaction of mind and body, especially the workings of the endocrine system and the healing functions of the body that would take doctors over forty years to discover for themselves. Cayce restricted the use of his psychic talent, in fact, to medical diagnosis and prescription, until one fateful meeting.

Some twenty years after that first experiment hypnotizing Cayce, a wealthy printer named Arthur Lammer asked Cayce if he had ever sought out the mysteries of the universe through his psychic trance. Cayce hadn't even thought of the idea. Lammer's suggestion came as another challenge. He agreed to the experiment. Lammer asked many questions concerning metaphysics, reincarnation, and the spiritual nature of the human being. The answers that came from Cayce's psychic trance to such questions opened an entirely new horizon for Cayce's psychic vision. What followed was Cayce's teachings on the various ways that human beings are channels of divine energy and the significance of that spiritual potential.

The Suggestibility of the Subconscious During Hypnosis

It's common today to define hypnosis as a state of heightened suggestibility. This definition is another way of stating what Edgar Cayce explained was the essence of hypnosis—*communicating directly with the subconscious mind*.

The subconscious mind operates upon the principle of suggestion. It *accepts any* statement as being true. The conscious mind operates by reasoning upon sense impressions. It regards any statement, Cayce noted, as a *proposition* to be analyzed and evaluated.

If I suggest to you that there's an apple in front of you, your immediate reaction will be to compare that statement with the impression from your senses. Your conscious mind will disagree with me. The conscious mind can't accept suggestion, but first evaluates the statement.

On the other hand, if I suggest that you *imagine* an apple, or *pretend* that an apple is in front of you, your conscious mind will step aside and allow your subconscious to bring up an image of an apple. The subconscious mind readily accepts the suggestion concerning an apple and immediately complies with a suitable image.

While the subconscious mind is involved with the imaginal apple, the conscious mind may kibbutz from the sidelines. It may note that the imaginal image isn't like the experience of a real apple. It may note that pretending isn't the same as reality. If the conscious mind is distracted, however, from the activity of the subconscious, then there's nothing to interfere with the effective reality of the imaginal apple.

The process of hypnosis is like seducing the attention of the conscious mind and redirecting it elsewhere. Relaxation helps in this process. As the body relaxes, the sensory system also relaxes and the conscious mind grows dim. It's very much like what happens as we fall asleep. The only difference is that in hypnosis, the conscious mind doesn't dissolve because the hypnotist's voice has captured its attention and gives it a place of restful focus. If the hypnotist were to cease talking for a prolonged period of time, the conscious mind would lose that focus and the person could easily fall asleep.

As the person relaxes more fully, and the dimming conscious mind rests upon the pillow of the hypnotist's voice, the subconscious becomes uninhibited in its response to suggestion. Whatever the hypnotist suggests can be vividly imagined by the subconscious mind. And what it thus imagines, it takes to be reality. In this way hypnosis becomes both a state of heightened suggestibility and a state where the hypnotist can communicate directly with the subconscious mind.

Learning Self-Hypnosis Through Relaxation Imagery

You can learn to enter the hypnotic state yourself by learning to respond to your own suggestions. Focusing on images suggestive of relaxing is the basic procedure. Let's see how it works.

Get into a comfortable position, perhaps reclining in an easy chair or lying down on a bed. Rest your arms at your side. Take a deep breath, hold it momentarily, then let it out with a sigh. Now you're ready to work with suggestive imagery.

We've learned that we can control our body indirectly by imagining certain images. That's how we're going to enter a relaxed state.

Focus on your right arm. Notice anything about your right

arm that might feel like heaviness and say to yourself, "My right arm is heavy." Don't *do* anything with your arm, just let it lie there. Repeat the phrase to yourself several times, "My right arm is heavy." Allow yourself to experience your arm as feeling heavy. As you imagine your arm feeling heavy, notice how you *let go and relax* in your right arm. You are responding to the suggestion.

After about a minute, go through the same process with your left arm. Then focus on both your arms at the same time and repeat the phrase, "My *arms* are heavy." During the next minute, focus on your right leg, repeating the phrase, "My right leg is heavy." Then your left leg. Then both legs at the same time. Finally, spread your focus out over your arms and legs. Repeat to yourself, "My arms and legs are heavy." The more you experience your arms and legs as heavy, the more you let go and relax, the more you're responding to suggestion, and the more you're becoming absorbed in a self-hypnotic trance.

If you want to go further with this procedure, repeat all of the above steps, but this time use the word *warm* instead of *heavy*. When you're finished, repeat this phrase as an integrative suggestion, "My arms and legs are heavy and warm." To go deeper, begin to practice the meditation on the breath we learned earlier. Watch your breath without interfering with it. Repeat the phrase, "It breathes me." It's a very passive experience. Besides relaxing heaviness, you may also experience waves of tingling sensations as you move deeper into the self-hypnotic state.

By now you have become very relaxed. You will notice that your thinking is hazier and you may experience spontaneous daydreams, or have a tendency to fall asleep. You're bordering on the sleep state. You're beginning to directly experience the region of the subconscious mind.

Hypnosis and ESP

Recall that Cayce indicated that all subconscious minds are in contact with one another. If hypnosis is a means of communicating directly with the subconscious mind, we should expect that ESP would be more pronounced during hypnosis than during the normal, waking state. Hypnotic subjects should be mind readers. Experience and research proves this assumption correct.

In the original golden years of hypnosis of the 1800s, the psychic aspects of hypnosis were almost taken for granted. Hypnotized subjects could read books blindfolded. Hypnotists could deliver suggestions simply by thinking of them. In demonstrations of the "community of sensation," meaning the telepathic sharing of experiences, the hypnotist could bite into an orange and the subject would report the taste, think of the lyrics of a song and the subject would sing them, have himself be pinched and the subject would cry-ouch. In fact, some hypnotists could telepathically hypnotize their subjects even over great distances. Witnesses verified that the person, for no apparent reason, lay down on the couch and seemed to go to sleep. On other occasions, the person would stop what he or she was doing, make some excuse, and go to the telepathically suggested location.

Telepathic hypnosis is a controversial subject. The psychiatrist, Jules Eisenbud, in *Parapsychology and the Unconscious,* tells of his experiments sending suggestions to patients that they phone him. I have experienced myself the effect of telepathic hypnosis. Without my knowing that he was even thinking of me, a hypnotist telepathically induced analgesia in my arm. I was unaware of the effect until it was pointed out to me that I couldn't feel my arm being pinched. In my book, *Awakening Your Psychic Powers,* I give more details about this incident and provide other accounts of telepathically transmitted suggestions. Cayce reminds us that we affect people by our thoughts. The saying, "Don't say anything about a person unless you can say something positive" should be extended to what we think. Sending people thoughts of encouragement is a natural and positive use of telepathic suggestion.

Modern research in parapsychology, where ESP is statistically tested in laboratory settings, has confirmed that hypnosis often increases telepathic ability. Modern studies have also demonstrated the striking telepathic rapport that people in hypnosis can achieve with one another.

Hypnotic Imagery: A Channel of Self-Diagnosis

In his self-induced hypnotic trance, Edgar Cayce was able to clairvoyantly diagnose the medical problems of people who sought his help. Cayce indicated that we could diagnose ourselves if we would turn within.

Hypnosis has often been a catalyst for helping people to turn to the knowledge within. Marshall S. Wilensky, Ph.D., a Canadian psychologist, reported the use of hypnotic imagery to elicit self-diagnostic imagery in patients of varying medical conditions.

Wilensky used suggestive imagery, borrowed from Jean Houston's book, *The Possible Human,* involving a personification of the body's inner wisdom. His experiments demonstrate the evocative power of such imagery.

After entering a light hypnotic trance, the person imagines being on top of a mountain searching for a path down. After making a careful descent, the person discovers a door leading into the depths of the mountain, entering an atmosphere that has the vibrations of renewal and restoration. The person comes to a door with a sign upon it reading, "The One Who Knows Health." The person opens the door and meets someone who is completely knowledgeable about the person's body. The person sits down in front of this knowing one and asks questions. The One Who Knows Health answers, not just verbally, but also through images and bodily sensations that the person experiences.

Here are some brief descriptions of the cases Dr. Wilensky presents, showing that the imagery that comes through these sessions are surprisingly accurate, given follow-up medical examination.

One woman asked about her sore knee. The wise being answered her directly, "Forget about your knee. See somebody about your fatigue immediately!" She went to her physician the next day. The results of blood tests indicated that she had leukemia.

One man inquired about the night pains in his legs. His wise being gave him an image of two oxygen tanks strapped to his legs. When he went to his physician, examination revealed a circulatory disorder, starving his legs of oxygen.

A man suffered from a kidney and prostate infection. Treatment with antibiotics had cleared the infection, but the man complained of fatigue and physical distress and hadn't been able to resume working. His wisdom figure appeared as white light and as a sensation of movement in his lower abdomen. The information given was that the infection was indeed gone and the discomfort was an excuse not to work. His wisdom appeared as a sensation of movement, it explained, because it was a "call to action." Subsequent examination bore out the truth of this message.

A woman suffering from fainting spells had been diagnosed by CAT scans, but the source of her problem couldn't be located. Her wisdom figure appeared as a star and as a crystal. When asking about the problem, she touched the right side of her head, just above her ear. A repeat CAT scan located a glioma in just that location. A subsequent reexamination of the original scan also revealed this problem.

In Wilensky's opinion, the inner wisdom figure is an image representation of a state of consciousness, an internal awareness that has proven therapeutic value. Once again we see the value and power of the personification. Using an image of a person, or being, can unlock hidden powers within the mind.

The Power of Hypnotic Role Playing

Role playing allows us to take on the characteristics of the role, to channel whatever characteristics the role suggests. Role playing is a process of pretending. It engages the channel of the subconscious mind through an act of the imagination. By neutralizing any interference of the conscious mind and providing more direct access to the subconscious, hypnosis can increase the power of role playing to an incredible degree.

In his book, *The Laws of Psychic Phenomena*, Thomas J. Hudson describes a very revealing experiment in hypnotic role playing that he witnessed in the company of many well-educated people. The hypnotist, Dr. Carpenter, hypnotized a man and told him that Socrates was alive and standing right in front of him. Soon the young man said, "Oh yes, I see him there now." Dr. Carpenter told the man that Socrates was very eager to speak to him and would answer any question that the young man would care to ask. The young man began asking some questions and found that Socrates did answer. He relayed these answers to Dr. Carpenter. Members of the audience also suggested some questions to ask Socrates. As the man relayed answer upon answer, he gradually came to play Socrates himself. He amazed the audience with his eloquence and profundity. Hudson noted that these speeches, for they were becoming that, were delivered in a spontaneous manner with no hesitation. He proceeded to provide a complete account of the universe, a compelling spiritual philosophy worthy of the speaker's role. Even though the audience had witnessed the artificial creation of Socrates, the man's performance was so convincing, his utterances so inspiring, that many people even took notes!

The demonstration dumbfounded the audience. In his waking state, the man, although college educated, wasn't an impressive intellectual or speaker. Yet his Socrates was genuinely gifted. The audience genuinely believed that Dr. Carpenter had enabled the man to contact the spirit of Socrates. In later experiments, Dr. Carpenter suggested to the hypnotized man that he was in communication with a disembodied spirit of supreme intelligence. Once again, the man proceeded to expound the most spellbinding and marvelous spiritual philosophy, exceeding even his Socratic performance. Hudson remarked that a transcription of the discourse, had there been one, would have made a very credible book.

Hudson told this story to demonstrate one of the powers of the subconscious mind that we vastly underestimate. He calls it "deductive reasoning power." If you give the subconscious mind a certain assumption, that Socrates is present, for example, it can take that premise and instantly draw out its implications. Using the powers of the imagination, the subconscious begins with the person's own unconscious memories to fabricate its performance. Being in contact with other subconscious minds, it can also draw upon other person's memories. Conceivably, it could also attract actual spirits as a resource. It could tap into a universal level of awareness, accessing the Akashic Records of all knowledge. Whether it's accessing a disembodied pattern of thought forms, or simply the unconscious knowledge of the person, it's not possible to determine in a given instance. What is clear, however, is that the initial premise has a lot of power to generate a surprising performance. The subconscious was able to deliver on cue in a very convincing manner.

The story of channeling Socrates has a double-edged *good news, bad news* lesson. On the one hand, by demonstrating how the subconscious mind is capable of amazingly creative improvisation, we're reminded that the appearance of channeling a spirit doesn't necessarily mean a spirit is involved. On the other hand, the demonstration also shows the power of personification, how proposing an image of a being can open a profound channel of inspiration. We might wonder, therefore, if it's possible that given the right image, one could actually open up a valid channel of universal intelligence. What might this right image be? Cayce suggests that we choose according to our ideals, that it be an image of the higher self. Cayce's own experience serves as an instructive example.

Edgar Cayce's Hypnotic Journey

There have been a couple of references in this book to the fact that when Cayce went into trance, he experienced going to what he called the Hall of Records and getting his information from an old man. Although his trance source didn't describe the process in such concrete images and personifications, the waking Cayce did. Here's a verbatim account of Cayce's waking description of his journey in the trance state, taken from comments he made at a public lecture:

"I see myself as a tiny dot out of my physical body, which lies inert before me. I find myself oppressed by darkness and there is a feeling of terrific loneliness. Suddenly, I am conscious of a white beam of light. As this tiny dot, I move upward following the light, knowing that I must follow it or be lost.

"As I move along this path of light I gradually become conscious of various levels upon which there is movement. Upon the first levels there are vague, horrible shapes, grotesque forms such as one sees in nightmares. Passing on, there begins to appear on either side misshapen forms of human beings with some part of the body magnified. Again there is change and I become conscious of gray-hooded forms moving downward. Gradually, these become lighter in color. Then the direction changes and these forms move upward and the color of the robes grows rapidly lighter. Next, there begins to appear on either side vague outlines of houses, walls, trees, etc., but everything is motionless. As I pass on, there is more light and movement in what appear to be normal cities and towns. With the growth of movement I become conscious of sounds, at first indistinct rumblings, then music, laughter, and singing of birds. There is more and more light, the colors become very beautiful, and there is the sound of wonderful music. The houses are left behind, ahead there is only a blending of sound and color. Quite suddenly I come upon a hall of records. It is a hall without walls, without ceiling, but I am conscious of seeing an old man who hands me a large book, a record of the individual for whom I seek information."

On other occasions, Cayce "felt himself to be a bubble traveling through water to arrive at the place where he always got the information," according to records in the A.R.E. library. In another instance, he "went up and up through a very large column''; passing by all the horrible things without coming in contact personally with them, and came out where there was the house of records. It, the column, wound around on a wheel like the Rotarians have. He felt very secure traveling that way.

That was Cayce's experience of the imagery that accompanied his psychic trance. We might wonder, what would happen if that imagery were used as a series of suggestions to someone in a hypnotic trance? Would it lead to the same type of psychic, universal awareness Cayce obtained?

Henry Bolduc, the hypnotist I referred to in the beginning of this chapter, has tried that experiment. In his book, *The Journey Within: Past Life Regression and Channeling,* he tells the story of what happened when he turned Cayce's description of his trance into a script for hypnotic suggestions.

His first experiment was with Daniel Clay, a lay minister whom Henry had trained in self-hypnosis, and who initiated the idea of following in Cayce's thought patterns.

After Clay was in the hypnotic state, Henry began by turning Cayce's first statement into a suggestion: "You will see yourself as a tiny dot out of your physical body, which lies inert before you." That suggestion was easy for Clay to follow. At the next suggestion, "You find yourself oppressed by darkness and there's a feeling of terrific loneliness," Clay's face drooped in sadness. Clay's facial expressions showed appropriate responsiveness to each of the remaining suggestions. At the end of the sequence, Henry gave Clay the name of someone and it was suggested that the old man would produce that person's record book. Clay made a few statements about the person in question. Afterward, Henry was able to verify that some of what Clay indicated was correct. They decided to continue this line of experimentation.

Each time they repeated the experiment, Clay's body seemed more adjusted to the sequence. There was less physical torment expressed during the passage by the grotesque figures, and the clairvoyant information was clearer and more accurate. The result was that Clay began to channel what appeared to be a universal consciousness called "The Eternal Ones." This source identified itself as a state of consciousness within us all. It distinguished that source from spirit mediumship, a channel the Eternal Ones discouraged in no uncertain terms. Clay has since built a reputation for accurate and inspiring channeled readings.

I have met with Clay on numerous occasions and have interacted with the Eternal Ones. What has impressed me the most isn't how different or spellbinding the Eternal Ones might appear, but how much resemblance I sense between the spirit of Clay's sincerity of purpose and gentleness as a human being and the effect of being in the presence of his trance channeling. That resemblance has confirmed for me Cayce's perspective that channeling, when it's not "trick shooting," is an expression of the channel's own growth in consciousness.

Henry describes a second experiment, with a woman named Eileen Rota. Using the same procedure, Eileen ultimately channeled a source called "Pretty Flower," yet whose self-description and style of teaching was quite different from the Eternal Ones. Pretty Flower's work has since been published as a book, *Welcome Home: A Time for Uniting*.

What's particularly interesting about Eileen's experience is that soon after Pretty Flower appeared, she told Henry that it would be better for Eileen to use her own imagery rather than Cayce's. She suggested images that were more in keeping with Eileen's own style of higher self consciousness. When Henry shifted to using these images, the work accelerated.

Improving trance channeling by using the person's own imagery parallels Cayce's story of his development as a trance psychic. Under hypnosis, when he, rather than the hypnotist, was allowed to design the suggestions, Cayce finally made some progress.

Henry reports a third experiment that sounds an important note of caution. A woman wanted to learn trance channeling and Henry asked her first to master the preliminaries of self-hypnosis and its use for general self-improvement. She was impatient, however, and asked her husband to give her hypnotic suggestions following the Cayce imagery. Although she showed some signs of modest success, she began suffering from a skin irritation that required her to give up the experiments. It's easy to speculate that opening herself up to channeling stimulated some unresolved emotional problems. Her story serves as a warning against moving too fast into such experiments.

My Experiments With Trance Channeling

To use Cayce's imagery as a basis for suggestion, to test its effectiveness as an approach to trance channeling, makes a lot of sense. I wanted to experience it for myself. I called up Henry Bolduc and asked him if he would demonstrate his method with me. He readily agreed.

The only thing about Henry that fits the popular stereotype of the hypnotist is that he has a beard. A man of tremendous warmth and enthusiasm, I trusted him the moment he walked up to my door. Besides making a house visit for our first session, he also went into our kitchen and taught me how to make a quick and easy soup for lunch afterward.

I was anxious to try the Cayce imagery, but he insisted that we move slowly. His plan was to start with recapturing childhood memories and then past life recall before attempting channeling. We followed his plan.

I had been hypnotized several times before, by different hypnotists, and found nothing unusual about Henry's induction. I did find his personal warmth, however, to add to my feelings of comfort and relaxation.

At the end of our first session, I emerged with a past life memory that pleased Henry immensely. I was skeptical, however, that I had recalled an actual memory, or even anything meaningful. As the weeks went by I had to admit, however, that as an allegorical story, my "memory" did reveal some important themes in my life.

Henry encouraged me to practice with a self-hypnosis tape that included the induction of hypnosis and some positive suggestions about self-confidence. I worked with that tape several times a week.

A couple of months later, Henry again led me through a past life recall experience. This time he suggested that I would remember my *very first* lifetime. I experienced something very strange, as if out of a science fiction fantasy novel. It concerned souls working with God's creative forces to make a material world and inhabit it with bodies. Part of the soul's discovery process was learning what *physical feeling* was like and what it added as a channel of awareness.

Again, I was skeptical about the experience, except that the story was an intuitively inspiring one that has stayed with me. Recently, when Ken Carey published his channeled book, *Return of the Bird Tribes*, I found that some of his descriptions of the primordial life of Native American souls were similar to my own story. More than I realized, I must have been tapping into a universal level of the imagination. It's so easy to undervalue your own experience.

In my third session, I told Henry that I thought that I could contact a higher self plane of consciousness. My intuition visualized it as the process of rising up on a blue flame. Henry agreed to try that image and we proceeded. During that session, I became so deeply relaxed, my body felt very heavy and I seemed to float within it. I found that the effect of dissolving into blue flame gave me a sense of a very quiet confidence, an expanded sense of being all-knowing.

When Henry asked me to speak, I hesitated. No matter how relaxed I might be, or confident I might feel, I was getting in my own way. It was like I had a sense of stage fright, and I was blocking the ability of the expanded awareness to speak out. Henry suggested I relax and then encouraged me to simply start talking. Once I began, by surrendering the need to make sure I would say something wise, the words flowed easily. In that respect, it was much like the process of inspirational writing.

As agreed, Henry gave the suggestion that I would speak about my book. I did so, particularly about my attitude toward writing it. Using a humorous and noncritical example, I teased the compulsiveness in my approach to writing the book. I also provided some alternative images and early childhood memories to remind myself of what it was like for me to approach work in a more casual manner. I described several different exercises I could do to keep my attitude positive and help the work proceed smoothly. I kidded myself about wanting to receive the text of the book effortlessly through this trance state, saying that I wasn't really the sort of person who would enjoy taking dictation.

Henry was very excited about this session. My wife was in attendance and she, too, thought I had said some very important things about my writing. I was skeptical, as usual. I assumed that I remembered most of what I had said, and it didn't seem like any big deal. Henry encouraged me to listen to the tape, try the suggestions, and keep practicing with the self-hypnosis tape.

I didn't listen to the tape of my channeling session for several weeks. One day, my wife pointed out to me that I had been complaining regularly about the progress of my writing and perhaps I should listen to my tape. I did and was quite surprised. There were many key statements that I had forgotten. They spoke directly to my feeling stuck in my writing and were just the sort of counsel I needed to hear. What particularly impressed me was the tone of the reading. It was like listening to myself being a wise and loving big brother and my best friend. Nobody else could know me as well and know just what to say to get me back up on my feet. It was a record of a state of consciousness that restored me to myself. I began practicing its advice, with good effect.

A few months later, Henry conducted me in a fourth session. In the middle of my trance talking, I suddenly announced, "There're entities that would speak." I sensed something like a ball of energetic knowing just above my head, and I experienced it as wanting to open up. I heard myself say, "There's a plant entity. There's a bird entity. There's an angel entity. There's an extraterrestrial entity." I felt apprehensive, nervous.

Henry seemed calm and took my announcement in stride. He began to suggest that I might allow them to speak. I heard myself advise him, "The channel's blood flow is constricted . . . warming the hands will open the channel." I must have been referring to the physical consequences of being nervous. Henry suggested that my hands and feet would become warm and they did. One by one, I allowed the "entities" to speak.

Each character had something interesting to say, each provided food for thought. I later discovered some Cayce readings that resembled what the plant told me about the creative forces, what the bird told me about intuition and what the angel told me about celestial music. The angel also gave me some interesting advice about combining the exercise of walking with singing silently to myself, which I have continued to practice with good effect. The basic message of the extraterrestrial was for me to grow stronger in the earth before I allowed my imagination to soar so high.

Afterward, Henry was enthusiastic, as usual. I was intrigued, probably because of what Cayce would call the "wonderment" of it all. During the channeling process, I didn't feel possessed, or out of control. Rather, it was more like I had become suddenly inspired to speak as a plant, to speak as a bird, and so on. It felt like role playing in trance, a way of giving expression to various intuitions. It was hard, but I tried not to be too skeptical, or analytical.

Subsequent sessions were more like the third. I practiced speaking improvisationally from a trance state of higher consciousness. No more characters appeared. Instead, I continued to give myself advice about writing and about developing my channeling abilities.

In this trance work, and while applying the advice I received, I learned an important lesson. My tendency to become fascinated with the phenomenon of trance channeling got in the way of my being a graceful channel. It became clear that it was important to integrate what I experienced in trance into my daily life. If I approached trance channeling as a way to overcome my sense of inadequacy as a person, it was easy to become attached or addicted to the apparent power of the trance state. On the other hand, as I incorporate the trance insights, including the experience of feeling confident in approaching life in a spontaneous manner, the trance state itself becomes less a compelling need. Instead, trance channeling feels more like simply taking time out, as in meditation, to honor and focus exclusively upon a state of awareness that's always there.

PART IV

Becoming a Channel
of Blessings

CHAPTER TWELVE

The Channel of Cooperation in a Group

"Yes, we have the group—as a group—as gathered here, seeking to be a channel that they, as a group, as individuals, may be—and give—the light to the waiting world. . . . First let each prepare themselves and receive that as will be given unto each in *their respective* sphere of development, of desire of ability. The first *lesson*—as has been given—learn what it means to cooperate in *one* mind, in *God's* way; for, as each would prepare themselves, in meditating day and night, in "What wilt thou have me do, O Lord?" and the *answer will* be *definite,* clear to each as are gathered here, will they seek in His name; for He is *among* you in this present hour, for all as *seek* are in that attitude of prayer."

—Edgar Cayce, 262–1

"In cooperation *is* the offering of self to be a channel of activity, of thought . . . for he that would have life must *give* life, they that would have love must show themselves lovely, they that would have friends must be friendly, they that would have cooperation *must* cooperate by the *giving* of self *to* that as is to be accomplished."

—Edgar Cayce, 262–3

> "Father, as we seek to see and know Thy face,
> may we each—as individuals and as a group—
> come to know ourselves, even as we are known,
> that we—as lights in Thee—may give the better
> concept of Thy spirit in this world."
> —Edgar Cayce, 262–5

Cooperation is an excellent form of channeling. We set aside exclusive focus on ourselves and act in harmony with others toward a common goal. Learning to cooperate in a group is a good way to learn channeling.

The power of the group is much more than that of any one of the individuals. A group of novices can work together to channel astonishing psychic effects. Experiments in group channeling allows you to discover that your own contribution, although apparently minor when considered by itself, is actually quite significant. Such experiences can help you learn to appreciate the hidden value of ordinary moments of channeling, moments that you might otherwise disregard.

A Group Channels an Artificial Ghost

For an interesting story about the power of a group, as well as the deceptive nature of spirit guides, read the book, *Conjuring Up Philip*. It makes a Ouija board seem like boring child's play.

Members of the Toronto Society for Psychical Research conducted an experiment attempting to create an artificial ghost. They began by inventing a fictitious character. One member of the group started by telling a brief story of "Philip."

Philip lived in seventeenth-century England. He was unhappily married and fell in love with a gypsy. His wife found out about the affair and accused the gypsy woman of being a witch. Philip was afraid of losing his social status, so he did not come to his lover's defense. The authorities burned the gypsy woman and in his remorse, Philip committed suicide.

Given that brief description of Philip's identity, the group playfully filled out the details. In brainstorming sessions they invented his physical appearance, his clothing, and his home environment. They also discussed the political climate of the time, how Philip got along with his neighbors, his relationship with the king, and his religion and politics. They read books about the conditions in that period of English history. They studied the music and the arts and steeped themselves in the lore of the time. Through their study, imagination, and conversation, they made Philip become very real to them. That was the plan—to materialize Philip. They hoped that he might appear as a ghost that they could all see.

For over a year, they met once a week and sat in meditation trying to tune into Philip. Various members of the group would have individual impressions that Philip was present or that he had said something to them. The group, however, did not encourage these individual experiences. What they were after was a group experience that they could all share.

The purpose of the experiment was not to develop mediumship on any one individual's part, but to have it be a group effort. Nobody had any claims to any special psychic ability. That was the way they wanted it.

They met for a whole year without any results other than having convinced themselves in their playful way of the reality of Philip. He manifested within the group in no manner at all except within their shared imagination.

In their second year, they tried a different approach. Research by Kenneth Batcheldor, a British parapsychologist, showed that a group of people can create psychokinetic (mind over matter) effects by an indirect method. Rather than meditating, they must proceed more in the spirit of the original Victorian-era seance. Simply visit with one another in a relaxed atmosphere, he advised. Sing songs, tell jokes, have conversations, tell stories, make it a social occasion. The Toronto group decided to follow Batcheldor's advice.

They had always meditated and focused intently when they got together. They had difficulty letting go of that structure. Although they were friendly with one another, it felt awkward to visit on purpose. Gradually they caught on to the new approach. Sitting around a table, with the lights on, they'd visit and gossip. They'd sing songs, laugh, and have a good time while they waited for Philip to appear in some form. By the fourth such social gathering, they heard a rapping on the table.

They weren't sure if it was for real. They resumed visiting and soon there was another rapping sound. Everybody heard it. They were suspicious, of course, that somebody in the group had deliberately, or accidentally, rapped the table.

Then the table started to slide a little bit. Apparently it was sliding by itself. As all could see, the only part of their person touching the table was their fingertips making light contact with the tabletop. The loud raps on the table and the sudden violent movements further convinced them that it was a spontaneous event not created by any of the members.

Someone said aloud, "I wonder if Philip is doing this." Immediately there was a very loud rap on the tabletop. The group moved rapidly to a code: one rap for yes, and two for no. Thus they established communication with Philip.

In subsequent meetings, they sat as a group, visited, and soon the rappings would begin. They began to ask Philip yes/no-type questions about his life and corroborated all the "facts" they knew about him.

Several weeks later, they tired of these questions and paid more attention to Philip's physical manifestations. Not only could he rap the table, but also he could shake it, make it vibrate, lift it up on its side, and move it about the room. They had to keep up with the table's movements to keep their fingertips touching the tabletop. Sometimes this was difficult as the table would move fast and unexpectedly in different directions.

Many of the group members smoked and there was one member who objected to smoking. When asked if he minded smoking, Philip would answer yes if the objecting nonsmoker was in the group. He'd also tilt the table to dump the ashtray into the lap of one of the smokers. If the nonsmoker was absent, Philip would say he did not mind smoking.

On a couple of occasions he levitated his table completely off the floor about a half inch and held it there momentarily. Another levitation trick involved pieces of candy. They'd place cellophane-wrapped candies around the table for each person and one in the center for Philip. Philip turned over the table and all the candy fell to the floor except Philip's candy, which remained suspended in place on the tabletop.

The group made a home movie and a videotape of Philip's antics. They even took Philip and his table to a couple of television shows. On one such occasion, Philip made the table climb the stairs to the podium where the master of ceremonies was standing.

In reviewing their experiment with Philip, the group noted that he showed no more knowledge than the group. Where their imagined scenario about Philip differed from factual, recorded history, Philip followed their version. Philip remained faithful to their imagination, not to the facts.

Philip was clearly not a spirit. They interpreted Philip as an artificially created thought form. This creation of their group mind, however, was obviously capable of producing quite dramatic as well as seemingly intelligent physical phenomena. It had apparent psychokinetic ability.

The group hired an engineer to record the rapping sound and do an acoustic analysis of its characteristics. He reported that the waveform characteristics of Philip's rapping were unique. They were unlike any of the other patterns produced by the sound of people using their fingers, fists, pencils, and other things to hit the table. Philip's psychokinetic energy produced its own special effect.

The Toronto group instructed a second group of people to attempt the same experiment. This group invented an entirely new character named Lilith and developed the details of Lilith's life. They proceeded to the visiting part of the experiment, and Lilith soon appeared. She behaved much like Philip.

What is the significance of the Philip experiment? We certainly see some suggestive evidence about the reality of thought forms and their ability to mimic the presence of an actual spirit. It shows that such thought forms can take on a life of their own and exercise power on the physical world. It also shows that the source of a thought form can be the conglomerate of several people's thinking.

The Toronto experiment is a dramatic demonstration of the power of cooperation within a group. When group members set themselves aside from the tendency to make deliberate efforts, they can open up a forceful psychic channel.

The Channel of Cooperation

Cayce delivered an important series of psychic readings on developing psychic ability. He said the first step should be to learn how to cooperate within a group. He then proceeded to outline a course of study for such a group endeavor. Today, A.R.E. "Study Groups" around the country participate in *A Search for God,* as this material is entitled. These manuals contain several lessons on developing spiritual awareness, psychic ability, and becoming a conscious channel.

If you doubt that cooperation is fundamental to channeling, you are not alone. Although we all value cooperation, we underestimate its significance, especially because competition seems necessary to our survival. It's easy to value channeling as a way for us to get *ahead* in life, rather than to be *in harmony* with it. We all have a tendency, if we're honest with ourselves, to want to use channeling in some competitive fashion. Take the case of good sportsmanship. It's a tradition that expresses a valuable piece of wisdom: "It's not whether you win or lose, it's how you play the game that counts." When studying inspirational writing and creativity, we learned that this same wisdom applied. When it comes time to channel, we need to emphasize the process rather than focusing on the final product. Yet look what has happened to the value of good sportsmanship. Sports, once an honored arena for character development, has become an economic ballgame. Although we frown on a professional tennis player who throws tantrums, we find ourselves fascinated by the money he earns. The motto over the arena now seems to read, "The bottom line is *winning is everything!*" Has there been a similar deterioration in the valuing of cooperation?

We assume that competition improves performance; that it motivates us to do our best. That assumption may not be correct. In *No Contest: The Case Against Competition,* Alfie Kohn collected over two hundred studies demonstrating that cooperation breeds better performance than competition. Recall from Chapter Seven the study showing that students who focused on the joy of writing wrote more creative poems than students who focused on winning a prize. Kohn reports several studies of that variety. He also reports studies from the world of business. One study, for example, compared the sales performance of two groups within the same organization. One group worked competitively, where workers did not share with one another any information about their sales leads. The other group worked cooperatively, sharing information openly. The cooperative group grossed significantly higher sales than the competitive group. Cooperation can help the bottom line!

The popular dictum from evolutionary theory, *the survival of the fittest,* reinforces our assumption that competition is more natural than cooperation. Cayce stresses that nothing could be farther from the truth. Nature interacts in an overall pattern of cooperation. Each piece of creation plays a role and each has a purpose in the survival of the whole. The same holds true for each of us. Rediscovering the spirit of cooperation actually places us more closely aligned with a consciousness that promotes our better channeling.

Channeling requires setting oneself aside so a higher source of consciousness may manifest. Cooperation requires setting aside one's personal desires for contributing to a common goal. When we work toward the common good, we recognize and respond to something that transcends the artificial boundary of our separate self. Cooperation shows that there's no limit to what can be accomplished when no one is concerned about who's going to get the credit. The act of cooperation attunes us to the *transpersonal* level of our existence, joined with the rest of creation in a unitary expression.

These considerations show good reasons for Cayce beginning his teachings on psychic ability and spiritual channeling by the topic of cooperation. Channeling and cooperation are soul mates, two activities most closely resembling and belonging to one another. Furthermore, through learning to cooperate, we can also explore the meaning and significance of our individuality as we contribute to the common whole.

We as Lights in Thee

That channeling is essentially a cooperative process may appear paradoxical. We tend to perceive a conflict between expressing ourselves and cooperating to serve the needs of the whole. That conflict comes from the mistaken assumption that it's our ego that really needs to express itself. Instead it's the true self, the soul self, that needs expression.

It is the *individuality* of the soul, not the personality of the ego, that is the truly unique pattern of expression. In our personal hangups we are more alike than different. It is in expressing our true selves that we appear more individual. Our true selves can join with one another in cooperative expression.

Cayce gave a prayer about this principle, quoted at the beginning of this chapter. The prayer asks that we seek, both as individuals and as a group, to know God, to know ourselves, and one another, and to be able to express that knowledge in the world. The prayer expresses the desire to channel, through the way we live, our developing awareness of our individual mirroring of God. The prayer further states that we are "as lights" in God. As each star in the sky gives its own illumination in the darkness, each of us functions as a portion of God's awareness. Each of us is a unique channel of God's consciousness.

For years I have used this prayer to stimulate concrete ways to reveal this principle in practice. Following ''Cayce's Law,'' I sought to find experimental methods for groups of people to apply the principle to experience its truth. I finally had a dream:

''We are gathered for research and enlightenment. We are standing in the dark, not knowing how to proceed. Sudden-

The Dance of Coopeartion
Becomes a Channel of Inspiration

Figure 18

ly, we begin dancing together, each of us displaying an individual symbol. As we greet and celebrate one another in turn, the dance itself generates a fountain of sparks that light our path. We've found our way.''

The dream contains many of the images of the prayer. Each person displays an individual symbol, representing that person's uniqueness. We are cooperating in a dance where we honor and celebrate one another. Yet the cooperative dance creates a fountain of sparks, the light we need in order to find our way. Through cooperation we have generated something that transcends any one individual.

On the basis of this dream, I devised several different experiments in group channeling. I've conducted these on many different occasions and find that they do give people the experience envisioned in Cayce's prayer and my dream. They are each concrete examples of learning about one's channeling ability through cooperating in a group effort. In each case, a person's individual contribution proves to fit into the pattern of the group's cooperative effort. The group effect thus proves the value of the individual contribution that might otherwise go unappreciated. Each unique individual's expression combines harmoniously with a cooperative group effort.

The first experiment, developed in cooperation with Bob Van de Castle, of the University of Virginia Medical School, involves a group incubating telepathic dreams to help someone in distress.

The Dream Helper Ceremony

Imagine attending a "Dream Helper Ceremony." You find yourself among a group of strangers gathered together for an overnight healing service. We explain, "Tonight, you will not be dreaming for yourself, but for someone else. You will discover your telepathic healing ability by putting it to work serving the needs of someone in distress."

"Who among you is feeling troubled by a specific problem," we ask, "and is willing to ask this group for help?

Don't reveal the nature of your problem tonight. Keep it a secret until after tomorrow morning. When we give you our dreams, you may then tell us about it.''

Someone volunteers to be the focus of the group's dreams. This focal person leads the group in a silent meditation and then we prepare to go to bed.

We provide little explanation for how to obtain a helpful dream for a stranger in need. We do warn the helpers, ''Tonight your dreams belong to someone else. Don't lose them or censor any dream material you may recall.''

If you can imagine being in such a situation, you can appreciate how it might feel. You don't know what the person's problem is, but you are certainly curious and are trying to feel it out. You want to be helpful, but it's hard to believe that you could produce a psychic dream.

In fact, the next morning, very few people think that they've had dreams related to the focal person. Not until everyone has told their dreams do they begin to suspect that their dreams contain something meaningful for the focal person.

Consider the case of a dream helper group dreaming for a twenty-one-year-old woman, whom I'll call Mary. One helper dreamed of going to a supermarket. Another dreamed of going to a drugstore to purchase a ''pocket shower kit,'' but had difficulty paying for it. This helper also dreamed of going to a library. Another dreamed of a ''Jewish mother'' who never believed her child was well. Another helper dreamed of holding hands in communion with Mary, of going to a piano recital, and of a boy diving very deep into a pool of clear water. Another dreamed of being underwater, emerging to fly over our group, where she saw Mary, and heard a doctor's voice declare, ''Her diet is too tight—water is very important.'' This helper also dreamed of being at a fashionable poolside party.

I dreamed that I was lying on the deck of a sinking ship where the flooding water was beginning to enter my mouth to drown me. I choked, and woke up abruptly, with the inexplicable impression that Mary had been ill and almost died. I also dreamed I was in my childhood home, where "mom" was playing the piano. I also saw her in the bathroom taking a shower. Then I saw her standing in the kitchen, dripping from the shower, talking on the telephone to someone about how her piano playing was always interrupted. (I use quotes around "mom" because she didn't look like my mother at all.) Then I went outside to return a book to the library. On the lawn was my personal library—it was being soaked by a lawn sprinkler! Those were the dreams for Mary.

Once the dreams are reported, the group quickly notices some common elements. These commonalities and underlying patterns encourage the helpers to accept the possibility that their individual dreams may be related to the focal person after all.

In dreaming for Mary, for example, certain images had been repeated: shopping, the library, mother, and piano. The image of water appeared the most, often in conjunction with a health theme. The group guessed, therefore, that Mary's problem concerned health, for which water might be a critical factor.

Now it was Mary's turn to speak. She was obviously stirred by the dreams, and responded excitedly, saying something to the effect that we were wrong about the problem, but otherwise more right than we knew. She explained that she was concerned about her recently canceled wedding. None of our dreams reflected a marriage theme, but two did touch on matters that were involved in the breakup. The dream of the poolside party was the type of social function she frequently had to attend with her ex-fiancé and his family. She and he came from disparate social backgrounds, and this difference created problems for them. She said that the dream of the Jewish mother also reminder her of her ex-fiancé, for he had once been very ill, and his mother continued to treat him like a sick little boy. Beyond these two correspondences, she saw little in the dreams pertaining to her question about the canceled wedding. What impressed Mary was that the dreams were directly related to many other problems that confronted her. With regard to the water and health themes, Mary revealed her medical history, a secret she had kept to herself for many years. She had a chronic, epilepticlike condition, with seizurelike episodes brought on by tension. She said the themes of being underwater reminded her of how she would feel "flooded" before a seizure. She said that my drowning dream was a good image of what had happened to her during a recent stay in the hospital. As an unexpected side effect to some medication she had received for her condition, she developed a temporary partial paralysis in her sleep. As a result, while sleeping on her back, her saliva was not swallowed, but instead filled her throat, choking her, and she almost died from suffocation. My dream of going down with the ship was just the sort of nightmare of helplessness that might be provoked by an event in sleep such as Mary's. In regard to the other underwater dream, where the dreamer heard a doctor's comment on Mary's condition, she explained that her doctors had not yet diagnosed her condition to their satisfaction, and various treatment programs had been attempted. The phrase, "diet too tight—water important" reminded Mary of her fluid retention problem and she wondered if perhaps diet might indeed be a potential mode of therapy. Because Mary was anxious to reduce medication, perhaps this dream contained a needed clue for her treatment.

Mary said that the image of a library had recently been on her mind. It related to her ambivalence about going back to school because her parents would have to bear the expense. She frequently wondered why she couldn't learn what she really needed by reading in a library. It was interesting that my personal library, the one being watered in my dream, was actually borne out of just the sort of fantasy Mary had been entertaining. Concerning the piano theme, Mary said that everyone in her family was musical except her. She frequently went to piano recitals with her family. Her mother played the piano but found the responsibilities of the home disruptive to her practice.

Mary's reactions to the dreams is typical of a focal person's initial response. No obvious "answer" is perceived, but many correspondences to related critical areas in the focal person's life are recognized in the dreams. The purpose of the ceremony, however, is to be helpful, not merely to spot isolated facts in a person's life. Edgar Cayce consistently maintained that behind apparent psychic aspects in a dream, there is always an immediate and important purpose being served for the dreamer. Interpreting an apparent telepathic dream from the dreamer's point of view often shows how the underlying meaning of the dream reveals that purpose. What purpose was being served by our dreams for Mary?

I began the uncovering process by sharing my personal feelings about my own dreams. In going over with Mary my dream of being back in my childhood home, we discovered that although our home situations had some commonalities, the dream depicted her home more than mine. Both our mothers played the piano, and both complained about their playing being so often interrupted. The physical description I gave of the mother in the dream was unlike my own, but fit Mary's mother very well. In my home there was only one phone, in a vestibule; but in Mary's home there were several, of which her mother used only the one in the kitchen. Whereas my mother used the telephone only rarely, Mary said her mother was frequently in the kitchen talking on the telephone. This dream thus had the curious quality of being a literal representation of an aspect of Mary's home, but also portraying an emotional situation we both could recognize. If the literal details of the dream applied to Mary, I wondered if the emotional significance that might be revealed in the meaning of the dream might also be relevant to her. I therefore began to work on the dream relative to myself, to see if Mary would respond to any of my self-analysis.

The most salient aspect of the dream for me was seeing mother in the shower. This dream image recalled to mind an old childhood memory of walking in on my mother while she was taking a bath. I recall her getting terribly upset, complaining about her lack of privacy, and making me feel very guilty about invading her life. This memory seemed to have a strong emotional connection with memories surrounding my mother's piano playing. Listening to her play gave me an oceanic feeling of bliss. If she were to be interrupted, and get upset, I would somehow feel guilty, as if I were the source of her frustrations. From training in psychotherapy, I could recognize how such memories were part of my own particular mother complex. One aspect was an unresolved dependency that was both disguised and fed by guilt feelings about being the cause of mother's unhappiness. It had been with the task of "watering my books," a metaphor for allowing my feelings to flow through my storehouse of thinking patterns, that I was led to resolve this dependency.

Mary responded very intently to my self-analysis. She explained that her mother's frustrations were a frequent source of friction in the home. Mary realized that she too, like me, assumed that she was somehow to blame for her mother's unhappiness, and the discord between her parents. Mary also now realized how her guilt feelings paradoxically inhibited any tendency to leave home and begin a life of her own, thereby prolonging that dependency. Mary indicated that recognizing the relationship between her guilt feelings and her emotional dependency was a new realization for her.

Three other dream helpers supported this analysis by finding similar guilt and dependency themes reflected in their dreams. For example, the helper who dreamed of having difficulty paying for the pocket shower kit at the drugstore discovered that the theme of "paying for what you get" was exactly how she had to deal with her own difficulty in outgrowing her dependency on her mother. Mary responded to her by indicating that the library theme, which this helper had also dreamed about, represented the same type of problem for Mary, as she had not been able to face up to the responsibility of paying for her own education.

What emerged from the discussion was a definite pattern, reflected in the collection of dreams, revealing a hypothesis that Mary found very meaningful. Besides the possibility that diet might be a contributory factor in her medical situation, there was also a suggestion that there might be a psychosomatic component as well. Her feeling image of being flooded, before seizure, echoed her style of dealing with emotional tensions, especially conflicts associated with guilt. Fantasies of guilt concerning her mother perhaps served to help Mary avoid assuming the responsibility for resolving her need for dependence upon her mother. Further discussion revealed that Mary's ex-fiancé had a similar dependency conflict, a commonality with Mary that seemed to have played a strong role in the breaking off of their engagement.

The case of dreaming for Mary provides a good example of what happens in one of our experimental Dream Helper ceremonies. The group discussion becomes something like a self-help group. The emotional sharing reveals how the dreams are both relevant to the focal person's critical situation and to unresolved aspects of the dreamer's own lives as well. It is as if before going to sleep, each person engages his or her instinctive, projective empathy to intuit that aspect of the focal person's undisclosed problem that corresponds, naturally, with an unreconciled issue within the person's own life. Having been reminded of that issue, the person's dreams then perform their usual work of reconciliation, using both the person's own experiences and images telepathically received from the focal person's life. In that manner, the group's dreams collaborate on a common problem as perceived from individual perspectives.

The specific focus of the group's dreams is even clearer when we have enough people present at a ceremony to divide them into two groups, each dreaming for a different focal person. We can then compare the dreams between the two groups. The occurrence of distinct commonalities in the dreams of one group, as compared with the other group, suggests that the dreams are in fact being focused on something specific to the focal person.

In Mary's group, for example, several of the dreams contained the image of water. Water is a very common dream image, so we might expect it to occur in several of the dreams. At the same time I was involved with Mary's group, however, Bob was involved with another group, dreaming for a different woman. In that group's dreams, the image of water did not appear even once! Instead, that group had several dreams containing the theme of black vs. white and of related polarities. As it turned out, that focal woman was concerned about a biracial romance. There were no black-white or polarity themes in the dreams for Mary. Although both women were concerned with relationship issues, the common dream themes for each woman were definitely distinct and different.

Another way of telling if the dreams are helpful, or if we are simply spinning webs of illusion, is in the long-range impact of the ceremony upon the focal person. In Mary's case, for example, she wrote back a year later, indicating that she had found an apartment for herself. She was now on a special diet and off medication. She had lost several pounds. Most significantly, she was in a therapy group with her mother to work on their relationship. Her application proved the interpretation, as Cayce had often suggested was the best test.

Dream Helper is a powerful group ceremony for channeling dream guidance. It gives a group an opportunity to function as a "psychic consultant." In her book, *Dreams Beyond Dreaming,* Jean Campbell describes a special experiment I once conducted where the dream helpers' dreams proved to be more helpful and "on target" than a reading from a professional psychic hired to participate in the research.

Other psychics have since confirmed in their readings about Dream Helper the special "group oracle of healing" that results from this ceremony. It's a powerful way for a group to be a channel of blessing to someone in need, while at the same time learning something about themselves (not to mention discovering the telepathic power hidden in ordinary dreams). As portrayed in my dream of the "research dance," people sharing of themselves with one another can channel a fountain of enlightenment.

The Cotton Ball: Getting to Know You

In the dream helper ceremony, people with no previous experience can demonstrate psychic channeling ability. All it requires is remembering a dream. There are similar experiments, having the same "we as lights in thee" structure, but quicker to perform, that use the imagination as a channel. The two I will describe, however, require that participants have learned to trust in their spontaneous reactions. I have successfully performed these experiments in workshops, but first have had to train the participants in spontaneity.

I call the first experiment "Getting to Know You." In a small group of strangers, people take turns introducing themselves. Rather than saying anything personal, the person merely says, "Mary had a little lamb." While reciting this phrase, the person visualizes some favorite scene that expresses something positive in the person's life. Group members empathically attune to the sound of the person's voice and monitor their spontaneous responses. After a minute's contemplation of the person's voice vibration, group members share what they experienced. Some people have images, others experience feelings, others hear or see words.

As in the dream helper ceremony, most people doubt that their spontaneous reaction to the person's voice contains anything meaningful. As group members share their experiences, however, usually one or two common themes or images are present in what they say. We try to guess the nature of the scene the person was imagining. We are often wrong, although one group member may have hit upon it in his or her experience. On the other hand, the focal person usually notes that most group members have tuned into some aspect of the person's life. Group members' experiences often reflect commonalities they have with the focal person. Besides being an experiment in intuitive empathy, the sharing that results makes a great ice-breaker.

The "Getting to Know You Game" works on our natural curiosity about strangers. It achieves a certain level of spontaneous, lighthearted channeling. A more profound level of channeling occurs when the motivation serves a more pressing need, as in the dream helper ceremony. The second experiment, "the Cotton Ball Ceremony," serves that function.

In this experiment, one person in the group volunteers to be the focus. Like the Dream Helper, someone with an undisclosed personal problem asks the group for help. This person takes a large wad of sterile cotton out of an envelope. The person rubs the cotton between the hands while thinking about the problem. Meanwhile, the rest of the group meditates. Afterward, the focal person breaks the cotton into smaller pieces to give to each of the group members. They hold the cotton in their hands and tune into their impressions. They verbalize whatever comes to mind. After everyone has finished, the focal person responds to this outpouring.

Very often the focal person is in tears. The group members' statements touch deep feelings and prompt a release of emotion. The resultant sharing is very much like the dream helper ceremony, except that there are no dreams to interpret. The experience of closeness is much more immediate. Whether or not the group members' channeling contains any helpful advice, their evident deep attunement is itself a healing experience for the focal person. Members are so concentrated on the person's concern that they forget about noticing how well they channeled information. They've stepped beyond themselves. Their common concern for another person evoked their channeling ability. This cotton ball ceremony is a moving testimony to the power of cooperation.

Choir Practice: Channeling the Sounds of the Higher Self

I'll conclude this chapter with my favorite experiment in group channeling. Like Cayce, I find the sound of music to be a very special channel. I enjoy teaching people that they can make spontaneous sounds that free them to be themselves as well as raise their consciousness. Leading a group in what I call choir practice requires a Richard Simmons form of sustained, energetic leadership to help people overcome their shyness. The results, although they require patience, are invariably worth the effort.

We warm up with a jungle symphony. I ask everyone to make, all at the same time, the sound of their favorite animal. We do this a few times until people are comfortable enough to sound out loudly and for as long as a minute. Then I ask the animals to respond to one another's sounds, to interact, to communicate, and to harmonize, as they would in nature. The jungle symphony is great fun and reminds people that their inner child still enjoys to play with sound.

We then move on to mood music. I ask everyone to make, all at the same time, the sound of feeling good. We get a pleasant medley of *Aahhs, Oohhs,* and *Yeys.* Following Cayce's remarks about the importance of vowel sounds, I ask the group to express feeling good with *Aee* sounds, then *Eye* sounds, and so on, through the vowels. With each vowel sound, I ask them to experiment with the tone and quality until they find the pitch quality that makes their whole body vibrate or tingle with the sound. Now that they all have several sounds to express good feelings, I ask them to begin playing with these sounds, interacting with one another, to create a symphony of good feelings. The effect is somewhat like a jam session, a cooperative improvisational choir, making nonsensical sounds that feel good. In a playful way, it sounds good, too.

Without destroying the precious mood of playfulness, I then move the group on to a more purposeful effort. We practice making sounds of the higher self. I start them out with chanting *Om.* They practice chanting this sound at their own individual pace. At any given moment, some people are starting an Om sound, some are in the middle of the sound, and some are concluding the sound, so the effect is somewhat like a musical round, but less structured. We then experiment with inventing our own individual sounds to express the feeling of the higher self.

The final experience is an improvised choral piece with

everyone making a variety of uplifting sounds. We play off one another's sounds to create a flowing, ever-changing current of sound vibration. Every now and then you can hear a brief solo passage filtering through the choir, to which the group gives echo and changes the direction of the improvisation. People are obviously feeling the vibrations in their bodies, for they are swaying to the music and moving their arms.

By cooperating in this way, they give themselves an experience they couldn't achieve individually. Everybody gets to experience making a valuable contribution, in spite of feeling that they "can't sing." We also get to luxuriate in the pleasure of flowing together in a beautiful expression of harmony and higher consciousness.

There is a healing energy at work in this choir practice. Some people report flashes of past life memories. Some people are in tears as they experience deep emotional release through their sounds. Most people report intense tingling sensations in the body. Clearly we are opening a profound channel. By cooperating in sound, the group has become a channel of the creative forces.

Chapter Thirteen

Being a Channel of Healing Forces

"As the body attunes self, as has been given, it may be a channel where there may be even *instant* healing with the laying on of hands."

—**Edgar Cayce, 281–5**

"The nearer the body of an individual . . . draws to that attunement, or consciousness, as was in the Christ Consciousness, as is *in* the Christ Consciousness, the nearer does the body, or that body, become a channel for *life-living* life—to others to whom the thought is directed."

—**Edgar Cayce, 281–5**

"There are, as seen, many *various* channels through which healing may come. That as of the individual contact; that as of the faith; that as of the laying on of hands; that as will create in the mind (for it is the builder in a human being) that consciousness that makes for the closer contact with the universal, or the *Creative* Forces, in its experience."

—**Edgar Cayce, 281–6**

"Kindness, gentleness and prayer. These offer the channels through which the greater help may come."

—**Edgar Cayce, 1183–3**

"He that wishes his brother well, yet makes no
move to aid or supply, or to comfort, or to cheer,
is only fooling self. He that would know the way
must oft be in prayer, joyous prayer, *knowing*
He giveth life to as many as seek in sincerity to
be the channel of blessing to someone."
—**Edgar Cayce, 281–12**

May the Force be with you! The movie *Star Wars* made
this expression popular. What is this force? It was the force
that allowed Luke Skywalker to guide his spacecraft through
many dangerous obstacles. It is the same force that allowed
the blindfolded Zen archer to hit the bull's-eye with the
arrow. It is what Cayce calls the Creative Force, Spirit, the
one energy in creation.

Channeling the ideals of the higher self includes learning
to channel the Creative Force itself. Cayce taught that if you
can develop a conscious relationship with this force, creation itself is available to be within your care. You can
become a channel of healing.

The Secret of the Green Thumb

Luther Burbank, the famous American horticulturalist,
knew the secret of the creative force active in the life of
plants. In his *Autobiography of a Yogi,* Paramahansa
Yogananda, the influential Indian master, called Burbank an
American saint. Yogananda visited with Burbank on his
trips to America. He was delighted with Burbank's spiritual
orientation toward his plants. The results he achieved through
this orientation was evident in his experiments with plants.
Burbank admitted to Yogananda that he talked with his
plants. He developed thornless cacti, for example, by telling
them that they had nothing to fear and thus no need for such
protection. Although he knew that the will of a plant is
much stronger than the will of a human being who might
wish to bend the plant's habits, Burbank learned the secret

of blending new life patterns into a plant's structure. "The secret of improved plant breeding," he told Yogananda, "apart from scientific knowledge, is love."

Burbank was a practiced meditator. It was by meditating with his plants that he learned their secrets. He noted that sometimes during such communion, he felt close to what he called "the Infinite Power." At such times, he admitted to Yogananda, he was able to heal the sick, as well as the plants.

Edgar Cayce was an avid gardener. Many of us share with him a love for gardening. It is a pastime that is enjoying great popularity today. We seem to have a native instinct for wanting to get our hands in the earth, to mingle with and be surrounded with plants and flowers. As we nurture our gardens, it rejuvenates us. Developing the green thumb is good for our health, as well as our plants.

Cayce was a believer in the power of our thoughts and feelings on plants. Besides watering, fertilizer, and other care, plants need our love! In one of his psychic readings, he pointed out that vegetables grown by a grouchy gardener are hard on our digestion! Better, he said, that the gardener tell jokes in the garden, even if they were dirty jokes, than to grumble and grouse!

Awareness of the Unseen Forces in Creation

Have you ever suspected that lurking within the scenic garden, hidden behind the veil of the visible leaves, flowers, and fruits, there was a great activity of unseen forces? If you're out in nature, it's something you can almost feel. You can almost hum along with the silent voices that are singing songs of Mother Nature. A secret delight, a joy, nudges you to a quiet dance. Perhaps you've been on the verge of becoming aware of these unseen forces. The invisible forces, the intelligence of the creativity at work in plant life, in all life, is what Cayce called the *Creative Forces*.

In her book, *Behaving as if the God in All Life Mattered:*

A New Age Ecology, Machaelle Small Wright told her personal story about how spending time in nature taught her about meditation. She tells how nature instructed her how to meditate, and then introduced her to the invisible forces at work in the plants, animals, and insects. Her term for these forces was the "overlighting intelligences." Others have called them *devas, nature spirits, elementals,* or *fairies.*

Wright's approach to experiencing the creative forces parallels what Cayce taught. In particular, she sought contact with these forces *from within herself.* Not that these forces don't exist independently of us, for they do. At the same time, however, humans, being *one with* nature, contain these forces *within* us as well. They are first met within and then we can cooperate with their activity beyond ourselves, in the external world.

Rather than seeking the creative forces with instruments directed outside ourselves, the secret is to look within. Cayce taught that they are to be found, and worked with, through working on our state of consciousness.

In my own experience I've confirmed Cayce's state of consciousness approach. Many times I've sought to *see* or to *hear* elementals as I walked in nature or worked in my garden. Never have I been successful. On the other hand, I once encountered the consciousness of these elementals, quite by surprise, not through intent. It was from within myself that they greeted me. I was working in a garden, weeding, when, for some reason, I had stopped to rest. My state of mind was more like goofing off. I had not only stopped *working* in the garden, but also in these moments I had stopped *any kind* of *striving.* I was merely being there, lying about on the ground, pleasantly idle.

I was absentmindedly staring into the squash plants, musing over their large yellow blossoms, daydreaming, when I noticed that I was being subtly filled with a mood. It was as if a soft, melodic mood began to color my emotional frame of mind. Suddenly I realized that I was not alone. It wasn't as if I was aware of the smell of someone's breath, or the sound of breathing, but it was intimate contact. I felt an emotional presence.

As soon as I became aware of it, I was so startled I'm sorry to say I lost the contact. Only the faintest glimmering in my inner vision provided me with a brief impression of their smiling faces. In other words, I saw them in my imagination. The imagination, if you recall from our discussion in Chapter Eight, is the channel, par excellence, for receiving impressions of unseen forces.

As if to confirm for me the reality of my image impressions, I later encountered a book, *Beauty Unknown,* self-published by an anonymous psychic author. It contained paintings of various spirit guides the psychic had seen. Among these luminaries I found a picture of a face I immediately recognized. It had the same look, the same expression on its face as what I had encountered in the garden. I was dumbfounded to see on the facing page that the author had identified it as a *squash deva.* The message the psychic had channeled from the deva was, "Have you been too busy to enjoy the joy that exists in the garden of God's happy people?" The author's psychic impression, shared in the drawing, the association with squash, as well as the message to take a moment's pause from labor to enjoy the garden, all corroborated my own experience.

Girded with the confidence of that external source of support, I reflected long and hard upon my experience. I realized that it was through my state of consciousness that I made the contact. I also realized that the contact was made from within. It wasn't by squinting my eyes in some special way, or by closely scrutinizing the squash blossoms, or through any externally directed maneuver.

Cayce also taught that by merging intuitively with plants, becoming one with them, we can develop an awareness of the unseen forces at work. His method for doing so derives from his approach to teaching the creative arts, where, as we learned in Chapter Seven, he regarded nature as the master teacher of creativity. Here is an exercise I developed based on his suggestion about how to attune to a plant to make contact with the unseen creative force.

Find a plant that attracts you and become that plant in your imagination. I'm going to use a rosebush. I approach the plant respectfully, acknowledging that it is expressing its creative nature with no reservations. I thank it for being willing to share its secrets with me openly. Approaching it as a living being puts me into the proper frame of mind for receiving the plant's lesson. I stand in front of the rosebush and begin to imagine what it is like to be a rosebush. I imagine being a stem, rising from the earth and branching outward. I imagine growing thorns and leaves. I imagine being a new little leaf, reddish purple in color and changing to green as I mature. As I look at the roses themselves, in varying stages of growth, I can imagine being a tiny bud, growing larger, then opening bit by bit, until I totally surrender myself, my petals lying limp, then falling to the ground. I take in the rosebush as a whole, and imagine drawing nutrients from the ground, from the air, and from the sun.

As you imagine being the plant, allow your images to work themselves into your body. Mimic the feeling of the plant in the position and movements of your body. As I empathize with the creative miracle of the rosebush, I spread my feet apart, feeling the earth feed me. I spread my arms out like branches and feel energy rise up through my feet and out through my outstretched hands. My hands circulate in the breeze and my fingers play with sunbeams. My head becomes a rosebud. It begins bowed, with my eyes closed, but gradually it rises up toward the sky, my eyes open, and my mouth breaks out into a smile as the rose blooms. My head falls back, then bows again to begin another rosebud to blossom cycle.

As you join your plant in its *dance*, allow your mood to express itself in sound. Sing the plant's song. It's a matter of improvising in sound to the attunement you feel with the plant. I begin with a silent hum, as I feel the nutrients rising up my stems. I begin making an *ahh* sound as the leaves dance in the sunlight. As my head rises to the sky to blossom, my smile breaks out into the sounds of *Ah so!* Then I begin the cycle again. I'm feeling happy, I'm dancing happy and singing happy. I've my place in the sun and I'm enjoying it. By giving myself over to the spirit of life, I express that life in my own way, openly, fully. It's a quiet exuberance, yet charged with energy.

The point of joining with your plant in song and dance is not to create an artistic performance. It is to join the plant in spirit. It requires being able to let go of worrying about how you might look. In setting yourself aside and joining the plant in the spirit of love, you become a channel of creative energy in harmony with the plant.

Afterward, sit quietly with your plant. Just be there with it in the afterglow of your communion. You may notice that you experience the plant differently now. Perhaps you can sense variations in the plant's vitality, how the stem, for example, is dense and sturdy, while the new leaves are delicate. Compared to the base of the stem, there is a vibrance in the growing edges of the plant, such as around the new leaves and buds.

You've experienced within yourself the energy pattern of the plant. You've empathized with the plant's energy body and perhaps now you can almost imagine, if not quite see, radiations of energy around the plant. Don't squint your eyes, for the eyes are not the primary channel for perceiving the plant's *aura*, or energy body. Don't try too hard, as if there were a great gap between you and what you want to see. Your loving attunement to the plant, your active, imaginative joining with the plant is the vital channel for perceiving this subtle, etheric level of the plant's existence. What you want to see is within you. As you remain relaxed and joined with the spirit of the plant, the mood of the moment may bring you a sensation of the unseen forces, or the etheric intelligence, patterning the life of the plant.

Awakening the Atomic Power of Healing Forces From Within

The Creative Forces at work in nature also flow through our bodies. This energy is available for healing and regeneration. We can learn how to awaken this force and become channels of healing.

Cayce indicates that there is consciousness all throughout our body. Psychologists have demonstrated, in fact, that with a little training, subjects can make contact with individual cells within the body and affect their functioning. Cayce would have us realize, however, that consciousness within the body exists at an even finer level than individual cells. Every *atom* in the body has consciousness.

When we meditate, the ideal we focus on shapes our awareness. This altering of our consciousness filters down to every cell in the body and to every atom. Cayce explained that to become a channel of healing, it is important to set as the ideal the Christ Consciousness, or as Jesus said, "The Father and I are One."

The closer we are able to attune ourselves to the ideal of conscious oneness with God, the greater effect this ideal has upon the body. As explained in Chapter Five, meditating upon the ideal of the Christ Consciousness causes a pattern of awakening in the Kundalini forces within the endocrine system. The consciousness of every atom within the body becomes filled with the awareness of God. That consciousness that is aware of itself as being one with creation is thus able to be a channel of the force of creation.

The effect of this awareness, Cayce reveals, is to alter the very rotary forces themselves within the heart of the atom. His referring to these rotary forces proved to be quite prophetic. Modern physics has learned, as discussed in Chapter Two, that atoms are in instant communication with one another. Specifically, what they seem to communicate is the information contained in the rotary activity within the atom. It is something about the spin of energy within the core of the atom that serves as an instantaneous telepathic link between all atoms. Thus, Cayce's linking the effect on the rotary forces within the atoms of the body during deep meditation to the opening of the channel of the healing forces of creation has taken on more profound significance.

Try to imagine it for a moment. By allowing your conscious mind to become absorbed in the awareness of oneness with all life, with God, the atoms in your body also awaken to this consciousness. You, all the way from your conscious awareness down to the very atoms of your body, are resonating in harmony with the basic creative energy of life itself. You become a channel of the Life Force.

Having awakened this connection with the Life Force, we can then direct it. Cayce indicates that we can direct it through our hands, through touch. We can also direct it with our minds, by sending out prayers of healing to others. Cayce explains that through subliminal, telepathic influence, the subconscious mind of that individual will pick up the pattern in our prayers, and the atoms in that person's body will respond accordingly. The atomic structure of the receiver's body will realign itself in the direction of greater balance and harmony.

Thus we transfer the healing power expressed in our own meditative attunement. It's awesome to realize that we're able, by deciding to deeply concentrate upon our oneness with God, to awaken the atomic power of the life force that is alive within us. It's even more awesome to contemplate our ability to then become channels of this power, focusing it outside of ourselves to affect the atomic forces within another living being. As awesome as it may be to contemplate, research suggests that it's true!

Research on Channeled Healing

Healing through prayer and the laying on of hands has a long history. It is only relatively late in that history, however, that science has begun to investigate such healing. There is a growing body of research that confirms the healing power of touch and prayer.

Nuclear physicist Elizabeth Rauscher, for example, tested the ability of gifted healer Olga Worrell to affect bacteria growing in special laboratory containers. Olga would hold a container of bacteria in her hands and either attempt to enhance the bacterial growth or retard it. Dr. Rauscher would later count the bacterial population to determine the effect of the healer's directed touch. She found that Mrs.

Worrell could significantly affect bacterial growth, in whichever direction she desired. To make the task more difficult, Dr. Rauscher placed the bacteria in a biochemical environment that either retarded or accelerated their growth, and found that Mrs. Worrell's touch could counteract the effect of these chemical factors. For example, placing bacterial growth in an environment with antibiotics severely hampers the bacteria from multiplying. Yet Mrs. Worrell could lay her hands on the laboratory dishes housing these endangered bacteria and significantly improve their chances of surviving in their hostile environment. Conversely, Mrs. Worrell could retard the growth of bacteria in an environment that favored their growth.

Dr. Carroll Nash, of St. Joseph's University, conducted a similar study using college students as the healers. He found that these inexperienced young people could enhance the growth rate of bacteria through the laying on of hands. In a later, more daring study, he found that students could actually create *genetic mutations* in bacteria!

A most unusual experiment provided further evidence that the laying on of hands has the power to operate at the atomic level of the body. Stephen Schwartz, head of the innovative research organization, The Mobius Society, tested the effect of the healer's touch upon the atomic structure of water. In his experiment, healers laid hands upon human patients with real illnesses. During these treatments, the healers wore special gloves that had vials of distilled water sewn in their palms. Afterward, an engineer performed infrared spectrophotometric analysis of the water. This is a technique that determines the pattern of atomic structure of a material by analyzing the frequencies of infrared light that the material will reflect. The results of this analysis proved that the water in the palms of these healers during their work had been atomically altered. The healing energy had altered the nature of the bonding between the oxygen and the hydrogen atoms in the water molecules! In his study, Schwartz had employed both gifted, practiced healers, as well as novices with no previous experience. The results indicated that all participants were able to affect the water molecules, but the effect was greatest among the experienced practitioners.

These studies involved the laying on of hands, where the healer provides a channel of direct contact for the healing energies. Let's now examine studies of healing at a distance, through the channel of thought transmission, or prayer.

A study involving nearly four hundred coronary care patients at the San Francisco General Hospital revealed that receiving prayer aided recovery. Medical researcher Randy Byrd recruited people of all faiths from across the United States to serve as distant prayer helpers, giving them the name of the patient, the diagnosis, and condition, but no instructions in how to pray. Half of the patients received prayer (with an average of six prayer helpers), and half received no prayer. The patients receiving prayer recovered with significantly fewer complications than the patients who did not receive prayer. In reviewing the report of this research, several doctors replied that the results confirmed their own private opinion, as they themselves prayed for their patients and believed it to be effective.

In another study, involving strictly the psychokinetic power of mind over matter, Dr. William Braud, senior research associate with the Mind Science Foundation, asked laypeople to attempt to mentally "operate" on the blood of another person. The experimenter drew the blood from the patient before this "operation," so that the patient's frame of mind had no influence on the results. Dr. Braud found that people could mentally delay the breakdown of red blood cells (hemolysis). Within the blood system, this effect would enhance the blood cells' ability to fight off disease.

What these types of studies show is that healing effects, both through touch and thought, can operate in situations where the recipient's own belief system is not relevant. We are not dealing with psychological effects, such as positive thinking or the placebo factor. We are seeing in these studies that people can channel healing energies that operate upon molecular structures themselves. They add credence to

Cayce's statement that the awakening of the healing forces is something that is of the nature of atomic energy itself!

The Glad Helpers

Edgar Cayce gave a lengthy series of psychic readings on the healing power of meditation and prayer. They are sometimes referred to as the "Prayer Group" readings because they were given for a group of people who wanted to learn how to become healers through prayer and the laying on of hands. Although the membership of that group has evolved since it began in 1931, it remains active to this day. Every Wednesday morning at the A.R.E. headquarters in Virginia Beach, the "Glad Helpers," as they call themselves, meet for a period of meditation. After the meditation they pray for all those who have asked to be placed on their prayer list. They also lay hands on those people who have come to the meeting to receive healing.

The Prayer Group readings discuss several of the topics that we've already looked at in this book. The importance of meditation, especially its effect upon the atomic consciousness of the body, comprises a major portion of these readings. For a good resource book concerning the specific, practical, hands-on techniques of healing, I would recommend Dolores Krieger's fine guide, *The Therapeutic Touch: How to Use Your Hands to Help and Heal*. Cayce's complete prayer group readings are contained in Volume 2 of the Edgar Cayce readings, *Meditation, Part I: Healing, Prayer and the Revelation*. These readings approach the development of healing ability, not as a technique, but more as an opportunity for soul growth for the practitioner as that person develops an awareness of Oneness with God and is able to share that with others.

The nature of that sharing touches upon a potential controversy concerning the use of the word, *channeling*. Nowhere in the Cayce readings does that form of the word appear. Cayce never used the word as a verb suggesting that it was something that we actively *do*. He always used the word as a noun, reminding us that we *are* channels of energy. Although it is perfectly correct to talk in terms of how we might *channel* our energies, it can also be misleading. His avoiding using channel as a verb was an expression of the humility often seen in persons who are genuine channels of the spirit. If pressed, they'll admit to their personal dedication to serving, but they'll give the credit to God for the services rendered.

Some New Age philosophers might claim that this shyness is merely an old-fashioned unwillingness to assume personal responsibility for the immense energies at our disposal. Many experienced healers know that they can direct healing energy. Olga Worrell was able to either inhibit or support bacterial effort. Other healers can move healing energies to varying parts of the recipient's body. These experiences show that healing can be an active, channeling experience. I suspect, however, that the reticence of many healers to speak of it in such active terms is less shyness and is more rooted in other experiences while being a channel of healing.

Interviewing members of the Glad Helpers, for example, I discovered a uniformity in their description of what it was like during moments of healing. Specifically, I wanted to find out how it differed from meditation experiences, which is also a period of channeling spiritual energy. What does it feel like when one ends a period of meditation and *directs* healing energy to another person?

In meditation, it feels as if something is happening within you. The more experience you have entering deeper and deeper levels of meditation, the more feelings of relaxation become feelings of bliss. Experiences of deep peace can become so intense that it may feel like ripples of energy within the body, or explosions of joyful light. Although you are by yourself, you don't feel lonely because there is a definite sense of communion with a presence. It is a wonderful experience of *being alive*, of feeling *full of life*.

As meditation yields to prayer and the laying on of hands, the experience of being alive changes in a very definite manner. Many practitioners speak of the creation of a triangle. What had been a private experience between the mediator and God, or the Creative Forces, suddenly flows outward and includes another person. Including the other person creates a powerful new circuit and the energy, the joy, the peace, surges forth, as if it had suddenly found *a needed outlet* in order to express its true nature. One practitioner describes it as being *yoked* to the other person, intimately connected in such a way that *together* they are the channel of the healing energy. This formulation reminds us of a principle of channeling that we've encountered before in this book, that channeling flows better when there is a point of application ready to receive it.

Other practitioners focus less on images related to the completion of an electrical circuit and instead refer to a quite human, personable feeling. They say that their feeling of joy during meditation is simply made greater by being able to share it with someone else. This last formulation perhaps gets to the essence of being a channel of healing, which is overcoming the illusion of separation and returning to the shared experience of spiritual oneness.

Most of us have had the experience of being very happy about something yet finding ourselves alone, with no one around with whom we might share it. It's common to feel that happiness becomes greater when we have someone to share it with. Yet we don't experience ourselves as *trying* to shower the other person with our happiness, as if to improve that person's mood. Instead, our motivation is simply a desire to expand our boundaries and include another conscious being in what we are experiencing. The happiness we feel naturally spreads to the other person.

Healing doesn't mean that we *zap* the other person with a ray of energy as if we were a pest exterminator. Instead, what's important is for us to *recognize our oneness with others* and let that realization have its natural way with our actions. Being a channel of healing feels more like including other people in our experience of the joy of God. We actively seek an attunement, and include the other person in that attunement, but the healing is something that happens of itself.

The Little Things That Count

Although Cayce never described channeling healing as if it were an active effort where one *tries* to create an effect, he nevertheless insisted that to become channels of blessing, we must be willing to be active in life, ready to help out where needed. Moreover, Cayce indicated to the group learning to be healers that they couldn't restrict their practice to those special times of meditative attunement. Learning to be a channel of healing requires learning to act, on a daily basis, in a positive and constructive manner. He repeatedly pointed to the value of the little things that count.

Ever notice the value of a smile? It is one of those little things that can make all the difference. To Cayce, a smile was as valuable as a prayer.

Lending a hand, reaching out to touch someone, giving a hug—all these little acts are as valuable as the laying on of hands in a formal healing service.

Taking time to listen, rather than give advice, is also one of those little things that can make a difference to someone. Listening can be more effective in helping a person than all the suggestions we might conceivably offer.

To become a channel of healing, it's important that we understand that it isn't for us to *fix* or *rescue* people. Such an attitude is only a shade away from judging other people and their problems. Cayce insisted that it was important, not only that we not judge one another, but also that we keep our thoughts positive. Our thought are not private, but affect those around us. Thinking kindly of others is as important as acting in kindness.

Maintaining a positive attitude is important to our own personal health as well as in becoming a channel of healing. Cayce explained this relationship by referring to the effect of attitudes and emotions upon the endocrine system. Today we appreciate the value of his perspective. Modern holistic medicine now recognizes, through countless research studies, that a positive attitude has definite positive effects on the body's immune system.

In learning to be a channel of healing, all the other

principles that we've learned in other aspects of channeling apply. In particular, Cayce's model of channeling (attune to an ideal, set yourself aside, and allow the ideal to express itself) applies especially to being a channel of healing. When members of the original Glad Helpers group asked Cayce whether or not their healing prayers were being effective, he reassured them to keep their attention focused on the process, to have faith in the process, and to leave the results to God.

Nothing is achieved through self-doubt, he explained. He encouraged us, as we learn to become channels of blessings, to lay aside concerns about how well we're doing.

Above all, don't stand in your own way. The final secret of learning to be a channel is the hardest of all, yet it's also the simplest. It is that being yourself, your real, true, spontaneous, essential, genuinely individual self, is the best way to be a channel of blessing to others.

CHAPTER FOURTEEN

Being Yourself: The Ultimate Form of Channeling

"For to fulfill that purpose for which an entity, a being, has manifested in matter is the greater service than can possibly be rendered.

"Is the oak the lord over the vine? Is the Jimson beset before the tomato? Are the grassy roots ashamed of their flower beside the rose?

"All those forces in nature are fulfilling rather those purposes to which their Maker, their Creator, has called them into being.

"Man is in that position where he may gain the greater lesson from nature, and the creatures in the natural world; they each fulfilling their purpose, singing their song, filling the air with their perfume, that they, too, may honor and praise their Creator; though in their humble way in comparison to some, they each in their *own* humble way are fulfilling that for which they were called into being, reflecting—as each soul, as each man and each woman should do in their particular sphere—*their* concept of their Maker."

—Edgar Cayce, 1391–1

"For with God nothing is impossible, and the individual that may give himself as a channel

through which the influences of good may come
to others may indeed be guided or shown the way.
For the influences of such a nature are those that
all men seek, and for which there is a great cry
in the earth today—and *today IS* the accepted
time!''

—Edgar Cayce, 165–24

I'll always remember Diane's dilemma. An intelligent
and enthusiastic woman, she was well read in metaphysics.
Her knowledge, however, was primarily intellectual. One
summer years ago, at A.R.E.'s camp, she spent a night in
the dream incubation tent. Through this experience, she
gained a direct realization that her gut feelings and her
intuitive side were as intelligent, and perhaps as trustworthy,
as her intellect. She spent the next few years developing that
newfound part of herself. Her intuitive and creative gifts
blossomed. Gradually, she developed the ability to do trance
channeling.

During this time, she worked for a public service agency.
She had the responsibility for dealing with some very
challenging social problems. In one of her trance channeling
sessions, she gave a reading on how to deal with a particularly thorny type of problem, concerning families and their
children. Her channeled source gave some very good ideas
on how to approach this problem, both at the level of
philosophical policy as well as at the practical level. It was
a different approach from the way the agency was currently
handling these types of problems, but those of us who were
familiar with the matter believed that her channeled advice
was very good.

I suggested to her that she write up a memo based upon
the transcript of her reading and submit it to her superiors.
The agency needed to consider her ideas. Her response to
me was, ''How could I do that? I'd have to explain to them
about being psychic and doing trance channeling. They'd
never go for that!''

I could understand her reaction, but I replied, ''Why do

you have to say anything about trance channeling? Why don't you just say that these are some ideas that you think are valuable?''

She thought for a moment then said, ''I couldn't do that, either, because they wouldn't listen to *my* ideas. Besides, it's the trance channeling aspect that makes the ideas worthwhile.''

I was saddened to realize how much she was discounting herself. In further discussion, I heard her say that she had more confidence in what came through her channeling than she did in her own waking thoughts. Anything that came from her conscious mind couldn't be as good as her channeled insights, she thought. Only psychic insights were worth considering. I realized that it wasn't just that she didn't believe the agency would listen to her ideas. The problem was also that *she* didn't believe in herself either. She needed to insist on the channeled source of her ideas in order to give them credibility herself. By insisting on the psychic aspect of her ideas, however, she effectively prevented people in the public agency from having the opportunity to consider them. If *psychic channeling* was the necessary packaging for her ideas, then no one in the agency would open the package. Diane had placed herself in a frustrating dilemma.

Diane had learned well the art of trance channeling. Her channeled readings were quite inspiring and insightful. She could gather an audience of like-minded people to listen to her channel. Yet there was a block in her own waking ability to channel this channeled wisdom into the mainstream of society, where it was needed. The root of this problem was that her channeling ability had not yet touched the mainstream of her own self-image.

Diane wasn't a ''trick shooter,'' a dissociated channel of entities. She channeled her own higher consciousness. Nevertheless she still hadn't fully integrated the significance of her channeling ability into her self-concept. She devalued her conscious self in favor of her trance self. Her ego still needed to put trance channeling on a pedestal, so it could serve her ego's need to say, ''Look, isn't that special!'' The ability of her channeling to serve the real needs of others was thus diminished. The potential of her channeling ability to transform her self-concept, to bring about an acceptance and valuing of her total self, had yet to be realized.

Channeling Is Not a Substitute for Believing in Yourself

Diane's dilemma is not unique. I've encountered a similar attitude in many people I've counseled who, in becoming psychic, come to devalue any thoughts that aren't channeled in some psychic fashion. Discovering a new, fascinating genie, their underlying rejecting attitude toward their normal self becomes evident. Their predicament is something we all must face, for self-doubt is a pernicious pest.

A major theme in this book has been that you are spirit in a physically channeled form. You can experience that spirit by becoming aware of your channeling ability. If we approach channeling, however, as a *substitute*, rather than as a *means*, to become who we really are, it won't work. If we use channeling as a crutch, to simply *compensate* for a low self-image, rather than allowing it to *touch and heal* that problem, we cheat ourselves of the ultimate secret value of learning to be a channel.

As we've grown up from childhood, we've all suffered wounds causing us to doubt ourselves and our value. Psychologists who've studied the development of channelers find that these people used their wounds as a motivation to develop an alternative self that is confident, spontaneous, and trustworthy. But Diane's dilemma shows that at some point, the channeler's conscious personality, including the self-doubt, has to be touched by the free spirit that's the source of channeling. If learning to be an active channel is to bring blessings to others and to ourselves, we have to allow our channeling to heal our self-doubts and teach us that we are okay and worthwhile. Otherwise, learning to channel can be a self-defeating, self-deceptive exercise.

Channeling Can Teach Self-Esteem

Channeling is basically a creative process. Cayce's formula of creation, ''Spirit is the Life, Mind is the Builder, the Physical is the Result,'' provides the basis for channeling. The mind sets an ideal, which determines the pattern through which the spirit flows. The formula for channeling becomes, ''Set the ideal, then set oneself aside to let the idealized spirit express itself.'' The result is an inspiration and then an action that serves the ideal.

Channeling involves getting out of the way so that an ideal can express itself through you. Channeling intuition, for example, requires setting aside our rational mind to allow inner knowledge to materialize. Regardless of the channeling modality, learning to step aside, to remove oneself as a block to the channel, is part of the process.

By getting out of the way and opening the channel, you open a flow of spontaneity. Rather than being guarded about every word or action, you let go and talk and act freely without forethought. In many of the advanced forms of channeling, such as inspirational writing, visionary imaging, and trance channeling, we must trust our immediate experience, accept the first images that come to mind, the first words that reach our lips. We become totally open, transparent, letting the ideal we've attuned to shine forth without hesitation or censorship.

Being spontaneous is not that easy to do. It's not easy to ''watch yourself go by,'' as Cayce suggests we do. It takes trust and relaxation to meditate upon inspiration, letting yourself breathe naturally while you watch it happen. It requires that we be there in awareness but not be in the way.

It's not that easy to be conscious of self without being self-conscious. We constantly hedge our bets. We cover our light with all kinds of baskets. Our self-doubt gets in the way. We have insecurities. We're concerned about what others might think. Our pride won't let us risk making a fool of ourselves. We wish to remain invulnerable to criticism. We can't afford to lose control, or surrender protective mechanisms. It's hard to set self aside without resorting to doing away with the self.

The difficulty of watching ourselves be spontaneous is what makes "trick shooting," such as automatic writing and other dissociative modes of channeling, so attractive. Turning out the lights on the conscious mind is a convenient way to get the self out of the picture. "*Getting rid* of the ego" becomes the goal of this approach to channeling. It doesn't work. We can't use a trick to bypass the problem of self-doubt. We must heal this doubt.

Learning to be a channel of your higher self involves learning self-acceptance. When we meditate, for example, our typical thoughts and worries pass through our mind. Yet we continue meditating, returning to our focus. Gradually, we become more relaxed. Thoughts and worries continue to pass by, but we are so relaxed, we easily ignore them. They don't bother us anymore. They don't disturb the peace.

In a workshop I once led on psychic development and channeling, I taught many of the techniques discussed in this book. At the conclusion of the workshop, we discussed the implications of what we had learned. The participants noted that all the techniques could be summarized as learning *self-esteem*. They learned to trust the value of their initial reactions, thoughts, or images. They translated that lesson as a growth in self-esteem, an elusive combination of self-acceptance, honoring, and valuing oneself. Taking a cue from nature, we noted that a plant gives freely of its flower, but keeps its leaves for itself. A healthy self-esteem recognizes the difference between the flower and leaf parts of oneself.

Serving an Ideal Opens the Channel

"Don't just be good," Cayce frequently admonished, "be good for something." When entering meditation or self-hypnosis in preparation for channeling insights, it's easy to focus on being good, on being insightful. It can put our self-esteem at issue. Having a *need* for the insights, however, directs our focus elsewhere. The need actually opens the channel. Now we have something to be good *for*.

Cayce indicated often that his psychic readings were stimulated by the need of the questioner. The greater and more genuine the person's need, the better Cayce's psychic functioning.

It's the same for us. Whether we're serving a need or serving the expression of an ideal, when we respond to something more compelling than our own personal concerns, it's easier to set ourselves aside. We can thus thank the power of an ideal, or being needed, for pulling us out of ourselves. I think it's something you've experienced.

Haven't you found that your talents express themselves best when you're using them to make some kind of gift for someone else? Perhaps it's preparing a meal, sewing a piece of clothing, making a piece of furniture, or something as simple as doing someone a favor. Paintings I make as presents for other people are invariably better than paintings I make purely for display. Having someone to paint for actually inspires my creativity. I know I'm not alone. Many times I've heard people say that having someone to cook for inspires the gourmet chef's talent lurking within.

We'll often do better for someone else than when simply doing for ourselves. Focusing on the other person's need can inspire our ingenuity. Expressing our love of a person in our work often helps us enjoy the process even more. We are more likely to "whistle while we work," pouring our heart out into our efforts, our work of love. Enjoying the process in that way actually helps us get into a mode suited for channeling creativity.

What is surprising is that by offering our creativity to someone, by dedicating our effort to the service of another, we actually become creative. What we were willing to give away comes back to us as a present for ourselves. Cayce taught that this paradoxical fact is actually an important principle in life. What qualities we wish to have for ourselves, we need to give to others. By becoming a channel of blessings, we ourselves are blessed.

Service: the Misunderstood Secret

"Service is our most important product." Serving an expression of an ideal is a vital and important dimension to channeling. Having an application for the channeled information serves to complete a circuit of channeling energy. Testing channeled guidance by putting it into service, by applying it, helps test its validity and, if valid, increases our awareness of its truth. These are some of the principles of service we've looked at in this book.

We've also considered service from the standpoint of our oneness with all life. Cooperation is a good example, for through cooperating we express our sense of relationship with others. With regard to service, Cayce also reminds us of Jesus' admonition to love our neighbors as ourselves.

Serving another person in need also helps distract our attention away from ourselves so that we more readily open ourselves to channel.

Service is not only the purpose for channeling, it's also its stimulant and its means. Unfortunately, it's too easy to interpret service as a *should* rather than a natural, meaningful part of channeling.

That misunderstanding can be dangerous. If we channel as a substitute for self-esteem, rather than as an expression of it, and we see service as a should, we're likely to become martyrs. As Carmen Renee Berry describes so well in her book, *When Helping You Is Hurting Me,* a Messiah trap awaits anyone who feels that serving others means total self-sacrifice. It's a path to self-depletion, rather than self-renewal. It reinforces a low self-esteem, creating a vicious, downward spiral. It creates an addiction to pleasing others or rescuing them, rather than sharing with them your sense of self-worth.

Channeling as an expression of self-esteem, however, in the service of the ideals of our higher self, reinforces our awareness of our oneness with life. Serving others need not be cause for praise or applause because serving is its own blessing. We focus on the process because we enjoy the process. When we serve as an expression of our self-esteem, doing good feels good.

Social scientists are finding that genuine altruism creates good feelings in the people who express caring and volunteer to help. Alan Luks, director of the Institute for the Advancement of Health, has found that there's actually such a thing as the "helper's high." It's a definite feeling in the body, a pleasant sensation accompanied by a mood that some describe as calm, warm, or glowing. It may be the experience of radiating love. Whatever its underlying basis, it comes only when the person is *freely choosing to help*, not when it is *forced*, or when helping feels *obligatory*. As potent a relaxer and stress reducer as meditation, the helper's high comes from the experience of being able and wanting to help another person. It's one of the blessings of being a channel of blessings. It's the secret value of service.

Become a Conscious Channel

Trance channeling certainly appears to be a remarkable phenomenon. By now you probably realize, however, that it is but one example, although extreme, of a wide range of opportunities to express the reality of our spirit. If you recall, Cayce believed that through the arts we are capable of expressing spiritual truths in a more powerful manner than through any other means of channeling. He also stated that the highest form of psychic ability was intuition because it holistically combined ESP and values into a form ready-made for guidance. Intuitions are less dependent upon being in a trance than they are upon our desire to be a channel of service to an ideal. Certainly, trance channeling is not the ultimate in channeling. The ultimate experience is to become a conscious channel, capable of receiving inspirations and sharing them in a state of conscious awareness.

In preparing this book, I had the opportunity to interview Ray Stanford, the channel of *Fatima Prophecy: Days of Darkness, Promise of Light*. These psychic readings, conducted in 1971, reveal the nature of the secret message that the

Virgin Mary relayed to the Vatican via the children who saw her at Fatima, Portugal in 1917. Ray's *Fatima Prophecy* increased in significance when one of the predictions they contained, concerning as assassination attempt on the Pope, was unfortunately validated ten years later.

By that time, however, Ray had stopped his trance channeling. He stopped because of a dream. In his dream, he was with his friends at Virginia Beach when he spotted a white dolphin. The dolphin was jumping in the air and singing a song that filled Ray and his friends with joy. They realized the dolphin was a spiritual creature and swam out to greet it. The dolphin's singing communicated great insights and spiritual revelations to the people. Their hunger for the dolphin's revelations was insatiable, yet they were not really digesting anything it said. They were just asking for more. They decided to create a channel on the beach for the dolphin to swim ashore. When the dolphin swam ashore, they blocked its return. Ray watched the scene with great sadness. He realized that he and his friends had only the best of intentions, yet they were killing the dolphin. The song, "Born Free" ran through his mind. Finally, he persuaded his friends to allow him to return the dolphin to the ocean.

Ray explained to me that the dream was an intensely poignant and moving experience. He realized that truth isn't to be found in words, but in one's own heart. The spirit of truth has to be free. When we try to possess it with concepts, he explained, rather than living it anew each moment, that spirit dies.

His trance source confirmed this insight. It indicated that trance channeling was fine as long as that was the best he could do. It was time to grow to a new level of channeling. Thus Ray's trance channeling came to an end. He began what proved to be an eleven-year transition period learning to channel what he could from the conscious state.

When Ray recently made his first public appearance after those eleven years, it was obvious that although speaking in public did not come easily for him, he was still willing to be himself—willing to share his personal experiences, willing to share his feelings, willing to be led by his enthusiasm.

The audience could feel him reaching deep within himself to communicate the spirit of truth that once came through only in the trance state. It was an inspiring evening.

I mention Ray because his story is an interesting case study in the development of channeling ability. At a time when trance channeling enjoys such popularity, for someone who channeled as influential a book as *Fatima Prophecy* to give up trance work in favor of learning to serve the spirit through being himself, is quite a testimony to the value of simply being conscious.

I find myself coming to a similar viewpoint. I've practiced channeling with dreams and creativity for over twenty years. Whenever I reflected upon what I'd learned from these two channels, I came to the same conclusion. First, they taught me that I was something more than I suspected, that there was a spirit inside that connected me to the rest of creation. Second, they taught me that being myself was potentially a perfectly fine way to channel that spirit. I say *potentially* because I found that I had trouble being myself, at least the way I thought being myself should be.

Then I began practicing meditation. I learned from meditation a way of accepting things the way they are. I came to appreciate the subtle, enlightened humor in the double message Allan Watts, the gifted writer on meditation and Zen, gave us by titling his autobiography *In My Own Way*. It expresses the sublime sense of freedom and release that comes from realizing that one's ego is always going to be there, but that one need pay it no mind.

In the past couple of years I've been exploring trance channeling. I love the feeling of being entranced, of being able to verbalize intuitive knowledge. Even though I'll probably further develop this art form, especially if it continues to help me express more in writing, what I've gained that's more important is a more relaxed me, a more centered me, a more ''in tune'' me. Yet it's a me that's no more gifted in trance than the me who gets relaxed in the garden or on my bicycle. It's no more gifted than the me who gets centered in meditation, or by completely concentrating on the spirit in which I wish to express myself. It's no more gifted than the me who gets "in tune" through music or through interacting with other sincerely seeking individuals. Trance channeling has shown me, however, that the task ahead remains to learn how to love, to trust love, to be love, and to love being myself, in my own way. More trance channeling won't help me live that lesson any better.

To Be Yourself as Only You Can Be

Let's take a cue from cartoonist Ashleigh Brilliant who confides, "I'm trying to live my life—a task so difficult it has never been tried before." If you want to be unique, original, be yourself—your real self. There's no one else like it.

The only way you can be your unique self is in the conscious awake state, acting in a totally spontaneous manner. Just watch yourself go by and don't stand in the way.

If you go into trance, if you learn how to channel from the superconscious state of universal awareness, you'll sound pretty much like all the other trance channels who've tapped into that same source. When there's no ego at all, universal awareness and the same, timeless, unchanging message comes through. In some cases it can be almost as much a cliché as the familiar ego.

What gives universal intelligence a unique, individual flair is when it is channeled through a conscious person, someone whose ego is not running the show, but simply functions without calling attention to itself. What gives universal truth its vitality, and saves it from being a cliché, is the individual expression.

Cayce encouraged us to learn from nature. Each piece of nature serves its Creator's purpose by being itself. We serve the Creator's purpose, and thus render our greatest service, by knowing and sharing who we really are. No one else can be you the way you can. No one else can express the spirit of creation in the way you can. To express that spirit in your individual way is your purpose for being here.

Martha Graham, the dancer and choreographer, once

remarked, "There is a vitality, a life force, an energy, a quickening, that is translated through you into action and because there is only one of you in all of time, this expression is unique. And if you block it, it will never exist through any medium and be lost. The world will not have it."

God intends for the world to have your expression. Use your intuition to know your soul's identity, your heart's true desire, and let it be. Know that finding a way to express yourself in service to the world is what you really want. It's the ultimate purpose and the blessing of channeling your higher self.

THE A.R.E. TODAY

The Association for Reseach and Enlightenment, Inc., is a non-profit, open membership organization committed to spiritual growth, holistic healing, psychical research and its spiritual dimensions; and more specifically, to making practical use of the psychic readings of the late Edgar Cayce. Through nationwide programs, publications and study groups, A.R.E. offers all those interested, practical information and approaches for individual study and application to better understand and relate to themselves, to other people and to the universe. A.R.E. membership and outreach is concentrated in the United States with growing involvement throughout the world.

The headquarters at Virginia Beach, Virginia, includes a library/conference center, administrative offices and publishing facilities, and are served by a beachfront motel. The library is one of the largest metaphysical, parapsychological libraries in the country. A.R.E. operates a bookstore, which also offers mail-order service and carries approximately 1,000 titles on nearly every subject related to spiritual growth, world religions, parapsychology and transpersonal psychology. A.R.E. serves its members through nationwide lecture programs, publications, a Braille library, a camp and an extensive Study Group Program.

The A.R.E. facilities, located at 67th Street and Atlantic Avenue, are open year-round. Visitors are always welcome and may write A.R.E., P.O. Box 595, Virginia Beach, VA 23451, for more information about the Association.